INCOME INEQUALITY IN THE UNITED STATES, 1947–1985

Income Inequality in the United States, 1947–1985

Nan L. Maxwell

*Contributions in Economics
and Economic History,
Number 101*

GREENWOOD PRESS
New York • Westport, Connecticut • London

Library of Congress Cataloging-in-Publication Data

Maxwell, Nan L.
    Income inequality in the United States, 1947–1985 / Nan L.
Maxwell.
        p.   cm. — (Contributions in economics and economic history,
ISSN 0084–9235 ; no. 101)
    Bibliography: p.
    Includes index.
    ISBN 0–313–26411–2 (lib. bdg. : alk. paper)
    1. Income distribution—United States.   2. Labor market—United
States.   I. Title.   II. Series.
HC110.I5M37   1990
339.2′0973′09045—dc20   89–11971

British Library Cataloguing in Publication Data is available.

Library of Congress Catalog Card Number: 89–11971
ISBN: 0–313–26411–2
ISSN: 0084–9235

First published in 1990

Greenwood Press, Inc.
88 Post Road West, Westport, Connecticut 06881

Printed in the United States of America

∞

The paper used in this book complies with the
Permanent Paper Standard issued by the National
Information Standards Organization (Z39.48–1984).

10   9   8   7   6   5   4   3   2   1

Contents

Figures and Tables

FIGURES

TABLES

Preface

This book reports results of a systematic, empirical study of how deindustrialization, population age structure, female labor force participation, and government spending on social insurance affect income inequality and distribution. It directly addresses the two issues of income polarization (bottom-to-top income movement) and the declining middle class by analyzing yearly income data from 1947 to 1985. Because of the study's empirical nature, theoretical distinctions in welfare theory and normative judgments about ideal income distributions are not included. Since the study focuses on relative changes in the income distribution, discussion of absolute changes in the level of living are minimal.

Since the definition of equality is inherently subjective, discussions of income inequality often evoke much normative debate. This study minimizes normative judgments. Income inequality and distribution are quantified with the most widely recognized statistical measures, the Gini coefficient and quintile income distributions. These measures quantify the relative dispersion of the frequency distribution of income without referencing "goodness" or "badness" (e.g., no parameters are fit to a selected distribution). Of course, without a normative basis, this study can only describe one outcome of society—the income distribution—and cannot describe associated societal welfare.

The Gini coefficient is used to measure the deviation from "perfect equality"—roughly defined as each fifth (quintile) of the population receiving one-fifth of the income. To restrict normative interpretations of inequality, the Gini coefficient is not used as an absolute inequality measure at any point in time but as a comparative measure estimating income inequality movement. Because differing income distributions can produce similar Gini coefficients, quintile income share is used to measure income distribution. This distributional analysis allows comparison of the top-quintile income share with the bottom-quintile income share and provides a definition of middle class: the middle three quintiles (i.e., middle 60 percent of the population).

Any empirical study cannot examine all factors underlying the changing income distribution. In fact, no empirical study can quantify the totality of the impact on inequality of deindustrialization, population age, female labor force participation, and government spending. Because each factor's impact is too complex and multifaceted for concise quantification, the measures used in this study represent trends which are much more complex than their empirical specification. The complexities underlying the impact of each factor on income inequality are outlined using theories and previous research. By integrating the multidimensional facets of each factor shown in theory and previous research with results of this study, we can further our understanding of income inequality changes.

Throughout this study, I incurred many debts. The Affirmative Action Program and University Small Grant Program at California State University, Hayward, provided partial funding at various stages of the project. Chuck Baird, Eleanor Brown, Greg Christainsen, Lu Ann Duffus, Frank Levy, Wendy Max, Frank Mott, Jim St. Clair, William Serow, Steve Shmanske, and Ray O. Werner all provided comments and suggestions at various stages of the project. Kathy Dulkie typed (and retyped) tables without complaint. Trudi Amundson and Heather Konrad provided countless library hours in research and data collection. Michael Silva provided technical assistance with the figures. Richard Barbieri, Michael Dawson, and Lorraine Richards also provided research assistance at various stages. Most importantly Ronald D'Amico provided inspiration, comments, criticism, and emotional support throughout the project. His meticulous reading (and rereading) of each chapter was above and beyond the call of duty. Many, many thanks to each. Of course, I take full responsibility for remaining errors.

INCOME INEQUALITY
IN THE UNITED STATES,
1947–1985

1

Introduction

Income inequality increased in recent years. Concurrent with inequality increases, real wages fell and poverty increased. Since decreased real wages, increased poverty, and increased inequality did not affect all individuals uniformly, the changing income distribution has been increasingly scrutinized. Declining real wages focused attention on the potential decline of the middle class. Are middle Americans losing their ability to maintain their status? Increasing poverty focused attention on income polarization. Are we becoming a nation of haves and have-nots?

All three issues (inequality, middle class, and income polarization) are related but involve separate issues. Since changes in income inequality result from underlying changes in the income distribution, the issues are related. Since different distributional shifts can produce the same (measured) inequality fluctuation, the related issues necessitate separate study. For example, inequality increase can result from either income movement from the bottom of the distribution to the top and a stable middle or from income movement from the middle of the distribution to the bottom and top.[1]

Throughout this book the term "increasing income polarization" designates bottom-to-top movements in income and the term "declining middle class" designates decreased income share of the middle 60 percent of the income distribution (i.e., middle three quintiles). While both changes create increased income inequality, a declining middle class arouses more concern from middle America while increasing income polarization haunts those concerned with poverty.

With the resurgence of interest in the income distribution, the academic community, lay journals, popular press, and politicians all have devoted attention to distributional issues. Much of the focus has been on the extent to which economic factors (shifts in industrial and occupational employment) or demographic factors (relative increases in the nonworking (dependent) population and female-headed families) create distributional shifts. If economic factors play a predominate role in distributional shifts, inequality upswings will be more permanent than if the more transitory demographic factors predominate.

Academic studies are notable in their inconsistent interpretation of income inequality movements. These inconsistencies arise with differing factors under study, units of analysis, or methodology.[2] Thurow (1987) contends that the recent inequality surge stems from increased international competition, a rising proportion of female workers, and the feminization of poverty, while Bradbury (1986) argues that the latter two forces offset each other without a net impact on inequality. Levy (1987b) argues that living standards are stable with offsetting forces in decreased real wages, increased numbers of working women, and decreased birthrates. Studies show a shrinking middle class with growing service-sector employment and current changes in the population's age structure.[3]

The popular press has focused attention on the disappearance of the middle class. Some articles simply outline a declining middle class trend. Some call for solutions in government intervention.[4] All increase concern among middle Americans for their potential loss of living standard.

Policymakers have acted on increased distributional concerns from their constituents and the academic community. Congress enacted plant closure legislation enabling workers to have more flexibility in pursuing alternatives in the face of pending layoffs and considered extensive welfare reform for the first time since its implementation in 1935. Congress also requested that the Congressional Budget Office (CBO) study trends in family income. Using adjusted family income as a basis, the CBO (1988) found that median family income increased for most family types from 1970 to 1986.[5] There was, however, differential income growth among family types. Single mothers fared the worst, with their adjusted income, always just above poverty level, declining over this period and their poverty rates increasing. Conversely, the elderly fared the best, with falling poverty rates and above-average income growth. This uneven income growth among different family types resulted in greater inequality in 1986 than 1970. CBO cited government transfers, macroeconomics and employment, and demographics as the important determinants of income trends.

Levy (1987a) provides an overview of many of the CBO-cited factors influencing income inequality and changes. His thorough review describes within-group changes in level of living and income inequality and distribution for both families and unrelated individuals. He provides a review of postwar changes in industrial employment, geographic movement, labor force composition, and family and household structure. His focus, therefore, is on changing levels of income (defined as changes in average income around which the distribution is centered) and changing sources of income. Confirming the CBO findings, he shows that average income levels rose for families and unrelated individuals over the postwar period; however, he finds that the composition of income changed dramatically. These (offsetting) compositional changes (e.g., increased income from wives and decreased real wages) caused over-time stability in the living standards of the middle class.

Although Levy's book provides an outstanding discussion and elaboration of many of the inequality-increasing trends cited by the CBO, his conclusions differ slightly. The CBO shows differences *between* each family and unrelated individual by focusing on disaggregate units. Levy focuses on aggregates (families or unrelated individuals) and discusses income changes *within* each distribution. Neither the CBO or Levy show the relative contribution to income distribution changes of shifts in employment, population age, income-receiving unit composition, the macroeconomy, and government spending. This study examines the relative weight of each of these factors on income inequality changes from 1947 to 1985 within each family type and for unrelated individuals (as does the CBO) and in the aggregate (as does Levy).

INCOME INEQUALITY AND DISTRIBUTION TRENDS

Table 1–1 shows trends in income inequality (Gini coefficient) and quintile share distribution between 1947 and 1985. In the aggregate (all families and unrelated individuals), income inequality remained fairly constant until it began a slow upturn in the late 1960s that accelerated in the early 1980s.[6] Both middle-quintile income share (middle 20 percent of the population) and the top-to-bottom quintile share ratio were stable until the early 1980s, when the top-to-bottom share ratio increased and the middle-quintile share decreased. Although numerous problems exist in examining these aggregate trends, the pronounced inequality increase, middle-quintile share decrease, and top-to-bottom share ratio increase in the 1980s caused increased concern over income distribution changes.[7]

Each measure tells a different story. The Gini coefficient (the inequality measure) measures the deviation from "perfect equality," roughly defined as each fifth (quintile) of the population receiving one-fifth of the income.[8] The Gini coefficient can range from 0 to 1 with 0 indicating "perfect equality"—each fifth of the population receiving one-fifth of the income. Thus, as the income distribution moves further from equality, the Gini coefficient increases.

The Gini coefficient is not, however, a perfect indicator of income distribution since the same Gini coefficient can accompany different income distributions. This deficiency is rectified by examining share distributions along with the Gini coefficient. Since quintile share distributions indicate the share of income received by each fifth of the population, "perfect equality" would be designated with each fifth of the population receiving a .20 income share and the top-to-bottom share ratio would be one. Increases in the top-to-bottom share ratio show distributional shifts in favor of the top quintile at the expense of the bottom

Table 1–1
Inequality, Demographic, and Economic Characteristics, 1947–1985

	Mean	Standard Deviation	1947	1960	1970	1985	Maximum[1] Percent Change
Inequality[2]							
Gini coefficient	.407	.019	.401	.405	.424	.433	–
Top-quintile income share							
Bottom-quintile income share	13.5	–	13.2	14.0	14.2	15.3	–
Middle-quintile income share	.165	.014	.166	.168	.161	.147	–
Income-Receiving Units (Percent)							
Husband-wife families	67.4	4.25	71.2	70.3	66.5	58.0	-18.5
Female-headed units	21.8	3.09	17.9	20.1	22.8	27.8	55.3
Unrelated individuals	20.4	3.64	10.6	15.0	18.8	27.7	161.3
Blacks in husband-wife units	–	–	–	–	48.5	34.8	-28.2
Blacks in female-headed units	–	–	–	–	36.2	43.9	21.3
Demographic Characteristics							
Median age	29.4	1.02	29.8	29.4	27.9	31.5	12.9
Dependency ratio[3]	72.6	7.80	61.4	81.5	78.0	62.0	32.7
Total fertility rate[4]	2700	760	3274	3654	2480	1785	-51.1
Economic Characteristics (Percent)							
Female labor force participation	41.7	6.61	31.8	37.8	43.4	54.7	72.0
Blue-collar employment	38.2	4.63	46.4	40.2	37.0	28.1	-39.4
White-collar employment	49.2	3.40	43.8	47.6	50.5	55.1	25.8
Manufacturing employment	28.4	4.68	35.4	31.0	27.4	19.9	-43.8
Service sector employment	15.6	3.31	11.3	13.4	16.5	21.3	88.5
Government							
Percent of GNP as social insurance[5]	5.2	2.7	1.8	3.8	5.6	9.7	438.9

[1] Computed as the maximum difference over the period divided by the initial period (times 100).

[2] Computed using the income-receiving unit as the unit of analysis.

[3] The dependency ratio is the summation of individuals under 18 and over 64 divided by those between 18 and 64 (times 100).

[4] The total fertility rate is the number of children 1000 women would have if they lived through the childbearing years and gave birth at prevailing age-specific fertility rates.

[5] Social insurance payments include social security, railroad retirement, public employee retirement, unemployment insurance, disability insurance, and workers' compensation.

quintile (income polarization). Decreases in the middle three quintile shares (declining middle) show a loss of income share for the "middle" middle class (middle quintile), lower middle class (second quintile), or upper middle class (fourth quintile). Since the top-to-bottom share ratio was about fifteen in 1985, the "richest" fifth of the population had fifteen times the income share as the "poorest" fifth. Since the middle quintile had a share of about .15, the "middle" middle class and lower middle class had disproportionately low income shares while the upper middle class had a disproportionately high income share.

POSTWAR DEMOGRAPHIC AND ECONOMIC CHANGES AND THEIR RELATIONSHIP WITH INEQUALITY

As both the CBO and Levy illustrated, changing income inequality accompanies changing economics (employment and increased female labor force participation), demographics (income-receiving units and population age structure), and government spending trends.[9] Between 1947 and 1985, dramatic economic and demographic changes occurred. Today, increased imports are blamed for our declining steel, automobile, and textile industries and for moving our economy from a manufacturing to service orientation. The aging baby boom (individuals born between 1946 and 1964) decreased the proportion of nonworking-age (dependent) population when they entered the labor market in the 1970s. Since the 1960s, women increasingly participated in the labor market and increasingly headed their own households. The level of government intervention in the marketplace increased dramatically over the period. Each change had a major impact on the income distribution.

Changes in industrial employment become more apparent daily. Reflecting a more service-oriented economy, from 1947 to 1985 employment shifted from the manufacturing to the service sector with a 44 percent decrease in manufacturing employment and an 89 percent increase in service-sector employment (Table 1-1). While manufacturing employment was nearly three times greater than service-sector employment in 1947, the sectors had nearly equivalent employment levels by 1985. These shifts raised concerns about the income distribution since economies with increasing service output often face slowing rates of productivity increase and, hence, productivity-associated wage increases become slowed or reversed.

Occupational changes accompanied industrial employment shifts. Low-skill service and white-collar positions replaced unionized blue-collar jobs. In 1947, blue-collar and white-collar employment was nearly equivalent (about 45 percent), with blue-collar employment having a slight edge (Table 1-1). By 1985, blue-collar employment decreased by 39 percent, white-collar employment increased by 26 percent, and white-collar employment was about twice as great as blue-collar employment.

Policymakers, union leaders, and the general public are concerned about the impact of these occupational employment shifts on the income distribution. As low-skill and high-skill positions in the service sector replaced well-paying, "middle-class" blue-collar employment, fears of an income-polarized society emerged. Because a continuation of past industrial and occupational employment shifts is projected, distributional concerns exist for the short run (current) and the long run (future).

The supply side of the labor market also changed dramatically as females increasingly entered the labor force and the baby boom aged. In 1947, under one-third of all women were labor force participants while over one-half were participants by 1985 (Table 1–1). This large influx of women into the labor market, particularly married women, altered the income distribution with wage changes accompanying increased aggregate labor supply and a changed composition of family income (e.g., higher proportions of wife's earnings in family income).

Population-driven labor supply fluctuations primarily reflect fertility changes associated with the arrival and aging of the baby boom. From 1947 to 1985, the total fertility rate peaked around 1960 with 3.7 children per woman (Table 1–1) and fell continuously thereafter. The combination of the fertility decline and the low number of childbearing-age women produced few children in the post-baby boom period (the baby bust). Although low fertility rates continued as the baby-boom women entered the childbearing years, the large number of women bearing children produced an echo boom. This large cohort of children will alter the nonworking proportion of the population in the late 1980s.

When the baby boom arrived, the median population age fell (1947 to 1970) and the dependency ratio (the ratio of the youth and elderly (nonworking) population to the working-age population) rose with the large cohort of young individuals (Table 1–1). As the baby boom aged, the median age began to rise (1970–1985) and the dependency ratio fell.

Since income and age have an inverted U relationship (i.e., income is lowest at young and old ages), an increase in the proportion of young and/or (i.e., increased dependency) increases income inequality. Thus, increased fertility rates (and, to a lesser extent, increased life expectancy) increased the population of low-earners. Optimistic economists and policymakers focus on the transitory nature of this phenomenon and argue that increased inequality during the early 1980s resulted from age configurations of the population and will not continue into the future. Pessimists argue that increased inequality reflects permanent changes in industrial and occupational employment that outweigh temporary age influences and, therefore, predict continued inequality increases.

Living arrangements also changed dramatically. From 1947 to 1985, the proportion of (often impoverished) female-headed households increased by fifty-five percent, the proportion of husband-wife families decreased by nearly twenty percent, and the proportion of unrelated individuals increased by over 161 percent (Table 1–1). The trend toward female-headed units was particularly pronounced for blacks, with the percentage of husband-wife units declining by nearly thirty percent while the percentage of black female-headed units increased by nearly the same amount from 1970 to 1985. This shift from husband-wife to female-headed families increased the number of children living in a single-earner family with income levels below the poverty line.

Policymakers consciously or unconsciously alter the income distribution with social and economic policy changes. As expenditures on social programs increased between 1947 and 1985, the percentage of gross national product (GNP) devoted to social insurance increased by over 400 percent (Table 1–1). The primary policy change was the implementation, expansion, and modification of the Great Society programs. Most of these programs targeted aid to the disadvantaged—women, minorities, elderly, unemployed, or impoverished. Expansion also occurred in the liberalization of Social Security benefits when Congress linked benefits to the consumer price index (CPI) in 1972. This dramatically increased Social Security benefit levels during the high-inflation years of the 1970s and greatly reduced elderly poverty rates.

Disaggregate Distribution Impacts

Since labor market and policy changes do not uniformly affect all individuals, these economic, demographic, and policy changes differentially altered the income distribution of individual income-receiving units (e.g., households or families). In the labor market, for example, decreased blue-collar employment may not impact greatly on women's labor market earnings since few women work in blue-collar jobs. Thus, female-headed income-receiving units may be unaffected by occupational employment change. Since increased female labor force participation came primarily from married women, the income distribution of husband-wife families may be more affected than female-headed units that showed little variation in participation probabilities.

For some income-receiving units, the government provides the primary source of income. Government income, however, is often tied to previous or present circumstances (e.g., retirement, unemployment, or impoverishment). Because government benefits are not uniformly obtained and their benefit structure is often intentionally redistributory, program alteration impacts more heavily on some income-receiving units than others.

Income determination and distribution also varies by race. Whether the cause is discrimination, cultural disadvantages, government-induced dependency, or inadequate education, nonwhites earn less in the labor market and are more likely to receive income from means-tested government programs than whites. Thus, changes in the labor market or in government policies may have differential racial impacts.

This study examines these issues. It is a systematic, empirical study of the influence of industrial and occupational employment, population dependency, female labor force participation, income-receiving unit composition, and social-insurance expenditure on income inequality and distribution. It specifically addresses the issues of increasing income polarization and declining middle-class income by analyzing yearly income data from 1947 to 1985 with respect to these five changes. These issues are examined separately for individual income-receiving units and for whites and nonwhites.

THIS STUDY

To achieve this goal, yearly income data from the Current Population Survey (CPS) from 1947 to 1985 were analyzed.[10] The CPS is a monthly household survey conducted by the Bureau of the Census that conveys labor force information for the civilian noninstitutional population. Supplementary questions are asked every March about money income and work experience in the previous year.[11] Income is self-reported and includes money income from all sources. In-kind transfers are not included.[12] Since the survey is household-based, income data are available for different income-receiving units (different families, households, unrelated individuals), for individuals (by age and residence), and for workers (by industry and occupation). Data on industrial and occupational employment, population characteristics, female labor force participation, the economy, and social spending were compiled from various government sources. Appendix 3 provides a complete listing of all data sources.

Gini coefficients and quintile shares computed from the CPS were used to measure income inequality and distribution.[13] Because economic, demographic, and government-spending changes occurred simultaneously over the period, regression analysis was used to separate the effects. Specifically, the following ordinary-least-squares (OLS) model was estimated:[14]

$$Y_i = a_0 + a_1\text{dependency}_i + a_2\text{occupation}_i + a_3\text{industry}_i \qquad (1\text{--}1)$$
$$+ a_4\text{government}_i + a_5\text{income-receiving unit}_i + e$$

where

dependency_i = the dependency ratio (times 100) in year i

occupation_i = the ratio of blue-collar to white-collar workers (times 100) in year i

industry_i = the ratio of service to manufacturing workers (times 100) in year i

government_i = the ratio of social-insurance expenditure to gross national product (times 100) in year i

$\text{income-receiving unit}_i$ = the ratio of female-headed units to husband-wife families (times 100) in year i.

The dependent variable (Y_i) took the form of a yearly Gini coefficient for estimation of inequality influences. For estimation of distributional impacts, five separate equations—one with each quintile's income share as the dependent variable—were estimated.[15] Over-time presentation of Gini coefficients and quintile shares, and over-time percentile distributions of employment, population dependency, female labor force participation, and government spending allowed direct examination of the trends, while regression analysis disentangled the simultaneous influences on income inequality and distribution changes.[16]

Regression analysis statistically partitions each economic, demographic, and governmental influence on income inequality or quintile share. Elasticities, summary statistics based on the regression analysis, show the relative magnitude of each influence (the independent variables) on changes in income inequality and quintile share (dependent variables).[17] Since elasticities reflect the percent change in inequality (or quintile share) for a one-percent change in the independent variable, they measure the relative importance of each economic, demographic, and government influence.

Changes in the income distribution can occur in three ways. First, *within* each income-receiving unit the income distribution can change. These within-group distributional changes then alter aggregate income distribution. For example, within husband-wife families, the income distribution may equalize as wives increasingly enter the labor market. This equalization of family income reduces aggregate income inequality, all else equal. Second, the income distribution *between* groups can change. These between-group changes then alter aggregate income inequality. For example, the distribution of earnings within each racial group may stay the same, but the (mean) discrepancy in white-nonwhite earnings may widen. All else equal, this increases aggregate income inequality, even without within-group distributional changes. Third, the composition of income-receiving units can change. Since income-receiving units have varying income distribution and mean income levels, compositional changes alter the aggregate income distribution. For example, female-headed units have lower income levels and more unequally distributed incomes than husband-wife families. Thus, increases in the relative number of female-headed units increases aggregate inequality, all else equal.

To detect both within-group and between-group income inequality and distribution changes, the income distribution was analyzed in the aggregate and for individual income-receiving units. The disaggregate analysis included husband-wife families (with and without wife participation in the labor force), male-headed and female-headed families, male and female unrelated individuals, and whites and nonwhites. To detect the impact of compositional changes, the income-receiving unit variable was inserted into aggregate and racially stratified estimates of equation 1–1.

By estimating the relationship between economic, demographic, and policy changes and income inequality and distribution, this study answered the following questions:

1. Is middle-class income declining? If so, is the decline due to the transitory aging of the baby boom or to permanent changes in industrial-occupational employment?

2. Has increased female labor force participation created a society of high-income, dual-earning families at the expense of low-income units or has it reduced distributional dispersion and equalized income?

3. Does government spending on social-insurance programs increase the income share of the bottom fifth of the income distribution while other fifths lose a significant income share?

4. Do employment, dependency, female labor force participation, and government spending changes influence income inequality and distribution uniformly among income-receiving units (husband-wife, male-headed and female-headed families, and male and female unrelated-individual units) and between the races (whites and nonwhites)?

5. What are likely future income inequality and distributions, given projected changes in the population age structure and industrial-occupational employment?

Results of the study show that for most income-receiving units, within-group income inequality decreased between 1947 and 1985 with increased inequality toward the end of the period. Inequality increases stemmed from increased income polarization (bottom-to-top income movements) and were dominated by the influence of changing industrial employment. Declines in middle-class income were due primarily to declines in the second-quintile income share (lower middle class). Both demographic factors (changing income-receiving unit composition and population dependency) and economic factors (changing industrial and occupational employment) increased income inequality. Increased female labor force participation and increased expenditures on social insurance offset inequality increases. These aggregate trends differed dramatically from within-race and within income-receiving unit trends, however. In the future, changing industrial employment will dominate distributional change, primarily because of its greater predicted numeric change. Projected changes in economic and demographic factors will continue to increase income inequality, particularly for nonwhite and female-headed units, unless countervailing forces arise.

Book Organization

Each chapter examines the relationship between a specific economic, demographic, or policy influence and income inequality and share distribution. Theory and previous research are used to explain the estimated relationships.

Chapter 2 examines compositional change in income-receiving units. Compositional changes altered aggregate income inequality since individual income-receiving units have different income distributions. Nonwhites, female-headed units, and unrelated individuals had higher poverty rates and more unequal income distributions than whites, male-headed units, and families. Since dual-earner, husband-wife families had the most equally distributed incomes, inequality increases resultant from increased (unequally distributed) female-headed units and unrelated individuals were partially offset by increased dual-earning families.

Chapter 3 examines industrial and occupational employment changes. While both industrial and occupational employment shifts increased income inequality, the impact differed dramatically between income-receiving units. Industrial employment shifts exerted a stronger influence than occupational employment shifts on aggregate income inequality and share distribution changes (i.e., between-group inequality). Occupational employment changes, however, were more likely influences on within-unit distributional changes.

Chapter 4 examines population age changes—primarily the baby-boom's alteration of the nonworking-age proportion of the population. Increased population dependency increased income inequality in the aggregate and for all income-receiving units. Increased inequality stemmed from income polarization. As the baby boom entered the labor market and reduced population dependency, inequality decreased. These effects had a stronger impact on the income distribution of unrelated individuals than families, dual-earning as opposed to single-earning families, and female rather than male income-receiving units.

Chapter 5 examines the impact of increased female labor force participation. Results differed dramatically within each income-receiving unit. For male-headed units, income inequality decreased as increased female labor force participation depressed male earnings in higher-paying occupations and left unchanged the male earnings in lower-paying occupations. Thus, female labor force participation reduced income inequality for male income-receiving units by decreasing the top-quintile income share and increasing the bottom-quintile income share. For female income-receiving units, increased female labor force participation had little impact on income inequality or distribution change. For husband-wife families prior to 1980, increased female labor force participation reduced income inequality. After 1980, the impact reversed as increased female labor force participation increased both the labor supply and relative (female) earnings of women in high-income families. Thus, while increased female labor force participation decreased income inequality for husband-wife families prior to 1980, it increased inequality after 1980.

Chapter 6 examines the relationship between income inequality and distribution and increased proportions of social-insurance expenditures. With redistributory benefit structures of social-insurance programs, increased spending reduced income inequality. This outcome is not consistent within individual receiving units. With increased outlays on social insurance, income inequality of female-headed income-receiving units fell as the lowest-quintile income share increased. Male-headed units showed decreases in upper middle-class income (fourth-quintile share) with increased social-insurance expenditures. For nonworking-wife families, income inequality increased with increases in the top-quintile income share. Dual-earning, husband-wife familes showed no change in their income distribution with increased social-insurance expenditures.

Chapter 7 examines white-nonwhite over-time differences in inequality and inequality influences. Between 1947 and 1985, differences in between-race income distributions widened while within-race distributions narrowed. This resulted from a larger convergence of the (already more equal) white income distribution than the nonwhite income distribution. From 1950 to 1960, aggregate inequality increased as nonwhite within-race inequality increased. From 1960 to 1970, within-race inequality fell for both whites and nonwhites. From 1970 to 1985, white and nonwhite income distributions stabilized. The 1950 to 1960 increase caused aggregate inequality to exceed both white and nonwhite income inequality from 1960 onward. Changes in occupational employment and income-receiving unit composition played a major role in within-race distributional changes. Changes in industrial employment, female labor force participation, social-insurance expenditures, and population dependency altered aggregate (between-race) distributions more than within-race group distributions. An increasing proportion of female-headed units polarized the income distribution and had a greater impact on increasing within-race inequality for nonwhites than whites. This results from both the greater impact of a given economic, demographic, or policy change and the greater numeric change for nonwhites. Shifts in occupational employment also increased within-race income inequality with the impact much stronger for nonwhites.

Chapter 8 summarizes the research findings, compares the totality of economic, demographic, and government influences, and predicts future income distributions. By relating economic and demographic associations to their percent change between 1947 and 1985, the greater influence of industrial employment changes on income inequality is shown. This stronger industrial employment influence results from its large percent change. Thus, while changes in industrial and occupational employment, female labor force participation, population dependency, income-receiving unit composition, and social-insurance expenditures all alter income inequality, industrial employment changes, because of their greater percent change, had the greatest impact. If past economic and demographic trends continue, inequality will continue to increase through the year 2000, again primarily because of shifting industrial employment.

Chapter 9 answers the questions raised in this chapter and proposes policies that might prevent future increases in income inequality and polarization.

NOTES

1. The following examples further clarify this point. Inequality can change without change in middle-class income or income polarization if middle-class income is rearranged. Inequality can decrease with middle-class income decreases if those in poverty gain. Income polarization can occur without a declining middle class if income moves from the "poorest" to the "richest." Of course, increased inequality can stem from decreased middle-class income and/or increased income polarization.

2. Kosters and Ross (1988) provide an excellent example of conflicting findings with different methodologies. When aggregate earnings are studied, results show increased inequality in recent years (cf., Harrison and Bluestone, 1988; Dooley and Gottschalk,

1984) but stability in earlier years (cf., Chiswick and Mincer, 1972). When disaggregate income sources are studied, results show stability in inequality (cf., Levy, 1987a; Porter and Slottje, 1985). Inconsistent findings also result in analysis of family inequality with differing emphasis on the labor market or school (cf., Layard and Zabalza, 1979; Jencks, 1972; Thurow and Lucas, 1972).

3. Harrison et al. (1986), Lawrence (1984b), and Steinberg (1983) all focus on employment shifts while Blackburn and Bloom (1985) focus on a changing population's age structure.

4. *The Economist* (1988), Ehrenreich (1986), Wessel (1986), Thurow (1984) and Kuttner (1983) all outline current trends in a declining middle while Thurow (1986) and Kuttner (1985) focus on interventionist solutions.

5. Adjustments to family income account for family size and a noninflationary price index.

6. The reporting of select years masks decreases in income inequality between 1947 and 1960 since 1970 was a high inequality year relative to years around it.

7. One major drawback in using aggregate measures is the heterogeneous nature of each income-receiving unit. For example, families have much greater income needs than a single unrelated individual and families with children have greater income needs than childless families.

8. Inequality measures have differing statistical (Slottje, 1987; Allison, 1978; Champernowne, 1974; and Atkinson, 1970) and welfare properties (Aigner and Heins, 1967) and produce differing results (Butler and McDonald, 1986).

9. CBO also found that changing macroeconomic conditions (specifically unemployment) influenced income levels. This study, however, consistently found unemployment to be an insignificant determinant of changing income inequality.

10. Radner (1982) discusses potential biases from this data.

11. See U.S. Bureau of the Census (1988) or any other P–60 series CPS publication for a complete description of the data.

12. The exclusion of in-kind benefits places limitations on this study, particularly with respect to government redistribution efforts. Since government in-kind transfers (e.g., food stamps, public housing, medical care) are not included as money income and accrue mainly to the poor, the degree of income inequality is overstated and is more overstated as in-kind transfers increased in recent years. These effects are overshadowed by the exclusion of wealth from the income measure. Since wealth is much more unequally distributed than money income, this study understates inequality by restricting the scope to monetary analysis. See Danziger and Portney (1988) and Thurow (1975) for a discussion of these issues.

13. Appendix 3 provides a listing of the computed yearly Gini coefficients and quintile shares for each income-receiving unit. Appendix 1 provides a detailed description of the computations.

14. See Table 1–1 for a precise definition of the variables. The rationale for the construct of each independent variable is discussed in the relevant chapter. Some variables that other studies (or intuition) suggest as determinants of inequality were found insignificant in this analysis. Specifically, unemployment rate and a time trend were never significant predictors in our models.

All regressions were tested for autocorrelation (Durbin-Watson and Von Neuman tests), heteroskedasticity (Goldfeld-Quant and multiplicative tests), and multicollinearity (Haitovsky test). While the models showed no signs of heteroskedasticity, multicollinearity exists and many Durbin-Watson statistics were in the uncertain range. Since multicollinearity inflates standard errors and makes it difficult for variables to gain significance, our results *under report* significant relationships. Models were reestimated using generalized least squares (GLS) to detect potential autocorrelation problems. Since GLS and OLS results did not differ, OLS estimation is appropriate. Since similar magnitudes appeared under several specifications, any potential estimation problems did not influence the consistency of our estimators.

15. Browning (1979, 1976) and Smeeding (1979) discuss the relationship of income definitions, methodologies, and inequality measurement and Horrigan and Haugen (1988) discuss the sensitivity of the "middle-class" definition.

16. Lewis-Beck (1980) or Berry and Feldman (1985) intuitively discuss regression analysis while Mansfield (1988) discusses elasticities.

17. Full regression results are located in Appendix 4.

2

Household Structure Changes:
Income-Receiving Units

Income-receiving units vary dramatically in their level of income received and in their distribution of income. Female-headed units receive less income than male-headed units. Unrelated individuals receive less income than families. Husband-wife families without working wives receive less income than dual-earning families. Units with lower income levels—unrelated individuals, female-headed, and nonworking-wife families—also have more unequally distributed incomes.

Because of these within-unit income differences, aggregate income inequality changes as the composition of income-receiving units changes and as the income distribution within each unit changes. While the remaining chapters examine a specific economic, demographic, and government influence on within-unit income inequality and distribution, this chapter focuses on the impact of compositional change in income-receiving units on income inequality and distribution.

Throughout the book, all terminology used is based on Census definitions. A household includes all persons occupying a housing unit (separate living quarters). The household head is the designated adult male. In absence of an adult male, the household head is the designated adult female.[1] A family is a household comprised of the head and one or more persons living in the same household who are related by blood, marriage, or adoption. An unrelated individual is (1) a household head living alone or with nonrelatives, (2) a household member not related to the head, or (3) a person living in group quarters who is not an inmate of an institution.[2]

Throughout this book, the term ''female-headed unit'' encompasses both female-headed families and female unrelated individuals. ''Male-headed unit'' encompasses both *nonwife* male-headed families and male unrelated individuals. Husband-wife families are not discussed as male-headed units but as husband-wife families. The general term "family" encompasses husband-wife, male-headed, and female-headed families. The term "unrelated individuals" encompasses both male and female unrelated individuals.

Since the measured level of inequality varies under different income-receiving unit definitions, selecting the appropriate unit of analysis is important. Economists, concerned with the distribution of labor market rewards, often study the worker as the unit of analysis and examine relative productivities in the marketplace.[3] Demographers, concerned with a more need-based income analysis, often study the family or household as the unit of analysis and examine the primary institution through which income is jointly generated, pooled, and redistributed.[4]

Since this study examines all money income and since some income accrues jointly to an entire receiving unit (e.g., interest income), a more demographic-based definition of income-receiving unit is used. Unfortunately, the household or family is not the ideal unit of analysis since families are not the totality of the population (only 67 percent of income-receiving units in 1985) and not all households pool their income (e.g., college roommates).

As a benchmark for defining the income-receiving unit, Kuznets (1976) delineated four criteria for establishing the ideal unit. Each of the four criteria operationally follows from income jointness—an ideal unit is economically independent, identifiable, inclusive of decisionmakers whose decisions influence the lifetime income chances and plans of all members, and inclusive of all members of the population. To conform as closely as possible to Kuznet's criteria, we begin our aggregate unit of analysis construction with the family and add unrelated individuals.

The family as a unit of analysis has (relative) economic independence from all other units. Consumption, production, and income flows are usually contained within its boundaries (or traded in the market). The family is a readily identifiable unit and includes the major decisionmaker (the head); however, it does not include all members of the population. By combining family units with unrelated individuals, the totality of the (noninstitutional) population can be studied. Unrelated individuals are identifiable and contain the (only) decisionmaker; however, they often are not economically independent. Resources often flow between (unrelated) household members in the form of expense sharing, household production, etc. Thus, Kuznet's ideal benchmark definition is neither met with the inclusion of unrelated individuals nor with their exclusion.

Because this study is concerned with the totality of the population, our aggregate analysis was constructed from the summation of all families and unrelated individuals. Racial analysis reflects the summation of all white (or nonwhite) families and unrelated individuals.[5] Family analysis reflects (the summation of) husband-wife, male-headed, and female-headed families. Husband-wife families were stratified by the wife's labor force participation for most analyses. Unrelated individuals were examined separately by gender.

Disaggregate analysis shows dramatic absolute and relative income differentials between income-receiving units. Since the absolute differences in income and income inequality lessened over the period, between-unit dispersion, and hence inequality, lessened. At the same time, however, the proportion of (relatively) unequally distributed income-receiving units increased. This increased aggregate inequality. These two conflicting forces produced insignificant results when examining the compositional impact of income-receiving units on aggregate income inequality.[6] Each of these (counteracting) trends—between-unit income convergence and a population increasingly weighted with units of unequal income distribution—will be examined in turn.

RELATIONSHIP BETWEEN INCOME-RECEIVING UNITS AND INCOME

Although this book focuses on relative over-time changes in the income distribution, this section also examines absolute income levels. It places the within and between-unit comparisons in perspective by providing comparisons to aggregate trends in inequality and level of income growth.

Relative income comparisons can take two forms: between-group comparisons of absolute income levels and within-group comparisons of income distributions. Absolute income comparisons simply examine income levels without "relative" comparisons to specific groups. While over-time relative analysis shows income changes between or within subgroups, it reveals little about economic well-being. Alternatively, over-time absolute income comparisons show the economic level of living, yet give no indication of how subgroups are doing relative to each other.

For example, there could be little difference between subgroups with respect to income level or within-group income distribution. Within each subgroup nearly all income-receiving units could have equivalent income levels and between-subgroup income differences could be minimal. This could be true if everyone in the population was impoverished or everyone was wealthy. Alternatively, income could be distributed very unequally within and between groups yet no one would be "poor."

Over-Time Changes in Income Inequality and Distribution

Table 2–1 shows changes in income inequality and share distribution from 1950 to 1985 in the aggregate and for income-receiving units. Panel 1 shows over-time Gini coefficients, panel 2 shows top-to-bottom quintile share ratios, and panel 3 shows the middle-quintile income share.

In the aggregate, income inequality decreased steadily between 1960 and 1980

Table 2-1
Trends in Income-Receiving-Unit Income Distribution

	Gini Coefficient					Top-Quintile Income Share / Lowest-Quintile Income Share					Middle Quintile Income Share				
	1950	1960	1970	1980	1985	1950	1960	1970	1980	1985	1950	1960	1970	1980	1985
Aggregate[1]	.466	.465	.424	.413	.443	24.2	14.2	14.3	14.6	15.8	.178	.168	.161	.158	.147
Total Families	.427	.369	.355	.365	.376	24.1	8.6	7.2	8.4	9.5	.174	.177	.139	.172	.167
White	.372	.357	.346	.355	.379	8.6	7.8	7.0	7.3	8.6	.172	.175	.177	.176	.169
Nonwhite[2]	.402	.414	.392	.411	.432	11.4	11.5	9.6	11.0	12.9	.179	.164	.168	.160	.157
Total Unrelated Individuals	.545	.491	.464	.427	.431	16.7	17.0	24.2	13.2	13.9	.116	.133	.148	.150	.149
White	.484	.487	.475	.429	.437	17.2	17.8	14.4	10.9	12.1	.135	.137	.138	.154	.154
Nonwhite	.475	.489	.470	.458	.469	12.0	11.5	13.7	28.6	16.5	.136	.136	.138	.143	.144
Total Husband-Wife Families	.430	.355	.367	.341	.352	11.9	8.2	8.0	6.7	7.5	.134	.174	.141	.175	.170
Wife in the Labor Force	.360	.294	.334	.290	.315	11.9	5.2	6.2	5.0	5.9	.151	.185	.153	.185	.175
Wife out of Labor Force	.417	.378	.396	.380	.383	10.8	8.7	11.2	9.2	8.8	.142	.172	.175	.155	.159
Males															
Male-Headed Families	.431	.395	.400	.374	.383	24.8	10.1	11.7	8.8	10.1	.137	.170	.172	.167	.164
Male Individuals	.520	.469	.468	.413	.423	78.3	17.4	19.3	12.9	15.0	.136	.149	.134	.156	.156
Females															
Female-Headed Families	.525	.434	.575	.405	.423	75.2	13.7	35.2	12.8	13.3	.115	.158	.195	.162	.154
Female Individuals	.567	.479	.480	.407	.420	90.0	16.3	21.4	10.6	11.8	.144	.133	.158	.150	.148

[1]The aggregates and totals were computed as a weighted average of the income-receiving-unit components.

[2]Nonwhites are not confined to blacks. Blacks were 95.5 percent of the nonwhite population in 1950, 94.3 percent in 1960, 89.6 percent in 1970, and 80.3 percent in 1985.

but increased dramatically between 1980 and 1985. This increase placed 1985 inequality below 1960 levels but above 1970 levels. The same general pattern held for both family and unrelated-individual income distributions; however, in both cases the decreases began in 1950. Although unrelated individuals had greater levels of inequality than families in each year, the post–1980 inequality increase was much greater for families. Thus, by 1985, income inequality differences between families and unrelated individuals had lessened greatly.

Income distribution changes contrast somewhat with inequality changes. In the aggregate, the top-to-bottom share ratio fell dramatically between 1950 and 1960, stayed relatively stable from 1960 to 1980, and increased from 1980 to 1985. This is consistent with an inequality pattern of decreasing inequality prior to 1980 and increases thereafter. Middle-quintile income fell continuously throughout the period, with the sharpest decline between 1980 and 1985.

Although unrelated-individual income was consistently more unequally distributed than family income, both had over-time changes that were inconsistent between each other and with the aggregate. The top-to-bottom share ratio dropped sharply for families between 1950 and 1960 and remained fairly constant thereafter. For unrelated individuals, the top-to-bottom ratio peaked in 1970. Middle-quintile income share was fairly stable for families (except 1970), with a slight downturn between 1980 and 1985, and was increasing for unrelated individuals until 1970, with stability thereafter.

White income-inequality changes mirrored aggregate income-receiving unit counterparts. Nonwhite inequality changes within units were more similar to patterns within the nonwhite races than to aggregate counterparts. This implies that race is a more dominant determinant of income distribution than income-receiving unit. For all nonwhite units, income inequality increased between 1950 and 1960 (with little change in the top-to-bottom ratio) and decreased between 1960 and 1970. The inequality ascent began in 1980 for nonwhite families and 1970 for nonwhite unrelated individuals. With only a few exceptions, top-to-bottom share ratios were fairly constant for nonwhite families and unrelated individuals. Middle-quintile income share steadily decreased for nonwhite families and (generally) remained constant for nonwhite unrelated individuals. For all measures and all receiving units, nonwhites consistently had more unequally distributed incomes than whites.[7]

Husband-wife families, particularly those with working wives, had the most equally distributed incomes of all income-receiving units. For both husband-wife family types, income inequality and top-to-bottom ratios decreased between 1950 and 1960 and between 1970 and 1980 and increased between 1960 and 1970 and between 1980 and 1985. Inequality in 1985 was above the 1960 levels. Middle-quintile income share fluctuated for both groups, with ultimate increases between 1950 and 1985.

The comparison of male and female families and unrelated individuals consistently showed more equally distributed income for male units, although over-time patterns were similar. Income inequality and top-to-bottom share ratios generally decreased between 1950 and 1960, remained constant until 1970 (with the exception of female-headed families), declined further between 1970 and 1980, and increased between 1980 and 1985. Middle-quintile income share ultimately increased for all units.

In sum, income inequality within all income-receiving units was lower in 1985 than 1950 but increased between 1980 and 1985. Inequality levels and over-time inequality change were not uniform between different income-receiving units, however. Families had (decreasingly) more equally distributed incomes than unrelated individuals. Males had more equally distributed incomes than females. Dual-earning husband-wife families had more equally distributed income than nonworking-wife families. Whites had (increasingly) more equally distributed income than nonwhites.

Poverty. One of the primary concerns that accompanies rising levels of ine-quality or an increasingly unequal income distribution is the "inequity" that exists with impoverishment. If poverty is viewed relatively,[8] high levels of poverty question the ability of the economic system since all individuals do not share in society's wealth. This is particularly troublesome if subgroups of the population represent a disproportionately high percentage of the poor.

Between 1960 and 1985, poverty rates for all units declined, with unrelated individuals and husband-wife families having the largest percent decrease (Table 2–2). Families consistently had less impoverishment than unrelated individuals, and male-headed units had less impoverishment than female-headed units. From 1960 to 1985, the proportion of poor who live in female-headed families grew tremendously. This feminization of poverty results from two factors. Between 1960 and 1985, female-headed families had the lowest percent decline in poverty rates (Table 2–2) and the largest growth in relative numbers (Table 2–1). These factors led to a 111-percent increase (from 18 to 38 percent) in the proportion of the poor in female-headed families from 1960 to 1985.[9]

The feminization of poverty contributed to the increasing impoverishment of children. Throughout most of the postwar period, the elderly were the most impoverished group. With increased government transfer payments to the elderly in the 1970s, their poverty rate declined. Concurrently, children's poverty rate increased. Today, children comprise the largest impoverished group primarily because they are caught in economically deprived female-headed families. These units receive less income aid than the elderly or their equivalent units in other countries.[10]

Even though an increasing proportion of children begin life in poverty, very few suffer impoverishment throughout their life.[11] Bane and Ellwood (1986) demonstrated that most poor are temporarily impoverished because the income of the household head fell. This income drop usually results from a transitory event such as unemployment, divorce, birth of a child, or establishment of a new household, and the reversal of the event results in exit from poverty. The transitional nature of poverty is not uniform across subpopulations. The sub-populations with greater poverty rates (nonwhites and female-headed families)

Table 2-2
Percentage of Income-Receiving Units Classified as In Poverty[1]

	1960	1970	1980	1985	Percent[3] Change
Aggregate[2]	22.2	12.6	13.0	14.0	-36.9
Total Families	20.7	11.0	10.3	11.4	-44.9
Total Unrelated Individuals	45.2	32.7	22.9	21.5	-52.4
Husband-Wife Family	15.4	7.1	6.2	6.7	-56.5
Males Male-Headed Families	-	-	11.0	12.9	-
Male Individuals	36.0	24.0	17.4	17.4	-51.7
Females Female-Headed Families	42.4	32.5	32.7	34.0	-19.8
Female Individuals	50.9	38.2	27.4	24.8	-51.3

[1]Poverty is defined as having money income below the poverty line (Orshansky, 1965). Consistent poverty definitions are not available for 1950. For 1960 and 1970 all male-headed households are classified under husband-wife families. Further disaggregation is not available.

[2]Aggregate and totals reflect a weighted average of income-receiving unit components.

[3]Computed as the difference over the period divided by the initial period (times 100).

also have increased probabilities of remaining poor.[12] That is, individuals in female-headed families and nonwhites have a higher chance of lifetime impoverishment than the typical indigent.

Including in-kind transfers in income raises some units out of poverty. By including food, housing, and medical transfers (costed out at market value) in income, poverty would be reduced by one-third. Alternatively, subtracting taxes paid from money income lowers some units into poverty. Although many impoverished units do not pay (personal income) taxes, inflation has eroded tax brackets such that a family of four with poverty-level income paid about ten percent of its earnings in income and payroll taxes in 1984.[13] This reduces their post-tax income below poverty levels. These alterations in poverty status created by taxes and in-kind transfers make the poverty line less precise; however, they do not alter general trends in over-time comparisons and composition of poverty.

Poverty-rate differences between units exist for three reasons: labor markets, demographics, and government policy.[14] Labor market conditions affect poverty rates only for income-receiving units with able-bodied workers—primarily nonelderly unrelated individuals, husband-wife families, and male-headed families. While able-bodied heads of poor households have demonstrated strong labor force attachment, their employment tends toward low-paying work or less than full-year, full-time employment. For these individuals a deteriorating labor market, with high unemployment and reduced real wages, increases poverty. The decreasing (or low) poverty rates from 1960 to the 1970s for income-receiving units with able-bodied workers, therefore, resulted from an expanding labor market. When the expanding economy slowed during and after the 1970s, poverty declined less rapidly for these units.[15] Wilson (1987) asserts that a declining job market is especially problematic for blacks. Since blacks are more likely than whites to face high levels of unemployment, to have unstable employment with low earnings, and to be employed less than full-time and full-year, a deteriorating labor market intensifies poverty-related problems for already marginal black workers.[16]

Changing demographics also altered poverty rates. Since unrelated individuals and female-headed families have the highest incident of poverty, their increasing proportion of the population increased aggregate levels of poverty. Since delayed marriage and remarriage and increased divorce created much of the increase in unrelated individuals and female-headed families, these demographic events increased poverty. Female-headed families resulting from divorce suffer declines in economic well-being with the loss of the major income source (husband income) and often fall into poverty. Remarriage is the most frequent path out of poverty for female-headed families since lost husband's income often cannot be replaced with labor market earnings without entailing child care expenses. Black women (and children), with higher divorce rates and lower remarriage rates than whites, are particularly hard hit by these trends.[17]

Government redistribution efforts also altered poverty rates. While increased government spending on the elderly (primarily Social Security) diminished their poverty rates, increased spending on the nonelderly poor was not as successful. During the postwar period, the federal government tried to eradicate (nonelderly) poverty through four types of social welfare and social insurance programs:[18] accelerated economic growth; human resource, human capital, and employment programs; social institution restructuring; and direct cash or in-kind support.[19]

The tax cut in 1964 exemplified accelerated economic growth attempts. While the tight labor market during the 1960s resulted in both economic growth and low levels of unemployment, its impact on poverty was limited in scope.[20] Economic growth had greater distributional impacts (and poverty reductions) for husband-wife families, male unrelated individuals, and nonwhites. To a large extent, female-headed income-receiving units and aged individuals were isolated from their "trickling down" benefits.

A myriad of human resource policies attempted to change the characteristics of the poor by closing the poor-nonpoor gap in work skills or by removing spatial discrepancies between the poor and jobs.[21] Most programs were targeted toward specific groups of disadvantaged workers. Success was mixed at best.

Social institution restructuring programs attempted to increase the poor's access to jobs, goods, and social services and were less concerned with the indigent's personal characteristics.[22] Equal employment opportunity legislation, housing policies, and medical and legal assistance attempted to provide a "middle class" culture to the poor. While some progams showed moderate success (e.g., employment) and others were failures (e.g., housing), the in-kind nature of the programs did not directly alter the income distribution.

Direct redistribution of income came from cash support to particular categories of poor people, primarily Aid to Families with Dependent Children (AFDC). While initially (1935) designed as a program to aid the transitional (widowed) female-headed family, the program evolved into a guaranteed income for all female-headed families with dependent children. Because close to ninety percent of AFDC cases have an absent father and a one-hundred percent implicit tax on earnings,[23] program critics argue that AFDC perpetuates dependency by providing payments to nonworking female-headed families.[24] The incentives to establish and maintain female-headed families increase poverty since female headship often leads to poverty. The implicit tax on earnings provides incentives to reduce or eliminate labor supply. Thus, labor market earnings and spousal income, the obvious income alternatives to governmental support, are less likely given AFDC incentive structures. Most studies find negative labor supply effects with AFDC, although no consensus exists as to the magnitude of the effects. No consensus exists on the role that AFDC plays in marital breakup.

Thus, results on poverty-reducing government interventions are mixed.[25] While the income (and in-kind) support moved some impoverished income-receiving units above poverty, the price—pecuniary incentives for dependency with resultant loss of autonomy—is high. Emerging consensus argues that government programs should increase work responsibility so that labor market earnings substitute for government transfer payments among the poor. Comprehensive reform packages, including increasing the minimum wage, establishing work incentives in AFDC, and providing for day care availability are currently being considered by Congress.

In sum, an expanding labor market prior to the 1970s reduced poverty among income-receiving units with able-bodied workers while increased government spending reduced poverty rates for the elderly. Increasing divorce and separation rates and decreasing remarriage rates increased the number of (impoverished) female-headed families and children in poverty while government spending on these groups had limited (at best) success at alleviating their poverty.

Over-Time Changes in Absolute Income Levels

Income inequality and distributional change cannot describe changes in the level of living without analysis of income levels. The preceding analysis showed that both relative and absolute levels of inequality and poverty changed during the postwar period. This section shows that absolute and relative levels of income also changed.

From 1950 to 1985, all income-receiving units increased real median income levels by fifty to one hundred percent (Table 2–3). Most of this increase came prior to 1970 with little change thereafter.[26] Unrelated individuals in the lowest quintile showed the largest percent income increase, probably due to increased Social Security benefits for the elderly.

There was little between-unit variation in top-quintile real income growth, although top-quintile nonwhite families had above-average income growth and top-quintile female-headed families had below-average income growth. Bottom-quintile growth was substantially greater than top or middle-quintile growth. Within middle and bottom quintiles, however, unrelated individuals (especially females) had disproportionately large income growth. This differential income growth between high-growth, low-income units and low-growth, high-income units reduced aggregate income inequality by decreasing between-group income dispersion. It also raised many units out of poverty.

In sum, between-group differences in income level, inequality, and poverty caused aggregate income inequality to alter with compositional change. Aggregate income inequality decreased with an increased proportion of (equally distributed) dual-earning, husband-wife families and with decreasing dispersion in between-unit income levels. Aggregate income inequality increased with an increased proportion of (unequally distributed) unrelated individuals and female-headed families. These compositional changes offset each other and produced little net change in aggregate inequality.

TRENDS IN INCOME-RECEIVING UNITS

Because of between-unit differences in income level, inequality, and distribution, over-time shifts in the composition of income-receiving units in the population cause shifts in the aggregate income distribution. Unfortunately, the analysis is not this straightforward since the factors that determine the composition of income-receiving units are intertwined with the income distribution.[27] Within the family, income is often jointly produced, shared, and redistributed, yet how families are structured is affected by the way incomes are produced and distributed. Thus, the way income is generated influences family formation and dissolution and family formation and dissolution influences income distribution. This section examines both over-time compositional changes in family and unrelated-individual income-receiving units and the reasons underlying the changes.

Families

Between 1950 and 1985, the percentage of families declined steadily, particularly from 1970 to 1980 (Table 2–4).[28] The more rapid decrease for whites led

Table 2–3
Trends in Absolute Median Income Levels for Quintiles

	Top Quintile						Middle Quintile						Lowest Quintile					
	1950[1]	1960	1970	1980	1985	Percent Change[3]	1950	1960	1970	1980	1985	Percent Change	1950	1960	1970	1980	1985	Percent Change
Aggregate[2]	–	–	–	–	–	–	11347	16088	23082	19993	21614	90.5	1453	1700	3954	4841	4999	244.0
White	–	–	–	–	–	–	13885	18633	23950	22604	22972	65.4	2606	3365	5490	5924	5763	121.1
Nonwhite	–	–	–	–	–	–	7059	9482	14365	13680	14760	109.1	1229	1627	3146	3242	3242	163.8
Total Families	32172	39297	54167	57858	63102	96.1	14832	20414	27336	27446	27735	87.0	3903	5922	7511	7942	8056	106.4
White	37012	44468	60556	71213	85000	129.7	15395	21195	28358	28596	29152	89.4	4217	6589	9807	9780	9231	118.9
Nonwhite	17861	28480	40197	47071	48465	171.3	8352	11733	18052	18072	18635	126.1	1620	2693	5151	4943	4429	173.4
Total Unrelated Individuals	15649	20247	25157	29642	32155	105.5	4670	6248	8691	10831	11808	152.8	893	1088	2328	2540	3437	284.9
White	16085	20657	27616	30316	34456	114.2	4983	6756	9095	11440	12249	145.8	925	1168	2558	3577	3731	303.4
Nonwhite	12340	15972	21689	21440	25459	106.3	3651	3879	6214	7552	8782	140.5	738	756	1639	2022	1999	170.9
Total Husband–Wife Families	32711	41104	55854	60787	72390	121.3	15516	21418	29129	30315	31100	100.4	4653	7006	10684	10351	11053	137.5
Wife in the Labor Force	32999	51491	57378	63455	73161	121.7	17967	25122	34005	35211	36431	102.8	6695	10165	16183	15308	15829	136.4
Wife out of Labor Force	32401	37252	50143	57127	61340	89.3	14871	20103	25772	24853	24556	65.1	4217	6135	8854	8041	8527	102.2
Males																		
Male-Headed Families	33564	35857	50907	57640	63551	89.4	13933	17694	24963	22950	22622	62.4	3295	4734	7233	7216	6584	99.8
Male Individuals	17716	23977	33079	34737	35039	97.8	6985	9033	12576	14330	14339	105.3	1179	1525	2881	2999	3544	200.6
Females																		
Female-Headed Families	22896	29387	33597	33852	38407	67.7	8579	10804	14108	13634	13660	59.2	1488	2264	4120	3674	3383	127.4
Female Individuals	13738	17259	21589	23302	27244	98.3	3882	5033	6878	8735	9865	154.1	759	923	2067	2375	3385	346.0

[1] All income in 1985 dollars. All medians were found through interpolation. The top quintile median is the income level associated with 10 percent of the population above the top quintile lower limit. The middle quintile median is the median income level of the total population. The lowest quintile median is the income level associated with the lowest 10 percent of the population.

[2] Aggregation at the open-ended income level makes accurate top quintile medians for "totals" difficult to measure accurately. Aggregate and totals reflect the weighted average of income-receiving unit components.

[3] Computed as the difference over the period divided by the initial period (times 100).

Table 2–4
Percentage of Income-Receiving Units, 1950–1985

	1950	1960	1970	1980	1985
Aggregate[1]	100	100	100	100	100
Total Families	81.2	80.7	77.0	69.0	67.0
White	81.8	81.4	77.6	69.3	67.0
Nonwhite [2]	73.4	74.3	73.6	66.9	66.7
Total Unrelated Individuals	18.8	19.3	23.0	31.0	33.0
White	18.2	18.6	22.4	30.7	33.0
Nonwhite	26.6	25.7	26.4	33.1	33.3
Total Husband-Wife Families	70.5	70.3	66.3	56.4	53.7
Wife in the Labor Force	16.8	21.3	26.0	28.3	29.0
Wife out of Labor Force	53.7	49.0	40.2	28.1	24.7
Males					
Male-Headed Families	2.5	2.1	1.9	2.2	2.5
Male Individuals	8.2	7.4	8.8	13.9	15.1
Females					
Female-Headed Families	8.2	8.2	8.8	10.4	10.4
Female Individuals	10.5	11.9	13.9	17.2	17.9

[1]Aggregate and totals reflect the weighted average of the income-receiving-unit components.

[2]Nonwhites are not confined to blacks.

to nearly equivalent proportions of family income-receiving units between the races by 1985. The declining percentage of families stemmed from reductions in husband-wife units with nonworking-wives—the percentage of dual-earning, husband-wife families actually increased over the period and the percentage of male-headed families remained fairly constant. Female-headed families increased from 8.2 to 10.4 percent of all units.[29] The compositional change from non-working-wife, husband-wife families to female-headed families resulted from demographic trends (lower marriage rates, higher divorce rates, fewer children), increased female labor force participation, and employment and policy altera-tions.[30]

Marriage rates declined from 13.9 to 10.5 per 1,000 individuals from 1947 to 1985 while divorce rates increased from 3.4 to 4.9 per 1,000.[31] Neither trend was linear. Marriage and divorce rates both reached a low of 8.4 and 2.1, respectively, in 1958, in part because of changes in population age-composition (e.g., a population with a large number of individuals under 18 and/or over 65 has very low marriage and divorce rates since these groups typically do not marry or divorce). Nonetheless, the time trend toward later marriage and increased divorce is well-documented.[32]

Over-time changes in the relative costs and benefits of family formation lead to changes in marriage and divorce rates and, hence, the proportion of husband-wife and female-headed families. The new home economics explains family formation using market and household production within an economic paradigm.[33] Families form when individuals gain more from household production of income and nonmarket goods and services than from individual efforts in the market and at home. Family gains are expected since the production-oriented household achieves specialization gains associated with division of labor in market and nonmarket production. To maximize (constrained) lifetime production of goods and services, an individual searches for a marital partner whose traits, in combination with his/her own, can best help to achieve this goal.[34] When the (marginal) cost of this search (e.g., time spent searching) exceeds the (marginal) benefit (e.g., household production), a husband-wife family is formed. Breakdown of this household (i.e., divorce) occurs as joint (household) gain disappears or when partners received flawed information during search and do not obtain bargained-for benefits.[35]

Within this paradigm, increased female labor force participation and decreased fertility contributed heavily to change in family formation. Increasing female employment in the labor market diminished household specialization since previous specialization gains stemmed from the wife's nonmarket work (e.g., fertility) and husband's market work. Increased female labor market worth increased the cost of home production (foregone labor market earnings) and decreased fertility lessened the need for home production. Diminished gains from household formation resulted in delayed marriage and increased divorce and, hence, a decreased proportion of husband-wife families, particularly nonworking-wife families.

The same forces, combined with employment shifts and changing government policies, increased the proportion of female-headed units.[36] Wilson (1987) argues that decreased manufacturing and blue-collar employment, increased (technical) service-sector employment, and the movement of jobs from central cities to suburban rings increased unemployment of disadvantaged workers. Since marriageable males are noninstitutionalized and working, shifting employment patterns increased the proportion of unemployed and out-of-the-labor-force men. This increased the proportion of females to marriageable males and, hence, decreased marriage and increased divorce. The result is increased female-headed units and decreased husband-wife households.

In a counterargument, Murray (1984) posits that decreased marriage incentives accompany increased government spending. Government programs increased the cost of marriage by providing benefits for female-headed families.[37] Because eligibility for many means-tested programs requires a household with children and no male, females responded by having children out of wedlock. The result is increased (low-income) female-headed units and decreased husband-wife families.

In sum, decreased gains from marriage resultant from increased female labor force participation, decreased childbearing, changing employment structures, and liberalization of government means-tested policies, reduced the relative number of husband-wife families and increased the relative number of female-headed units from 1950 to 1985.

Unrelated Individuals

These same forces also facilitated the dramatic growth in unrelated individuals—from about nineteen percent of all units in 1950 to thirty-three percent in 1985 (Table 2–4). This increase affected whites, nonwhites, males, and females, although the magnitude of the increase differed. The larger percent increase in white unrelated individuals over nonwhites led to a convergence in the proportion of unrelated individuals between the races. The two-percent differential favoring females over males existed in both 1947 and 1985, although the percentage of both male and female unrelated individuals increased over the period.

The percentage of unrelated individuals in a population fluctuates with a number of factors.[38] The proportion increases as people move from families into group quarters (e.g., dormitories and barracks), solitary living, or nonrelatives (roommates) living arrangements. Life-cycle events (e.g., entering school or military) and increased marital breakup (from either death or divorce), in absence of children, contribute to this movement. The proportion of unrelated individuals decreases with increases in marriage, out-of-wedlock childbirth, extended families, and death.

While unrelated individuals are a diverse group, about eighty-six percent are individuals living alone and the majority are young adults or elderly.[39] The propensity to live alone increased greatly for both young adults and the elderly over the period.[40] Rising income levels, particularly increased Social Security benefits for the elderly, were primarily responsible for increases in living alone. For young adults, a changing social climate—changes in privacy norms, dormitory rules, and tastes—facilitated growth in single unrelated individuals. Delayed marriage (from decreasing marital benefits) increased the number of young adult unrelated individuals. Since delayed marriage and earlier movement away from the parental home (the desire for "semiautonomy") increased more for males than females, males are a larger proportion of young unrelated individuals. Since increased longevity increased the number of elderly unrelated individuals and life expectancy is longer for females than males, elderly unrelated individuals are primarily women. Although both youth and elderly unrelated individuals generally have low income levels, the dramatic increase in their proportion indicates that the psychological benefits from living alone may outweigh the reduced level of living.

In sum, the percentage of unrelated individuals increased dramatically during the postwar period. Since most unrelated individuals live alone and are either young adults or elderly, rising personal income levels, changes in attitudes toward privacy and autonomy, and changing marriage, divorce, and life expectancy facilitated this increase.

SUMMARY

The composition of income-receiving units changed dramatically during the postwar period. Increasing divorce and decreasing marriage and remarriage rates decreased the relative number of nonworking-wife, husband-wife families and increased the relative number of female-headed families. Increased female labor force participation and decreased birth rates reduced household specialization gains and increased the proportion of dual-earning, husband-wife families. Concurrently, a reduced supply of "marriageable men" associated with a deteriorating labor market and increased government transfer programs, increased the benefits of female headship by reducing marriage gains for women. This decreased the proportion of husband-wife families and increased the proportion of (impoverished) female-headed families.

The proportion of unrelated individuals also increased over the period. These individuals generally live alone and fall into two categories, the elderly and young adults. For the elderly, increased income (Social Security) and life expectancy increased the propensity to live alone. For young adults, delayed marriage, earlier (parental) home leaving, and taste changes (including relaxing of dormitory rules) increased the proportion of unrelated individuals.

These compositional changes altered aggregate income inequality since income distributions of individual income-receiving units vary. Nonwhites, female-headed units, and unrelated individuals have higher rates of poverty and more unequal income distributions than whites, male-headed units, and families. Since low-income income-receiving units with relatively unequally distributed incomes increased in proportion, aggregate inequality potentially increased. This inequality increase was offset with relative increases in dual-earning, husband-wife families—the units with the most equally distributed incomes.

Between-unit changes in the income level also offset potential aggregate income inequality increases. Income-receiving units with the lowest initial income levels had the fastest income growth. Thus, poverty rates decreased. Decreased poverty did not affect all income-receiving units equally. While the tight labor market during the 1950s and 1960s decreased poverty levels for units with able-bodied workers (families and male-headed units) and increased Social Security payments decreased poverty for the elderly, neither a strong labor market nor government programs had a great poverty-reducing impact for female-headed units (and nonwhites). Although poverty in these units was reduced absolutely, nearly one-third of all female-headed families were poor in 1985 and an increasing proportion of the impoverished were female.

NOTES

1. The 1980 Census definition does not prerestrict gender in designating head of household where both adult males and females are present. The household head is either the designated adult male or female or designated as joint headship. The distinction between our (pre–1980) definition and the post–1980 definition does not alter the composition of our stratified income-receiving units.

2. A primary individual is a household head who lives alone or with unrelated persons. Although this definition is similar to the unrelated-individual definition, it does not include those living in group quarters. The U.S. Bureau of the Census (1983) gives a thorough description of all definitions.

3. Sahota (1978), Atkinson (1976), and Mincer (1970) summarize income distribution and varying labor market productivities.

4. Kuznets (1976) discusses definitions for income-receiving units based on income jointness while Danziger and Taussig (1979) link different units of analysis and economic welfare.

5. Family racial classification is based on the race of the head.

6. The insignificance of the income-receiving-unit variable in aggregate analysis is seen in Appendix 4. Treas and Walther (1978) and Bartlett and Poulton-Callahan (1982) support offsetting compositional changes during the 1950 to 1971 period. Racial disaggregation produces significant within-race inequality changes with compositional changes in income-receiving units (Chapter 7).

7. Changing racial composition within the nonwhite population ambiguously altered nonwhite income inequality (Reimers, 1984; Thurow, 1970).

8. Poverty is officially defined as having below-minimum income. Minimum income is based on a multiple of food expenditures adjusted for family size (Orshansky, 1965). Hagenaars and Vos (1988) discuss varying definitions and their impact on "poverty."

9. Fuchs (1986) discusses the feminization of poverty.

10. During the early 1970s, Social Security benefits expanded and became indexed for inflation and Medicare and Supplemental Security Income were introduced. This decreased poverty among the elderly (Danziger et al., 1984). Concurrently, impoverishment of children increased as divorce increased the number of low-income female-headed families. Easterlin (1987) discusses these compositional changes while Moynihan (1987), McLanahan (1985), and Nelson and Skidmore (1983) discuss impoverished children. Torrey and Smeeding (1988) compare aid to impoverished female-headed families across countries.

11. Duncan (1984) found that only 2.6 percent of the population was impoverished eight out of ten years, but 24.4 percent was poor for at least one year. Ruggles and Williams (1986) show that only eleven percent of the population had below-poverty-level annual incomes, but twenty-six percent of the population had below-poverty-level incomes in at least one month. Bane and Ellwood (1986) show that about forty-five percent of all poverty spells end within a year, seventy percent are over within three years, and only thirteen percent last longer than eight years.

12. Chapter 7, Smith and Welch (1987), and Danziger et al. (1986) discuss race and poverty. Danziger and Gottschalk (1986a) discuss the interaction of race and gender in poverty.

13. Sawhill (1988) and Paglin (1980) discuss the role of taxes while U.S. Bureau of

the Census (1987), Smeeding (1982), and Smeeding and Moon (1980) discuss the role of in-kind benefits.

14. See Sawhill (1988) for discussion.

15. Easterlin (1987) and Danziger and Gottschalk (1986b) examine the labor market-poverty relationship while Blank and Blinder (1986) discuss the economy-poverty relationship.

16. Ellwood and Summer (1986) discuss nonwhite-white poverty issues. Blacks and other nonwhites also face discrimination in labor, education, and housing markets that facilitates a poverty environment (Schiller, 1976).

17. Ross et al. (1987) discuss the relationship between income-receiving-unit compositional changes and poverty. Bane (1986) and Bradbury et al. (1979) discuss the role of marriage and divorce. Wilson and Neckerman (1986) discuss the marriage, remarriage, divorce, and poverty relationship for blacks.

18. Chapter 6 discusses the two types of programs.

19. Haveman (1977) elaborates on these attempts. During the postwar period, expenditure expansion of social welfare programs was greater under Republican presidents, with Eisenhower and Nixon each increasing spending about ten percent (Browning, 1988). The exception to this trend is Ronald Reagan, under whose administration welfare spending was reduced through the Omnibus Budget Reconciliation Act (OBRA) (Hutchens, 1984).

20. See Danziger and Gottschalk (1988c), Treas (1983), and Anderson (1964).

21. Examples of human resource policies include Manpower Development and Training Act (MDTA), JOBS, WIN, Job Corps, Neighborhood Youth Corps, Head Start, Upward Bound, the consolidating Comprehensive Employment and Training Act (CETA), and the most recent Jobs Training and Partnership Act (JTPA). Bassi and Ashenfelter (1986) discuss the success of human resource programs.

22. Wallace (1988) discusses the success of social restructuring.

23. Over-time and state variations exist. Some states adopted AFDC-UP, allowing participation with an unemployed male in the household. Few husband-wife households participate. From 1935 to 1967 the implicit earnings tax of AFDC was one-hundred percent. The 1967 Social Security Act amendment lowered the tax to sixty-seven percent; however, the enactment of OBRA again increased the tax to one-hundred percent (Garfinkel, 1988).

24. Kniesner et al. (1988) discuss the AFDC incentives to maintain impoverished female-headed families while Murray (1984) and a 1986 issue of the *Cato Journal* (Dorn, 1986) criticize the welfare system. Wilson (1987) and Greenstein (1985) provide direct counterarguments to Murray while Ellwood and Summers (1986) and Wilson and Neckerman (1986) support the welfare system. Cain and Wissoker (1987), Darity and Myers (1984), and Bradbury et al. (1979) refute the marital break-up incentives of AFDC. Danziger et al. (1981) review empirical studies on labor supply effects of AFDC.

25. Danziger and Gottschalk (1985) discuss poverty-reduction aspects to government programs while Darity and Myers (1987) discuss the high costs to participants. Handler (1988) advocates built-in work incentives in reform legislation. An age-old proposal, the Negative Income Tax, has been extensively evaluated, see Robins (1985) for a summary. Recent work-incentive programs are currently undergoing evaluation (see Blau and Robins, 1986; Friedlander et al., 1986; Levy and Michel, 1986a; Moffit, 1986). Danziger (1988) provides an excellent summary of interventionist welfare reform.

26. Levy (1987a), Levy and Michel (1986b), and Michel et al. (1984) support little

change in levels of living in the 1980s, although Levy and Michel note that young adults now face more binding income constraints than young adults did in the past.

27. Ben-Porath (1986) elaborates on the interrelationship between causes and consequences of family formation.

28. The absolute number of most receiving units increased over the period because of the age composition of the population and population growth (Sweet, 1984). Thus, although husband-wife families (for example) decreased in relative proportion, their absolute number increased.

29. This cross-sectional analysis understates the magnitude of the increase in female-headed families. Since female-headed families are a dynamic, transitional state, many women flow into and out of female-headed families; hence, many more experience this state than these numbers suggest. For a full discussion, see Ross and Sawhill (1975).

30. For an excellent summary of demographic changes and their effect on changes in the relative number of income-receiving units see Masnick and Bane (1980).

31. With the exception of marriage and divorce statistics, all statistics in this section are referenced in Appendix 3. Marriage and divorce statistics were obtained from the U.S. Bureau of the Census (1970, 1986a). Espenshade (1985) discusses these trends.

32. First marriage rate declines are much more dramatic than text statistics indicate since text statistics include second (and higher order) marriages. See Glick and Norton (1973) for elaboration.

33. Economic use of the term "household" in household production differs from the Census definition. Since the new home economics deals with jointness in consumption and production of "household" services and income, the more appropriate unit of analysis is the family. For consistency with this literature, however, the economic definition of household is used in this section. See Becker (1981) or Schultz (1974) for an elaboration of the new home economics.

34. Chapter 5 discusses the type of traits sought in a spouse.

35. Berk and Berk (1983) or McCrate (1988) provide critiques of the new home economics. England and Farkas (1986) and Ben-Porath (1980) expand the theory into within-family organization.

36. Ross and Sawhill (1975) discuss the relationship between increased female labor force participation, decreased fertility, and increased female-headed households while Slesinger (1980) discusses the particularly strong impacts of the economy and government on changing the composition of low-income households.

37. For a similar argument to Murray with differing policy conclusions see Moynihan (1987).

38. Masnick and Bane (1980), U.S. Bureau of the Census (1986a), and Kobrin (1976) discuss unrelated individuals. Unrelated individuals not living alone have boarders, lodgers, servants, or partners. Only a small percentage live in group quarters. The percentage of female unrelated individuals living alone exceeds males since more males live in group quarters (primarily military barracks).

39. Richards et al. (1987) discuss the relationship between age and unrelated individuals while Michael et al. (1980) discuss divorced and widowed unrelated individuals. These characteristics make unrelated individuals the most transitory income-receiving unit—irrespective of race (Farley and Hermalin, 1979)—with the median time of survival under two years (Richards et al., 1980).

40. Michael et al. (1980), Pampel (1983), Goldscheider and Waite (1986) and Kobrin (1976) discuss youth unrelated individuals and Masnick and Bane (1980) discuss elderly unrelated individuals.

3

Labor Demand Changes: Industrial and Occupational Employment Shifts

Both labor market earnings level and variance differ by industry and occupation of employment—even for full-year, full-time workers. Since industrial and occupational employment, relative earnings, and earnings dispersion shifted between 1950 and 1985, the aggregate income distribution fluctuated with sector changes.

While agriculture and service industries consistently had the lowest (mean) annual earnings between 1950 and 1980 (Table 3–1), industries with the highest earnings fluctuated. In 1950, the mining and finance industries had the highest earnings while, in 1980, mining, trade, and transportation (communication and public utilities) paid the highest earnings. The shifts in relative-earnings rankings result from differential earnings growth across industries. The 1980 high-earnings sectors all had above-average growth between 1950 and 1980. Although earnings growth in the service industry exceeded other sectors, it was not sufficient to raise the relative ranking. The large service-sector earnings growth did decrease dispersion in industrial earnings.

Greater over-time consistency exists in earnings rankings for occupations between 1950 and 1980 (Table 3–1). Professionals, managers, and craftworkers consistently had the highest earnings while service workers, farmers, and laborers consistently had the lowest earnings. Some compression in the occupational-earnings distribution occurred, with earnings growth slowest for professionals and managers and greatest for service workers and laborers. Offsetting this compression, farmers, with the lowest relative earnings in 1950, had the slowest earnings growth over the period.

Table 3-1
Annual Earnings, Unemployment Rate, and Unionization by Industry and Occupation

	Mean Annual Earnings[1]					Unemployment Rate[3]				Unionization[4]		
	1950	1960	1970	1980	Percent Change[2]	1950	1960	1970	1980	1959	1970	1980
Aggregate	13374	17217	23897	22959	71.7	6.0	5.7	4.8	7.1	31	22	23
Industry												
Agriculture	8639	8693	15293	13712	58.7	9.0	8.3	7.5	11.0	–	4	8
Mining	15256	22985	27625	30782	101.8	6.7	9.5	3.1	6.4	40	35	34
Manufacturing	13268	19445	24461	24336	83.4	6.2	6.2	5.6	8.5	49	37	36
Construction	13705	18883	26341	24386	77.9	12.2	13.5	9.7	14.1	58	38	34
Trade	12966	14396	22455	27231	110.0	6.0	5.9	5.3	7.4	10	11	11
Transportation, Communication, Public Utilities	13601	19797	25580	26153	92.3	4.7	4.6	3.2	4.9	54	50	51
Finance, Insurance, and Real Estate	15920	19117	24953	23872	49.9	2.2	2.4	2.8	3.4	13	4	5
Service	6613	13568	16217	22049	233.4	6.4	5.1	4.7	5.9	10	17	19
Public Administration	14081	19471	27592	24967	77.3	3.0	2.4	2.2	4.1	10	–	35
Occupation												
White Collar												
Professionals/Managers	21014	25979	32817	30144	43.4	–	1.6	1.8	2.5	–	8	17
Clerical/Sales	11462	11411	20188	19020	65.9	–	3.8	4.0	5.1	–	11	14
Blue Collar												
Craft	14943	20190	25630	24367	63.1	–	5.3	3.8	6.6	–	42	39
Operatives	10984	14363	19126	19109	74.0	–	–	–	–	–	45	42
Laborers	8582	11239	17473	17396	102.7	–	12.6	9.5	14.6	–	33	32
Service	6475	7950	1087	14780	128.3	–	5.8	5.3	7.9	–	10	15
Farm	8915	8327	13191	12410	39.2	–	4.0	4.0	6.9	–	3	2

[1]All earnings are in 1985 dollars. Earnings reflect year-round, full-time workers.

[2]Computed as the difference over the period divided by the initial period (times 100).

[3]Occupational unemployment rate data for 1950 are not available. Operative unemployment rates are available only in 1985. Unemployment rates reflect unemployment from industry or occupation of last job.

[4]Unionization represents the percentage of all workers with union membership. Unionization data exclude public-sector unionization for all years and, in 1950, exclude farm workers.

Earnings variance of year-round, full-time workers also differed by industry and occupation. Differential unemployment and unionization patterns across industries and occupations account for much of the differential earnings dispersion. High levels of unemployment reduce (annual) sector earnings and increase the relative dispersion of labor market income while high levels of unionization usually decrease earnings dispersion.

Between 1950 and 1980, the agriculture and construction industries consistently had the highest unemployment rates while transportation, finance, and the public sector had the lowest rates (Table 3–1). This lowered the relative earnings of agricultural and construction workers, raised the relative earnings of transportation, finance, and public-sector workers, and decreased industrial earnings dispersion. Since professionals and managers consistently had the lowest unemployment rates while laborers consistently had the highest unemployment rates, unemployment increased dispersion in occupational earnings. Clerical and sales workers, with low relative earnings, increased in relative-earnings rankings with below-average unemployment rates.

Since earnings level and dispersion differ by industry and occupation, employment shifts alter the income distribution. This is significant since the postwar United States saw industry shift from a manufacturing employment base to a combination manufacturing-service base. Occupational employment shifted from (unionized) blue-collar employment to low-skill white-collar and service employment.[1]

Employment shifts were only one over-time labor market change affecting earnings. Rapid postwar productivity growth slowed dramatically in the early 1970s and government regulation of the business environment increased. Since productivity is a strong wage determinant and varies by industry and occupation, declining productivity significantly altered income inequality and distribution over the period. Government regulation directly altered employment and earnings as legislation and judicial decisions encouraged employment, education, and higher earnings for low-wage workers.

INDUSTRIAL AND OCCUPATIONAL SHIFTS

Either changing output or changing employment can be used to measure a shifting industrial base. While the two measures are interlinked, direct comparisons may not correspond since employment is only one factor determining output level. Output changes reflect changing demand for goods and services while industrial employment changes reflect shifting (final) demand for the product *and* labor's relative productivity. For example, with capital-intensive technological advances, output and productivity may increase with employment decreases.

Changing industrial output levels are measured in the percentage of national income generated. National income, the sum of income originating in each industry, measures the totality of income generated in the economy. In the aggregate, all measures of economic productivity and national income showed initially rapid postwar growth and dramatic slowdowns in the post–1973 period. Annual national income grew about 3.7 percent a year from 1948 to 1973 and about 2.6 percent a year from 1973 to 1979. It *declined* .54 percent annually from 1979 to 1982, and grew 1.8 percent annually from 1982 to 1985.[2] In response, real hourly labor compensation in the nonfarm business sector rose steadily until 1973, declined from 1973 to 1976, rose until 1978, fell from 1978 until 1982, and then began a slow increase. This left real unit labor costs lower in 1986 than 1980.[3]

Relative industry importance in contribution to national income changed from 1950 to 1985. In 1950, the manufacturing sector generated 31.6 percent of national income while the service sector generated about nine percent.[4] Manufacturing's contribution to national income peaked in 1955 (32.6 percent) and declined steadily thereafter. By 1985, less than twenty-five percent of national income was generated in the manufacturing sector. Income produced by the agricultural and transportation sectors also declined steadily; however, neither sector's share ever exceeded much more than five percent of national income. The government, service, and finance sectors increased their relative contribution to national income over the period.[5] In 1950, each sector accounted for nine to ten percent of national income. By 1980, the government produced 14.3 percent of national income, the service sector produced 13.6 percent, and the finance sector produced 11.6 percent. The remaining industrial sectors held a constant percentage of national income.

Over-time employment shifts reflect industrial changes in national income contribution (Table 3–2). Between 1950 and 1980, relative employment declined in manufacturing, agriculture, and transportation and increased in the service, finance, and government sectors. While the employment and output trends are consistent, the relationship is not absolute. The manufacturing sector produced a larger percentage of income than the service sector in 1985, yet employment was about twenty percent in each.

Since industries require different production skills of workers, industrial and occupational employment are linked and occupational employment shifts accompany industrial employment shifts.[6] The manufacturing sector contains a high proportion of blue-collar workers and the service, finance, and government sectors contain a high proportion of (low-skill) white-collar and service workers. Thus, relative white-collar and service employment categorically increased over the period while blue-collar employment categorically decreased (Table 3–2).

Explanations for Labor Market Changes

Two major explanations delineate the forces underlying the employment shift from manufacturing to service. The first, the "law of industrial growth," focuses on productivity declines in aging (manufacturing) industries and relative productivity growth in new (service) industries. The second, employment progres-

Table 3–2
Percentage of Industrial and Occupational Employment, 1950–1980

	1950	1960	1970	1980[1]	Percent Change[2]
Total	100	100	100	100	–
Industry					
Agriculture	13.3	9.6	7.2	4.9	-63.2
Mining	2.1	1.2	1.0	1.5	-28.6
Manufacturing	29.9	29.0	28.3	25.9	13.4
Construction	9.0	8.2	9.7	10.6	17.8
Trade	17.6	18.9	18.7	19.4	9.3
Transportation, Communication, Public Utilities	9.4	8.7	8.2	8.0	-14.9
Finance, Insurance, Real Estate	2.6	3.9	4.0	4.2	61.5
Service	11.5	14.8	17.4	20.3	76.5
Public Administration	4.8	5.7	5.6	5.9	22.9
Occupation					
White Collar					
Professionals/ Managers	18.8	23.8	22.5	25.9	37.8
Clerical/Sales	18.2	21.6	23.0	24.8	36.3
Blue Collar					
Craft	15.0	13.0	11.4	12.4	-17.3
Operatives	21.4	17.7	16.2	14.1	-34.1
Laborers	6.6	4.6	5.9	4.6	-30.3
Service	10.3	12.7	15.4	15.0	45.6
Farm	9.7	6.4	5.0	2.2	-77.5

[1]Data are presented only through 1980 since 1985 industry data are not available and 1985 occupational data are inconsistent with previous years.

[2]Computed as the difference over the period divided by the initial period (times 100).

sion, focuses on the "natural" employment shifts from agriculture to manufacturing to service associated with economic development. A third (minor) explanation focuses on the supply side of the labor market with employment changes resulting from the influx of low-productivity workers who typically do not work in manufacturing (baby-boom youth and women).

Relative declines in manufacturing employment and output growth are consistent with the "law of industrial growth"—industries mature when major technology gains end. The demise of technological advancements slows cost reductions, market expansion, and sales growth and leaves older industries vulnerable to the competition of younger rivals with faster productivity growth.[7] To many pre-Keynesian writers, this implied that long-term growth entails the eclipse of older industries by younger industries. To many contemporary writers, the issue centers around the question of why and how industries mature.

One thesis on industry maturation, consistent with "the law," is a cyclic appraisal of structural change—the best known being Schumpeter's "creative destruction." Schumpeter (1942) argues that declining investment and the rise of big business are not retardants since competition and technological innovation provide unlimited profit and growth opportunities within capitalism. This unlimited economic growth, however, is contained within 50 to 55-year Kondratieff cycles. Apparent vanishing investment opportunities in older industries (e.g., manufacturing) are actually the troughs of these cycles. Since these troughs serve to purge the economy of outworn practices and inefficient firms, the resultant creative destruction sets the stage for the rise of new industries (e.g., service). These new industries then spur the next long upswing of the cycle. Within these Kondratieff cycles, limitless economic growth exists; however, since the trough produces much "pain" as resources move from the older to the new sector, political and cultural impediments arise to ease the trough's "pain." Ultimately, a political climate develops that facilitates regulations aiding those harmed by the trough. These regulations impede capitalism's flexibility, stop economic growth, and eventually lead to socialism.

Consistent with the creative destruction view of new industries eclipsing the old is the retardation of industry growth thesis. Because of a narrowing scope for technological breakthroughs in aging industries, a large number of industries show declining value added with age.[8] The shift of technology into new industries, however, is hindered in maturing societies because of "social arteriosclerosis" (antiquated labor and management practices and big business politics), "polyarchy" (government by interest-group pressure), or an affluent, consumption-oriented society lacking in investment. Current manifestations of these impediments include upheavals in the American labor movement in response to Kondratieff cycle troughs and corporate flight abroad in search of increased flexibility in production.[9]

Three current labor market trends are consistent with current employment shifts in the face of a Kondratieff trough.[10] First, productivity has declined recently and the growth rate of the capital-labor ratio has slowed. During the 1948–1973 period, relatively high rates of investment resulted in a yearly growth of three percent in the capital-labor ratio. After 1973, investment declined and the yearly capital-labor growth rate fell to less than two percent. This reduced the rate of productivity increase by up to .5 percentage points per year.

Second, consistent with Schumpeter's view of government intervention as reduction of the trough's "pain," government regulation increased.[11] The increased constraints from government regulation (and associated litigation) shifted the firm's resources away from production. Because equity, a clean environment, and safety (for example) are not included in national income accounting, productivity measures declined.

Third, the proportion of gross national product devoted to research and development (R&D) declined during the late 1960s and early 1970s. While private (industry) expenditures on R&D increased throughout this period, real government expenditures peaked in 1967, with defense (Vietnam war) and the space program the leading recipients.[12] Thus, R&D accounted for three percent of gross national product expenditures in 1964 and for 2.2 percent by 1978. Baily and Chakrabarti (1985) argue that the slowing of innovation associated with R&D declines caused much of the productivity slowdown.

The second major explanation for employment shifts from manufacturing to service focuses less on cyclic productivity change and more singularly on employment movement. The systematic employment progression from agriculture to manufacturing to service often accompanies economic development. With rising productivity and limited appetites, employment naturally shifts from agriculture to manufacturing.[13] An extension of the same natural employment progression exists from manufacturing to service.

The employment progression thesis argues that productivity change is not the impetus for employment and output shifts; rather, shifts from goods (i.e., manufacturing) toward services causes productivity decline.[14] Potential productivity growth is less in the service sector than in manufacturing, with its inherently lower capital-labor ratios and lesser innovation capability.[15] The question then becomes, "why does employment shift from manufacturing to service?" Explanations vary.[16]

Shelp (1981) and Stanback (1979) argue that the production of goods and services are complementary; hence, initial expansion in manufacturing spawned service-sector growth. Complementary examples include the reliance of the production and consumption of goods on the development of services (e.g., transportation, retail sales, and repair). Such complementarity precludes a completely service-based economy without trade for manufactured goods. This argument is consistent with relative employment declines in manufacturing as opposed to absolute declines.[17]

Employment shifts into services also followed from changes in demand for products. Since the income elasticity of demand for services generally exceeds the elasticity for goods, increased income stimulates the demand for services faster than the demand for goods. Thus, as real incomes of Americans increased in the postwar period, the relative demand for services increased. In response, the relative price (and output) of services increased and the service sector increased employment. Since most government and nonprofit businesses provide services, increasing income levels also increased demand (and ultimately quantity supplied and employment) in these areas.[18]

The third (supply-side) explanation for shifting employment from manufacturing to service and declining productivity is compositional changes of the labor force. The entrance of the baby boom and females into the labor force led to an expansion in the proportion of inexperienced workers traditionally employed in the service sector. Since output per worker-hour is low among inexperienced workers, productivity fell. Darby (1984) argues that adjusting productivity for these demographic alterations eliminates any decline in technical progress while Urquhart (1984) argues that women's entrance into the labor force accounted for the majority of the increase in service-sector employment.

Other Labor Market Alterations

Industrial and occupational output and employment shifts are only one labor market alteration since World War II.[19] On the demand side of the labor market, the internal structure of firms changed with technological advancements and increased competition, while employee associations faced diminished employment and wage-setting power with declining unionization. On the supply side, the labor market became more female (Chapter 5), more educated, and younger (Chapter 4). Government intervention in labor market functions increased dramatically.

On the demand side, the firm's internal employment and wage structures and production processes continued their historical economic transformation with the evolution of a new internal production process in the 1970s and 1980s.[20] During the nineteenth century, wage labor became the dominant manner of organizing production. At the beginning of this century, factory owners used mechanization to control productivity and the pace of production. From the 1920s onward, owners fragmented the labor market to prevent a unified (and unionized) workforce. As competition increased during the 1970s and 1980s with increasingly international markets and deregulation, segmented labor markets began to decay and the internal production processes changed.[21]

"Sunrise" firms—those located in the emerging sector of the economy (e.g., service)—developed new internal structures based on professionalization and paraprofessionalization. These new internal processes reflect restructured mobility modules with worker movement occupationally oriented rather than firm-oriented. This decreases worker attachment to firms (and increases attachment to occupations), upgrades worker skill requirements, and elicits teamwork from employees.[22]

Changes also occurred in "sunset" firms—those located in the declining sector of the economy (e.g., manufacturing).[23] The mass-production model that built postwar prosperity used special-purpose (product-specific) machines and semi-skilled workers to produce standard goods. Increased competition threatened this inflexible production technique and flexible specialization emerged. This new technology, always existent in the craft sector, allows output flexibility with computer software adaptable to a multitude of environments. The result is constant reshaping of production components for tailored output in differing markets and economic climates.

Decreased unionization accompanied the internal restructuring of firms. While thirty-six percent of the nonagricultural labor force was unionized in 1954, the steady decline (accelerated in the late 1970s) left less than one-fifth of the nonagricultural labor force unionized by 1985. Counter to this trend, union formation increased in the public sector. Because the (declining) transportation and manufacturing industries and the (declining) blue-collar occupations had higher levels of unionization, employment shifts are associated with the unions' decline.[24]

On the supply side of the labor market, the labor force composition changed dramatically. Labor force participation increased for females (Chapter 5) and decreased for (older) men. The increasing proportion of females in the labor market coincided with industrial and occupational employment shifts. Analysis of labor flows among industries shows that employment into the service industry came predominately from new women labor market entrants and from two major occupations: managerial and professional workers, and sales, clerical, and service workers.[25] The increase in (low-wage) sales, clerical, and service employment facilitated women's continued employment in female-typed jobs. High-wage, male-dominated occupations, often located in manufacturing, had very little (female) employment increase (e.g., craft, operatives) or had stagnant or declining employment over the period. Thus, female employment in low-wage industrial and occupational sectors continued since their entrance coincided with growth in low-wage "female" employment.

Supply-side changes also occurred as occupational employment and internal structures of firms increased the demand for educated workers. Human capital theory shows that individuals undertake additional schooling as long as the present value of the benefits exceeds the present value of the costs (alternatively, if the rate of return to education exceeds alternative investments).[26] In the early 1960s, the increasing demand for professionals and managers increased the private (and social) rates of return to college education, the college-to-high-school earnings ratio, and the percentage of high-school graduates enrolled in college. By the mid–1970s, however, the supply of college graduates outstripped the demand and the returns to college education, college-to-high-school earnings ratio, and college enrollments (lagging behind economic reward changes) declined. This excess of supply over demand caused underemployment for college graduates and increased unemployment for educated workers.[27]

Government intervention in labor market processes increased dramatically from 1947 to 1985. Prior to 1960, legislation restricted only (minimum) wages and the union-management relationship. During the 1960s, real gross national product rose for nine straight years, inflation averaged below two percent annually, and unemployment rates were at "full employment." This prosperous economy facilitated desires to help the less fortunate members of society and the government enacted or expanded much labor market legislation to increase opportunities for the disadvantaged. This legislation directly constrained the firm's decisionmaking process.

The Civil Rights Act of 1964 initiated a series of government policies restricting a firm's hiring decisions by requiring more equal treatment of women and minorities. The Coal Mine Health and Safety Act (1969) and the Occupational Safety and Health Act (1970) further restricted a firm's production by requiring adoption of safety features. Firms' pension plans were scrutinized for proper funding under the Employee Retirement Income Security Act (1978) and minimum wage coverage continually expanded. Pollution and environmental concerns resulted in environmental regulations constraining waste disposal. Many labor market policies contracted in scope, with downturns in the late 1970s and early 1980s.[28]

Harrison and Bluestone (1988) argue that changing industrial employment, corporate restructuring, and government policy caused U-turns in positive labor market outcomes for workers. The primary response of firms to increased competition and the increased costs from the welfare state was to "zap labor" to reduce labor expenses. The response mechanisms dramatically altered internal employment and wage structures, including increased use of outsourcing (subcontracting), union-avoidance, two-tiered wage systems, and part-time contingent work schedules.

Employment changes also contributed to rising unemployment levels after the late 1960s.[29] As manufacturing employment declined and production-oriented skills became obsolete, workers trained in these areas found decreased demand for their services. Unemployment increased as plants closed and workers were laid off in manufacturing and production-oriented areas. With decreased demand for their services, reemployment was often slow and accompanied by wage loss.[30]

RELATIONSHIP BETWEEN EARNINGS, PRODUCTIVITY, AND EMPLOYMENT

Since labor market income depends on both labor supplied and hourly wage, alteration in either changes the income distribution. Since productivity and industrial and occupational structures both determine wages and employment, this section examines the link between wage determination, productivity, and labor market employment structures. Labor supply variations are discussed in the following three chapters.[31]

Two predominant explanations for wage determination exist: marginal productivity and structural theories. While marginal productivity theory focuses on the link between wages and productivity of the marginal (i.e., last-hired) worker, structural wage determination focuses on industry or occupation of employment as the key wage determinant.[32]

Marginal Productivity Theory

Marginal productivity theory focuses on marginal revenue product as a key determinant of labor demand and wage.[33] The firm hires labor until the cost of hiring the last worker (marginal factor cost) equals the additional revenue obtained from the worker's output (marginal revenue product). With the competitive market determining the marginal factor cost of hiring and the demand for the final product (i.e., marginal revenue), wage determination is based on individual productivity. Productivity and wages increase as (complementary) capital, technology, or human capital increases.[34] Productivity declines, therefore, lead to wage declines. Since labor productivity levels and growth are generally greater in manufacturing than services, shifting industrial employment increases low-wage workers by decreasing productivity.

Structural Theories

Structural theories posit that strong mobility barriers prevent outcomes associated with a competitive labor market—market clearing and productivity-determined wages and employment.[35] These barriers systematically exclude workers from a given market[36] and balkanize or segment markets, particularly along occupation and industry.[37]

At least two occupationally distinct labor markets exist.[38] The "primary" labor market consists of good jobs with high wages, employment stability, good working conditions, a high degree of unionization, chances for promotion, and equity and due process in employment.[39] The "secondary" labor market consists of bad jobs with low pay, no promotion opportunity, little job security, high turnover, and arbitrary management.

Industrially distinct labor markets also exist.[40] The core sector of the economy contains firms with political and economic power, high profit margins, capital intensity, monopoly elements, and unionization. These characteristics allow firms to raise wages above competitive levels. The periphery sector contains firms with low profit margins, extensive labor usage, and competitive product markets. Firms in this sector lack assets, size, and productivity potential, and cannot take advantage of economies of scale, research and development, or increased wages to attract quality workers.

Empirical classifications of segmented labor markets consistently place most manufacturing firms in the core sector and service firms in the periphery sector.[41] Skilled blue-collar occupations are located in the (high-wage) primary segment and low-skilled service occupations are in the (low-wage) secondary segment. A movement from manufacturing to service employment, therefore, increases (low-wage) periphery employment and decreases (high-wage) core employment. Since wages accompany industrial and occupational sector, the shifting economic base produces a shift from high-wage to low-wage employment.

Role of Unions

Unions are often "credited" with increasing the wages of their members and changing aggregate wage levels and dispersion.[42] By changing aggregate wages and dispersion, unions influenced wage inequality in five ways. First, unions decreased the dispersion of blue-collar workers by standardizing within-firm wages. Second, unions decreased blue-collar wage dispersion between unionized firms by establishing common wage scales. Third, unions altered differentials between white-collar and blue-collar wages, with ambiguous results.[43] Fourth, unions unambiguously increased the union-nonunion wage differential. While studies suggest the union-nonunion differential was nearly thirty percent during the 1970s, time-series estimates place the differential at ten to fifteen percent.[44] Fifth, increased union density (i.e., percentage organized) polarized the income distribution.

On balance, unionism reduced the overall dispersion of wages in the labor market by about three percent. This inequality reduction held across cities and industries.[45] Thus, changing employment patterns increased wage inequality directly by reducing union strength and indirectly with less unionization in new employment.

INDUSTRIAL AND OCCUPATIONAL CHANGES AND INCOME DISTRIBUTION

Although many labor market alterations occurred between 1947 and 1985, this section focuses on industrial and occupational employment shifts on the demand side and their relationship to income distribution. The major labor supply and government effects are held constant with our estimation technique and are discussed in Chapters 4 (baby boom), 5 (females), and 6 (government). While other demand influences—declining productivity and unionization—undoubtedly altered the income distribution, their impact is captured through changing employment patterns. Since statistical restrictions dictate brevity in variable selection, and industrial and occupational employment shifts encompass many of the demand-side labor market changes, this section focuses only on employment change.[46]

A general pattern of decreasing, increasing, and decreasing income inequality for workers exists between 1950 and 1980 (Table 3–3). For workers, the decline in income inequality between 1970 and 1980 did not offset the 1960 to 1970 increase. The top-to-bottom share ratio increased from 1950 to 1970 and fell between 1970 and 1980 to about halfway between its 1960 to 1970 level. These changes indicate potential polarization of workers' income beginning in 1960. Middle-quintile income share fluctuated between .13 and .16 and peaked in 1970, the year of the largest spread in the top-to-bottom income share. Thus, all measures show increased inequality for workers after 1970.

Blue-collar occupations and the mining industry consistently had the most equally distributed incomes between 1950 and 1980, perhaps because of heavy unionization (Table 3–3). Clerical/sales occupations and the government sector also had relatively equal income distributions in 1950 and 1960. By 1970 and 1980, professional/managerial workers and the transportation/communication/public utility and manufacturing sectors increased in their relative equality. Service workers and the service sector consistently had the most unequal income distribution. These between-sector differences in income distribution suggest that

Table 3–3
Industrial and Occupational Trends in Income Inequality and Distribution

	Gini Coefficient				Top Quintile Income Share / Lowest Quintile Income Share				Middle Quintile Income Share			
	1950	1960	1970	1980[1]	1950	1960	1970	1980	1950	1960	1970	1980
Aggregate[2]	**.461**	**.426**	**.504**	**.481**	**19.2**	**22.3**	**41.3**	**30.0**	**.155**	**.128**	**.162**	**.137**
Industry												
Agriculture	.552	.525	.613	.568	91.6	28.6	72.3	17.0	.078	.129	.092	.096
Mining	.330	.353	.348	.356	8.7	8.7	7.6	8.5	.227	.172	.142	.173
Manufacturing	.459	.383	.396	.393	21.1	14.3	12.0	11.9	.163	.150	.161	.166
Construction	.434	.355	.446	.420	18.8	10.5	22.1	17.2	.144	.146	.143	.158
Trade	.470	.491	.544	.531	19.9	21.8	62.2	29.7	.152	.117	.111	.119
Transportation, Communication, Public Utilities	.425	.399	.392	.376	9.7	8.7	13.8	11.3	.132	.151	.170	.181
Finance, Insurance, Real Estate	.469	.437	.469	.479	24.0	12.9	23.0	18.3	.156	.140	.148	.110
Service	.506	.498	.561	.510	73.6	52.5	67.3	42.4	.114	.162	.107	.136
Public Administration	.374	.346	.436	.396	11.2	7.0	20.5	19.8	.118	.182	.152	.182
Occupation												
White Collar												
Professionals/Managers	.505	.456	.456	.437	32.4	20.9	23.3	16.3	.112	.179	.108	.148
Clerical/Sales	.400	.414	.584	.460	15.7	19.8	84.6	25.1	.200	.198	.100	.161
Blue Collar												
Craft	.345	.367	.371	.358	8.4	7.2	10.1	9.0	.198	.144	.144	.180
Operatives	.358	.370	.416	.397	13.5	8.6	16.6	14.5	.211	.168	.173	.165
Laborers	.457	.435	.526	.493	11.1	15.6	108.4	36.0	.162	.164	.110	.139
Service	.566	.498	.577	.508	81.1	25.0	129.3	35.1	.129	.141	.114	.128
Farm	.516	.512	.636	.585	82.4	25.9	206.0	64.0	.141	.135	.074	.103

[1] Data are presented only through 1980 since 1985 industry data are not available and 1985 occupational data are inconsistent with previous years. Table includes only full-time, full-year workers.

[2] Aggregate and totals reflect a weighted average of industry (or occupational) components.

over-time shifts in employment increased aggregate inequality since employment increased in sectors with consistently unequal income distributions.

Table 3–4 shows the results of the multivariate analysis. Results represent estimation of equation 1–1 and are reported in the form of regression coefficients and elasticities. An elasticity represents the percent increase in income inequality (or quintile share) accompanying a one-percent change in the ratio of service-to-manufacturing employment (industry) or the ratio of blue-collar to white-collar workers (occupation). Thus, elasticities allow direct comparisons of the estimated reltaionship between industrial and occupational employment for each income-receiving unit.[47]

In the aggregate, industrial employment shifts increased income inequality with increases in the top-quintile income share and decreases in the second and lowest-quintile income share. Since neither the fourth or middle-quintile share altered significantly with industrial employment shifts, middle-class income is significantly reduced only for the lower middle class. This confirms suggested income polarization found in Table 3–3. Occupational employment shifts did not alter income inequality or share distribution in the aggregate. Occupational shifts did, however, influence within-unit income inequality and distribution.

The insignificance of occupational employment shifts on aggregate income inequality and the significance for specific income-receiving units suggests within income-receiving unit composition changes.[48] Since few women work in blue-collar occupations, relative blue-collar employment declines mainly affected employment probabilities of men, particularly low-wage earning men. With a lower employment probability, the number of "marriageable men" fell and the proportion of female-headed income-receiving units and unrelated individuals increased as the proportion of husband-wife families decreased.[49] Thus, while aggregate income inequality did not directly alter with occupational shifts, the composition of individual income-receiving units changed, which increased inequality. Compositional shifts also occurred as job displacement increased unemployment and lowered earnings of male heads of households. This drew females into the labor market. The increase in "additional workers" increased the proportion of dual-earning, husband-wife families and decreased inequality with compositional changes. These compositional effects associated with employment shifts may be offsetting and produce the insignificant aggregate occupational influence, but alter individual income-receiving units by changing the type of individual in the unit.

For families, industrial employment shifts increased inequality by lowering the second-quintile income share (lower middle-class income). Occupational employment shifts increased family income inequality by reducing (lower) middle-class income and increasing the top-quintile income share.

For unrelated individuals, industrial employment shifts increased income inequality by polarizing income (i.e., reduced lowest-quintile income share and increased top-quintile share) with no significant impact on middle-class income. While occupational employment shifts had the same distributional impacts for

Table 3–4
Industrial and Occupational Influences on Income Inequality and Distribution: Elasticities[1]

	Gini Coefficient	Top Quintile	Fourth Quintile	Middle Quintile	Second Quintile	Lowest Quintile
Industry						
Aggregate[2]	.490****	.466**	-.175	-.406	-.656***	-.988***
Total Families	.315**	.077	.485	-.115	-.695***	-1.16
Total Individuals	.368***	.400**	-.319	-.085	-.401	-3.23****
Husband-Wife Families	.276*	.113	.175	.140	-.621	-.643**
Wife in Labor Force	.434*	.119	.392	-.096	-.334	-1.03***
Wife out of Labor Force	.189	.049	.502	-.283	-.586**	-.337
Male-Headed Families	.358**	.128	.621	-.420	-.789**	-1.13****
Male Individuals	.258**	.310*	-.152	-.386	-.099	-1.94***
Female-Headed Families	.231	.225	.039	.172	-.889**	-1.08*
Female Individuals	.363***	.232**	.262	-.426	-.634*	-2.69****
Occupation						
Total	.283	.088	.190	-.338	-.435	-.025
Total Families	.452*	.595*	-.534	-.187	-.727*	-1.71
Total Individuals	.211	.501*	-.729	.004	.082	-3.54**
Husband-Wife Families	.663**	.728*	-.413	-.714	-.572	-.607
Wife in Labor Force	.589	.580	-.686	.168	-.416	-.800
Wife out of Labor Force	.513**	.616*	-.573	-.373	-.634	-.411
Male-Headed Families	-.194	.113	-.267	.042	-.008	.044
Male Individuals	-.146	.062	-.012	-.290	.454	-.847
Female-Headed Families	.025	.200	-.082	-.180	-.567	-.444
Female Individuals	.271	.481**	-.521	.250	-.975	-2.56**

[1]Elasticities reflect the percent change (at the mean) in the Gini coefficient or quintile income share associated with a one-percent change (at the mean) in the industry ratio (service employment/manufacturing employment) or occupation ratio (blue-collar employment/white-collar employment). Computations are based on regression results presented in Appendix Tables A4-1 to A4-6.

[2]Aggregate and totals reflect a weighted average of income-receiving units.

**** $p \leq .001$
*** $p \leq .01$
** $p \leq .05$
* $p \leq .10$

families and unrelated individuals, inequality (as measured by the Gini coefficient) is not altered significantly.[50]

The distributional impact of industrial and occupational employment shifts differed between husband-wife families with working and nonworking wives. For dual-earning families, industrial employment shifts increased inequality by reducing the lowest-quintile income share. Occupational employment shifts had no impact on income inequality or distribution for dual-earning, husband-wife families, however. For nonworking-wife families, industrial employment shifts reduced the second-quintile income share (i.e., lower middle class) while occupational employment shifts increased the top-quintile income share.

The income distribution of male-headed families and male unrelated individuals did not alter with occupational employment shifts; however, industrial employment shifts increased inequality with reductions in the lowest-quintile income share. For male-headed families, industrial employment shifts also decreased the second-quintile income share.

For female-headed income-receiving units, industrial employment shifts reduced the income share of the lowest and second quintiles. For female unrelated individuals, the top-quintile gained income share. Changing occupational employment did not alter income inequality or share distribution for female-headed families; however, it polarized income for female unrelated individuals.

In sum, relative shifts from manufacturing and blue-collar employment increased income inequality and altered the income distribution. Both industrial and occupational employment changes polarized income for female unrelated individuals while industrial changes polarized the income distribution for male unrelated individuals. Changing industrial employment reduced (lower) middle-class income share for husband-wife families with nonworking wives and male and female-headed families. For dual-earning, husband-wife families and male and female families, industrial changes reduced the lowest-quintile income share. For families without a working wife, employment changes polarized the income distribution.

Why Have Employment Shifts Increased Income Inequality?

While the correlation between changing employment patterns and increased income inequality is well-documented, no consensus exists as to whether the impact is: (1) large and the major source of increased inequality or small and dominated by other, primarily demographic forces (i.e., the result of labor demand or labor supply forces) or (2) the result of increased income polarization or decreased middle-class income.[51]

This study intensifies discussion of these issues. Although employment changes uniformly increased income inequality through income polarization (particularly after 1960), distributional changes varied in magnitude and significance depending on the income-receiving unit and type of employment shift under analysis.

Industrial employment shifts altered aggregate income inequality and distribution more than occupational employment shifts. Counteracting forces, however, may have offset aggregate occupation influences. Increased inequality resulted from (1) highly unionized blue-collar employment shifting to largely nonunionized white-collar employment, (2) high-earnings growth occupations having the highest unemployment rates,[52] and (3) compositional effects associated with an increased proportion of (unequally distributed) female-headed families and female unrelated individuals resulting from unemployment-induced reductions in marriageable men. Two forces offset the potential increased aggregate inequality. First, an overall compression of occupational earnings occurred as service workers had the fastest earnings growth over the period and professionals and managers had slow earnings growth. Second, some compositional changes equalized the aggregate income distribution. As unemployment of household heads increased with occupational employment shifts, spouses entered the labor force (additional worker hypothesis). Thus, husband-wife family structure shifted from nonworking to working wives. This equalized the income distribution since dual-earning families have the most equally distributed incomes.

Industrial changes have no such counteracting forces. Increased competition and reduced unionization, both associated with shifting industrial employment, increased wage dispersion.[53] The movement of employment from a more concentrated manufacturing sector to a competitive service sector unambiguously increased the number of low-wage workers. This increased inequality with decreased income share for workers at the bottom of the distribution. Since unionization in manufacturing exceeds unionization in service, and unions decrease income inequality, industrial employment shifts, causing declining unionization, increased wage inequality.[54]

CONCLUSION

The repercussions from current industrial and occupational employment shifts are heavily debated. In the long run, decreased productivity, increased service-sector employment, and slowed economic growth resulted from creative destruction in the (mature) manufacturing sector or the natural (employment) progression of capitalism from an agricultural to manufacturing to service base. Creative destruction theories predict the economy regains growth at the upturn of the Kondratieff cycle. Natural progression theory predictions are uncertain since upturns depend on the potential for technological innovation and productivity growth in the service sector. In the short run, both analyses predict increases in "pain" (unemployment and lower wages) as the economy goes through the transition.

Increased inequality may result from this pain. While consensus exists that current employment changes increase income inequality, the magnitude of the effects, the distributional nature of the alteration (middle-class decline vs. income polarization), and the long-run predictions are less certain. Much of this confusion results from magnitude and distributional differences between income-receiving units and between industrial and occupational employment changes. Thus, the measured impact of employment changes will differ depending on the unit of analysis (e.g., worker, family, individual) or the specification of the change (e.g., industry or occupation changes).

While employment changes consistently increased inequality, industrial employment shifts exerted a stronger impact than occupational shifts. Increased inequality for families resulted from declines in (lower) middle-class income while increased inequality for unrelated individuals and individual family units stemmed from income polarization. While many of these changes are consistent with structural (demand-emphasis) models of earnings determination, further research is needed to uncover the underpinnings of these findings.

NOTES

1. Blue-collar employment includes craft workers, operatives, and laborers. White-collar employment includes professionals, managers, and clerical and sales workers. Service and farm workers are the remaining categories.

2. Unless stated otherwise, 1948 to 1982 growth figures are from Denison (1985) and post–1982 figures are from Fulco (1986).

3. In the late 1960s and 1970s declining productivity caused a larger decline in profit than in wages (Wolff, 1986). Reversal in profit levels may have occurred, however, with decreased labor costs in the 1980s.

4. Industry income distribution data are from Craves et al. (1980).

5. The financial sector also includes insurance and real estate.

6. For example, the manufacturing sector employs a smaller percentage of service workers and a larger percentage of operatives than does the service sector. While some occupations operate almost exclusively in a particular industry (e.g., farmers in the farming industry and skip operators in the steel industry), others span all industries (e.g., secretaries and janitors).

7. Alderfer and Michl (1942) discuss the law of industrial growth in more detail.

8. Kuznets (1930) shows the relationship between declines in industrial value and age.

9. Kindleberger (1980, 1974) discusses social arteriosclerosis, Olson (1982) discusses polyarchy, Thurow (1980) discusses a consumption-oriented society. Gorden et al. (1982) discuss the Kondratieff trough and unionization and Bluestone and Harrison (1982) discuss current corporate flight.

10. Mansfield et al. (1980) and Denison (1985) provide an overview of aggregate growth, Kendrick and Vaccara (1980) discuss sector growth, and Christensen et al. (1982) measure productivity decline.

11. Policy measures advocated for relief of the trough's economic stagnation include laissez faire, a comprehensive industrial policy (AFL-CIO, 1984), and flexible exchange rates (Lawrence, 1984a). Schumpeter advocates a laissez-faire policy to enhance long-term economic growth, while those emphasizing short-term growth advocate some type of government intervention. An industrial policy dismisses traditional macroeconomic

stimulation in favor of social and economic tools easing the worker's transition from manufacturing sector employment to unemployment or reemployment in the service sector. Alternatively, flexible exchange rates (and appropriate monetary and fiscal policy) provide stagnation relief from recent aggregate demand slowdowns, supply shocks, anti-inflationary policy residuals, and trade deficits. The former policy prescription emphasizes low productivity in unemployment among displaced workers while the latter emphasizes stagnation from macroeconomic conditions (cf., *Fortune,* 1987).

12. Mansfield et al. (1980) discuss government expenditures on R&D.

13. See Singelmann (1978), Colin (1940), or Fisher (1935) for agriculture to manufacturing employment shift explanations. The same argument is made with respect to manufacturing but with a slightly different conclusion. Heilbroner (1966) argues that increased technology, supplying increasing amounts of goods and services, steadily increases the average level of well-being and gradually brings to an end the effective stimulus for markets.

14. Productivity differences between the sectors may facilitate service-sector growth (Fuchs, 1981, 1968). With rapid productivity increases in the manufacturing sector in the postwar U.S., fewer workers produced an equivalent amount of manufactured goods (Lawrence, 1984a). In the service sector, however, productivity increases were slower (Mark, 1982) and the increased demand for services can be met only with increased employment.

15. Nordhaus (1972) discusses general restrictions on productivity growth in the service sector while Grossman and Fuchs (1973), for example, discuss the limited role of sector shifts in productivity declines, with only a small proportion of the manufacturing sector having steady output and employment declines (e.g., steel). The latter argument is consistent with relative shifts toward services, not absolute shifts (Kutscher and Personick, 1986). With nonexistent absolute manufacturing declines, service-sector growth potential was not responsible for recent productivity slowdowns (Kutscher and Mark, 1983).

16. Norton (1986) provides a summary and discussion of "natural" flow while Singelmann (1978) provides disagreement.

17. See Kutscher and Personick (1986).

18. See Mirvis and Hackett (1983).

19. Freeman et al. (1980) outline many of these changes.

20. See Gorden et al. (1980) for an historical analysis and Bluestone and Harrison (1982) for recent changes.

21. This upskilling and teamwork approach contrasts to the traditional view of segmented labor markets in which mechanization produced downskilling and isolation of workers (cf., Braverman 1974).

22. Noyelle (1987) outlines these changes. Pfeffer and Baron (1988) document decreased worker attachment to firms, Mangum et al. (1985) report changing levels of worker attachment and skill levels with differential sectorial response. Tilly et al. (1986) document decreased worker attachment associated with increases in involuntary part-time and part-year work schedules. Not all researchers agree with the changes (cf., Mellor and Parks, 1988).

23. See Piore and Sabel (1984).

24. Hirsch and Addison (1986), Goldfield (1987), and Freeman and Medoff (1984) discuss declining unionization. Goldfield (1987) argues that most of the decline results from employer opposition and government policy favoring employers. Hirsch and Addison (1986) adopt a monopoly model of unionization and argue that union success depends

on (declining) highly concentrated, capital-intensive, or regulated industries. Freeman and Medoff (1984) adopt a more institutional (voice/response) model showing favorable societal outcomes of unionization but negative firm outcomes. Supply-side factors also contributed to unions' decline. Females and college-educated traditionally are not union members and their increasing presence in the labor market may have facilitated the unions' decline.

25. Urquhart (1984) elaborates on the flows of employment between the sectors, Sheets et al. (1987) analyzes growth in the service sector, and Blau and Ferber (1987) discuss female employment.

26. This discussion focuses on the production side of education and ignores the vast consumption benefits accruing to both educated individuals and societies. Much of the returns-to-education analysis comes from Freeman (1980a,b, 1977, 1976a,b).

27. Although these aggregate trends do not represent all fields of study, individuals entering occupational submarkets responded to the same demand-supply forces. See Howe (1988) for elaboration.

28. Murray (1984) elaborates on the expansion of government's role in the labor market while Freeman et al. (1980) discuss firms' response in personnel practices.

29. While changing demographics and unemployment insurance account for some of the unemployment increase, changing world market conditions, particularly increased oil and natural resource prices, and worldwide unemployment increases indicate that changes in aggregate demand for labor are primarily responsible (Freeman et al., 1980).

30. Researchers have attempted to quantify the cost of involuntary job loss associated with employment and productivity shifts. Studies show that displacement costs are higher for females than males (Madden, 1987; Maxwell and D'Amico, 1986) and for older workers (D'Amico and Golon, 1986; Shapiro and Sandell, 1985; Levy and Michel, 1985). Numerous studies provide general estimates of the costs of displacement (Maxwell, 1989a; Podgursky and Swaim, 1987; Devens, 1986; Flaim and Sehgal, 1985; Martin, 1983; Blau and Kahn, 1981; Gordus et al., 1981). Madden (1988) provides a linkage of the studies by outlining measurement differences underlying varying results.

31. Most variation in labor supply exists across age (Chapter 4), gender (Chapter 5), and race (Chapter 7).

32. One major distinction between the two theories is the degree to which labor demand or labor supply dominates wage determination. In general, marginal productivity theorists place more weight on the supply side since individuals can increase their productivity, and hence wages, by investing in human capital (Becker, 1975). Thus, the distribution of labor market income is primarily determined by choices individuals make in the human capital market (see Sahota, 1978; Atkinson, 1976; or Mincer, 1970 for reviews). Alternatively, structural theorists argue that the demand side dominates the wage determination process. Since productivity resides in the job and not the individual, wage determination is contingent upon placement in the employment queue for productive jobs (Thurow, 1975). The distribution of labor market income is then determined by the industrial and occupational employment mix since wages are tied to a particular job and individuals queue up for the jobs.

33. Theorists usually invoke the simplifying assumptions of profit-maximizing firms, competitive markets, and market-clearing outcomes. While some relaxation of the assumptions yields the same results, many structural theorists argue that the invalid assumptions relegate productivity to a minor determinant of wages.

34. This assumes that relative factor prices and supply-side shifts in productivity are

constant. Technology and other productivity changes have a two-ringed effect on labor demand. Productivity increases allow firms to produce a given level of output with fewer laborers while lowering product prices. Lowered prices increase sales and the demand for workers. Mark and Waldorf (1983) find that, between 1948 and 1981, forty percent of the increase in labor productivity was due to an increased capital-labor ratio while sixty percent was due to technological advances.

35. The market-clearing assumption is increasingly under attack. Many researchers now argue that firms increase wages above market-clearing levels to increase efficiency. This increased (efficiency) wage prevents shirking and turnover and attracts a better quality worker. Akerlof and Yellen (1986) and Dickens and Lang (1988) provide discussion.

36. Most economists recognize mobility barriers; however, competitive models posit relatively porous barriers that new workers (given enough time to retrain, relocate, etc.) can easily permeate. Structural models posit a variety of impermeable barriers. Internal labor markets reward seniority by "hiring from within" or by paying efficiency wages. Discrimination excludes members of a certain race, sex, age, or socioeconomic status from competing for jobs. Labor market "rules," imposed by government (e.g., occupational licensing) or unions (e.g., union hiring halls), prevent open entrance into certain labor markets.

37. Cain (1976) provides a thorough discussion and critique of these theories. Proponents argue that these theories developed as a response to persistent poverty and unemployment among certain disadvantaged groups. As such, critics often overextend their premises (cf., Hodson and Kaufman, 1982 or Wachter, 1974), particularly with respect to the emphasis on barrier immobility (Doeringer, 1986).

38. Doeringer and Piore (1971) discuss fully the characteristics and outcomes of the primary and secondary labor market. Some theorists propose a three-layer occupational tier (cf., Piore, 1975).

39. Because productivity adheres to the primary labor market job and not to the individual, workers require much training after hiring. To obtain trainable workers, employers devise an employment queue ranking and screening applicants on potential trainability (Thurow, 1975). Screens (e.g., education, race, gender, age, background) proxy for (unobservable) trainability and systematically prevent primary labor market employment for some groups. The extent to which these "trainability proxies" serve as screens or actually increase productivity is heavily debated (see Wolpin, 1977; or Stiglitz, 1975). Chapter 7 discusses race screens within a segmented labor market.

40. Industry divisions arise because of the capitalist's interest in maintaining control over workers (cf., Edwards, 1979; Braverman, 1974; Baron and Sweezy, 1966), industry survival with declining average costs (Bluestone, 1970; Averitt, 1968), or cost minimization in a bureaucratic firm (Berger and Piore, 1980).

41. See Zucker and Rosenstein (1981) for a review. These theories lack explanation for hybrid firms (Bluestone and Stevenson, 1981)—firms without the core sector-primary job and periphery sector-secondary job linkage.

42. A union's ability to raise wages, without employment loss, increases with an elastic demand for labor. Because changes during the 1970s increased elasticity of labor demand, union power declined considerably and real wages fell. Four "laws" govern this elasticity (Hicks, 1966).

First, labor demand is more elastic the smaller the price elasticity of demand for the final product. Increased wages cannot be successfully passed on to consumers. As competition from abroad increased and deregulation increased internal competition, consumers gained product substitutes and increased their response to wage-induced price increases. This reduced unions' potential for achieving wage gains (Kaufman and Stephan, 1987; Freeman and Medoff, 1981) and lessened the probability that all major producers in the industry were organized. With a smaller percentage of firms organized, more low-priced substitutes existed for consumers and union strength declined further.

Second, labor demand is more elastic as labor's share of total production costs increases. If increased wages dramatically increase total production costs, managers are more likely to oppose increases. Since most service-sector firms are more labor intensive than manufacturing firms, the shifting employment base erodes unions' power.

Third, labor demand is more elastic the greater the substitution for labor since firms can easily replace high-wage workers with substitutes. Since workers in low-skill, white-collar positions are more easily replaced by other workers than their skilled counterparts, occupational employment shifts toward increased low-skilled and white-collar employment negates some of the unions' power.

Finally, labor demand is more elastic the greater the elasticity of competing factors. This also increases the ability to substitute for high-wage laborers. With increased female labor force participation, the labor market entrance of the baby boom, and historically high unemployment rates, firms have increased ability to substitute for higher-wage workers.

43. Although the white-collar/blue-collar wage differential compressed during the 1970s, Freeman (1980c) found no support for the role of unions.

44. See, for example, Freeman and Medoff (1984), Moore and Raisain (1983), or Ashenfelter (1978) for cross-sectional estimates and Lewis (1986) or Pencavel and Hartsog (1984) for time-series estimates.

45. See Rubin (1988) or Freeman and Medoff (1984) for an overall discussion, Hyclack (1979) for an intercity analysis, and Hirsch (1982) for an interindustry analysis.

46. With limited years of data, the multivariate model only has 37 degrees of freedom and, therefore, can only support a limited number of independent variables without greatly increasing the probability of estimating chance correlations. That is, as the number of independent variables approaches the number of years of data, very large multiple correlations can be obtained with random fluctuations. For an elaboration, see Blalock (1979).

47. Elasticity comparisons between quintiles are more difficult since small income shifts represent a large proportion of the lowest-quintile income share and a small percentage of the top-quintile income share.

48. These within income-receiving unit composition changes are consistent with Blackburn and Bloom (1987).

49. See Wilson (1987) or Chapter 7 for an elaboration.

50. Since the same Gini coefficient underlies differing income distributions, the lack of significance between the Gini coefficient and changing employment is not inconsistent with significant changes in the income distribution.

51. McMahon and Tschetter (1986), Bell and Freeman (1986), and Harrington and Levinson (1985) estimate large demand-side influences while Shackett and Slottje (1987), Rosenthal (1985), and Lawrence (1984b) find small demand-side effects and large supply-side effects. Loveman and Tilly (1988) provide an excellent summary of the debate. The cause of income polarization and middle-class decline within the demand-side effects is also debated. Income polarization results from technological changes (cf., Leontief, 1983), increased competition from low-wage workers abroad causing corporate flight, increased unemployment and increased discouraged workers (cf., Bluestone and Harrison,

1982), or a service sector with heavy concentrations of better-than-average and poorer-than-average jobs (cf., Stanback, 1979). Researchers attribute the middle-class decline to trade imbalances and resultant dislocation of middle-wage earners from employment (cf., Harrison et al., 1986 or Thurow, 1984), replacement of mid-level jobs with capital (cf., Kuttner, 1983), or increased low-wage employment accompanying service-sector expansion (cf., Harrington and Levinson, 1985; Stanback, 1979).

52. Because increasing the percentage of workers working a full year increases the income share of the lower three quintiles and decreases the income share of the top quintile (Plotnick, 1982), increased unemployment (i.e., decreased full-year workers) reduced income share at the bottom and income polarization resulted.

53. Weiss (1966), Hodson (1978), and Beck et al. (1978) outline the relationship between industry concentration and wages while D'Amico and Daymont (1982) and Daymont (1980a) introduce the role of unions.

54. Davidson and Reich (1988) find increasing inequality over time associated with increased wage differentials between the high-wage and low-wage industrial sectors while Eberts and Groshen (1988) find initial wage differences between industrial sectors but equivalent earnings growth rates.

4

Labor Supply Changes: Population Age Structure

The preceding chapter focused almost exclusively on labor demand changes and income inequality and distribution. The next two chapters examine labor supply influences—the increase in the size of the labor force associated with changes in the population age structure (this chapter) and increased female labor force participation (Chapter 5).

Income varies dramatically with age, since age variation in both labor supply and income exists (Table 4–1). From 1950 to 1985, mean yearly income increased with age through age 64. These "age effects" show that those aged 16 to 19 and over 64 had relatively low income levels throughout the period. This is due, in part, to lower labor force participation rates (i.e., less labor supplied). Because of school attendance, only about half of all those aged 16 to 19 are in the labor market. For individuals over 64, retirement produces their lower-than-average participation probability and yearly income.

Changes in both age-related relative income and participation probabilities occurred over the period. These "period effects" are greatest for individuals over 64, with retirees having the largest percent increase in income and percent decrease in participation (both due to increasing Social Security benefits—Chapter 6). Participation probabilities increased most for (female) individuals age 25 to 44 (Chapter 5). Youth (16 to 19) had fewer over-time changes in both income and participation probability than other age groups. Their initially low relative income and participation rate and lesser over-time change further decreased their relative income over the period.

These age differences in income produce distributional changes with a changing population age structure. A population heavily weighted with the ends of

Table 4-1
Income and Labor Force Participation Changes by Age, 1950–1985

	Mean Yearly Income[1]					Percent Change[2]	Labor Force Participation Rate					Percent Change
	1950	1960	1970	1980	1985		1950	1960	1970	1980	1985	
Total	**8827**	**13254**	**14495**	**14407**	**15192**	**72.1**	**59.9**	**60.2**	**61.3**	**63.8**	**64.8**	**8.2**
16-19	2267	2497	3336	3230	2798	23.4	53.8	49.5	51.3	56.6	54.5	1.3
20-24	6241	8825	10110	9783	8822	41.4	67.7	68.3	72.2	77.2	78.5	16.0
25-44	10198	16354	18242	17486	18205	78.5	66.0	68.3	71.9	80.0	82.8	25.2
45-64	10348	15680	18682	18446	19347	87.0	62.2	67.3	68.4	65.6	65.9	5.9
65+	5280	7277	8919	9977	11451	116.9	26.7	20.9	17.0	12.5	10.8	-59.6

[1]Income is in 1985 dollars. Table includes all individuals 16 and over.

[2]Computed as the difference over the period divided by the initial period (times 100).

Table 4–2
Trends in the Age Structure of the Population[1]

	1950	1960	Percent 1970	1980	1985	Maximum Change from 1950 Percent[2]	Final Year
Total	100	100	100	100	100	–	–
15–19	5.2	7.4	13.2	11.6	9.9	153.8	1970
20–24	10.7	9.2	11.4	12.1	10.8	–14.0	1970
25–44	42.2	37.6	33.2	36.8	40.3	–21.3	1970
45–54	7.1	8.0	15.7	12.9	12.3	121.1	1970
55–64	12.9	13.2	13.6	12.5	11.3	–12.4	1985
65+	11.5	14.7	13.4	14.2	14.8	28.9	1985

[1]All individuals 15 years of age and older are included in the analysis.

[2]Computed as the difference between the initial and the final year divided by the initial period (times 100).

the age distribution will have a high degree of income inequality since these ages have a disproportionately large number of low (or zero) income individuals. All else equal, this increases income dispersion and inequality. Conversely, a population heavily weighted with working-age individuals will have less income inequality. Since period effects are examined in later chapters (primarily Chapters 5 and 6), this chapter examines only age effects on income inequality and distribution. Because some of the age effects are exaggerated by the cohort effects associated with the baby boom, the interaction between the age distribution and the aging baby boom is discussed.

TRENDS IN POPULATION AGE STRUCTURE

In a country with little in or out migration, life expectancy and fertility patterns determine the population's age structure. From 1947 to 1985, life expectancy at all ages increased and fertility fluctuated dramatically. These changes, particularly fertility fluctuations, continually altered the population's age structure and the nonworking proportion of the population (those under 18 and over 64) dependent upon workers (those aged 18 to 64). While increases in both dependent young and elderly alter the income distribution through their low (or zero) earnings, most youth eventually become productive earners while the aged continue their dependency.

The U.S. population's age structure changed dramatically from 1950 to 1985 (Table 4–2). The largest percent change in an age category came from birth fluctuations. This is seen in the large increase (153 percent) in those aged 15 to 19 between 1950 and 1970. Increased life expectancy increased the percentage of elderly (65 and older) by about thirty percent from 1950 to 1985. These relative increases in the percentage of youth and elderly meant relative declines in the percentage of "middle-aged" (20 to 64) population. These changes in the population's age structure altered the relative dependency of the population. The increased youth and elderly and decreased working-age population increased the relative proportion of nonworking population during the period. Because fertility patterns were not linear, this increased dependency was not permanent. With low incomes for individuals in the dependent population, dependency fluctuations, associated with fluctuating fertility and increased life expectancy, altered income inequality and distribution.[1]

Fluctuating Fertility

The number of births in a population depends on two factors: the number of women of childbearing age and the rate at which these women bear children. Both factors combined to produce the large cyclic fluctuations in births following World War II.

The most pronounced increase in births from 1947 to 1985 was the baby boom—individuals born from 1946 to 1964.[2] Four factors created increased births during this period. First, more women born in the 1920s and 1930s (potential baby-boom mothers) married than in previous birth cohorts. Although an increasing proportion of women had married for several decades, potential baby-boom mothers had historically high marriage rates, with over ninety-five percent marrying.

Second, once married, fewer women remained childless. Again, cohorts of potential baby-boom mothers historically altered demographic rates with only seven to nine percent of women not bearing children. Third, baby-boom mothers had children at younger ages. This increased the number of children born and overlapping childbearing, as preceding cohorts had not yet completed childbearing. Fourth, fertility rates increased. Although the total fertility rate had fallen for generations, it increased from 2.49 in 1945 to 3.09 in 1950 and reached a maximum of 3.71 in 1959.[3] Fertility rates increased in virtually all population subgroups and was not confined to groups with traditionally high birth rates.[4]

In 1960, coinciding with the authorization of the oral birth control pill (June 1960) and introduction of the intrauterine device (late 1960s), the total fertility rate began to fall. It exceeded the population replacement rate (2.2) until 1971— the beginning of the "baby bust" (the dearth of births during the late 1960s and 1970s). Because baby-boom women delayed marriage and childbearing, birth rates declined and the proportion of childless women once again increased.[5] In 1977, however, the *number* of births began to increase as the large number of (baby-boom) women entered childbearing age. Although birth rates are still at historic lows, the baby-boom women are producing an "echo boom"—a large cohort of baby-boom children.

Various reasons exist for fluctuating fertility rates. Richard Easterlin (1980) relates fluctuating fertility rates to immigration. Since immigration restrictions create favorable labor market conditions (i.e., high wages and low unemployment) when labor is scarce, a small birth cohort receives higher-than-anticipated earnings. In response, they have larger families. Although Easterlin's theory is empirically consistent with increased fertility associated with the baby boom (baby-boom parents were raised in the Depression, hence, their adult wages afforded a lifestyle better than adolescent memories) and with the low birth rates of the baby boomers (the large cohort produced low labor market wages contrasting with affluence in adolescence), it predicts an unlikely upturn of rates for the baby-bust cohort.

Butz and Ward (1979a), with an alternative cyclic theory, posit increased fertility with increases in husband's income and reduced fertility with increases in wife's income. Increased husband's income increases the couple's ability to afford children (income effect) while increased wife's income increases the (opportunity) cost of a child (substitution effect). The baby boom, therefore, resulted from postwar affluence increasing husband's income and low female labor force participation rates, creating little opportunity cost to childbearing. The baby bust resulted from increased female labor force participation, increasing the cost of childbearing, and decreased real wages associated with the baby-boom labor market entrance.

The "new home economics" places these fertility, income, and substitution effects into the economic demand and supply paradigm.[6] Because modern contraception yields a high degree of fertility control (timing and the number of births), the demand for children dominates the childbearing decisionmaking process.[7] The demand for child services is a positive function of income and a negative function of the price of children. The price of a child increases with increased opportunity cost[8] or quality of the child services. As the cost of children continues to increase with increased female labor force participation, the new home economics and Butz and Ward (1979b) predict continued low birth rates.

Changing Mortality

Mortality change in the post–1940 period falls into three characteristic periods: 1940 to 1954, 1954 to 1968, and 1968 to the present.[9] The introduction of antibiotic drugs in the 1930s, and their diffusion during the 1940s, began a steep decline in (age-adjusted) death rates associated with decreases in infectious diseases. The declines were highest at the youngest ages and lowest at the oldest ages. From 1954 to 1968, with infectious disease incidence at fairly low levels, mortality rates remained constant at all ages except those under fifteen. During this period, declining mortality at young ages slowed and mortality rates of males above fifteen increased.[10] In the post–1968 period, a new mortality decline began. Unlike the earlier decline, decreased cardiovascular disease decreased mortality at older ages. Infant mortality continued its decline at a pace equivalent to the earlier period.

With declining (age-adjusted) mortality rates, life expectancy increased throughout the postwar period (66.8 in 1947 to 74.6 in 1985).[11] Although decreased (age-adjusted) mortality rates increased life expectancy, much of the decrease stemmed from infant mortality (32.2 in 1947 to 11.2 in 1983). These reductions primarily increased dependency at younger ages (at least initially).

Both mortality trends (decreased infant mortality) and fluctuating fertility rates created postwar demographic changes that (initially) increased youth dependency more than old-age dependency. The increased youth dependency is significant since youth had smaller income increases over the period than other age categories and, hence, are losing ground in relative income comparisons.

DEPENDENCY AND INCOME DISTRIBUTION

The implicit relationship between the population age structure and income inequality and distribution is through the age-income relationship. Since the young and old both have below-average income levels, *individual* income inequality increases as the proportion of youth and elderly rise. Since the elderly are often separate income-receiving units, inequality based on income-receiving units will also increase. Dependent youth, however, are often subsumed within other income-receiving units, hence, their impact on income-receiving unit inequality is more indirect.[12]

A population weighted with children (under 18) represents a population with a high proportion of low-income income-receiving units.[13] Families with children have younger heads than families without children. Since earnings are correlated with age, a population heavily weighted with children indicates a population with a high proportion of workers in their "early career" with relatively low (lifetime) earnings. Second, the presence of (young) children reduces the probability of a woman's full-time employment.[14] Among husband-wife families, the increased presence of children lowers the proportion of dual-earner families and increases the relative proportion of (lower-income) single-earning families. Third, the presence of children in nonintact families dramatically increases the unit's probability of poverty and, hence, increases the proportion of low-income units in the population.

Thus, an increase in the relative proportion of the nonworking population (children and elderly) increases income inequality. The increasing presence of elderly directly increases the proportion of low-income receiving units while the presence of youth indirectly indicates a population more heavily weighted with low-income units.

Age-related income inequality and share distribution changed from 1950 to 1985 (Table 4–3). For all individuals over age 15, income inequality decreased dramatically over the period (panel 1). Individual age breakdowns reveal that the young and old consistently had the most unequally distributed incomes,

Table 4–3
Individual Income Inequality and Distribution: Age Trends[1]

	Gini Coefficient					Top Quintile Income Share / Lowest Quintile Income Share					Middle Quintile Income Share				
	1950	1960	1970	1980	1985	1950	1960	1970	1980	1985	1950	1960	1970	1980	1985
Aggregate[2]	.673	.542	.580	.517	.468	246.4	109.4	237.9	45.6	40.2	.048	.136	.110	.131	.143
15-19	.576	.698	.633	.515	.501	65.2	99.0	97.9	27.6	23.8	.043	.043	.034	.103	.123
20-24	.451	.514	.513	.448	.434	47.6	66.3	105.2	25.8	21.4	.164	.138	.130	.160	.161
25-44	.636	.468	.546	.469	.396	58.0	27.5	255.0	33.1	29.5	.073	.115	.146	.148	.176
45-54	.698	.511	.533	.505	.435	95.6	30.4	234.4	40.5	40.8	.044	.147	.132	.132	.161
55-64	.703	.539	.549	.518	.468	322.4	106.6	187.4	47.4	40.2	.037	.094	.132	.128	.143
65+	.724	.601	.527	.437	.402	416.7	109.2	36.3	13.4	10.3	.048	.112	.132	.135	.143

[1] All individuals 15 years of age and older are included in the analysis.

[2] "Aggregate" reflects a weighted average of individual age categories.

although the distributions became more equal throughout the period. The prime working-age population (20 to 54) had the most equally distributed incomes.

Because the baby-boom cohort intensified age differences throughout the period, aggregate inequality fluctuates as the baby boom ages. For persons over 15, aggregate inequality declined from 1950 to 1960—the years prior to the baby-boom cohort reaching age 15. As the baby boom entered the unequally distributed 15 to 19 age category in 1960, aggregate inequality rose. Aggregate inequality fell as the baby boom became a part of the more equally distributed working-age population.

The top-to-bottom share ratio (panel 2) fell dramatically over the period, indicating an overall reduction in individual inequality. The ratio was six times greater in 1950 than 1985. The ratio, however, retained the cyclic pattern associated with income inequality. Consistent with over-time inequality declines, the middle-quintile income share (panel 3) generally increased over the period (within the cyclic pattern). Although these share distribution patterns are generally consistent within all age subgroups, the patterns are strongest for individuals aged 55 to 64 and 65 + . Thus, the strength of the general decrease in inequality over the period (particularly top-to-bottom movement of income), resulted from equalization of the older population's income distribution.

Table 4–4 shows results of the multivariate estimation of the relationship between dependency (the ratio of the population aged 18 and under and over 64 to the population aged 18 to 64) and income inequality and share distribution. Results are presented in the aggregate and by income-receiving unit. In the aggregate, for families and for unrelated individuals, an increasingly dependent population increased income inequality with increases in the top-quintile income share and decreases in the second (for unrelated individuals) or lowest (for families) quintile share. Consistent with increases in the proportion of low-income, elderly units, the effects were stronger for unrelated individuals than families.

The same patterns held for husband-wife families. As the proportion of the nonworking-age population increased, income inequality increased with income shifting from the bottom two quintiles to the top quintile. Consistent with reduced female labor supply with the presence of children, these effects were stronger for families with women in the labor force than for families without working women.

For male-headed income-receiving units, the relationship between dependency and income distribution differed for families and unrelated individuals. Although increased dependency did not significantly alter income inequality for male-headed families (at least as measured by the Gini coefficient), it reduced the income share of the bottom two quintiles.[15] For male unrelated individuals, increased dependency increased income inequality with share increases to the top quintile and decreases to the bottom and middle quintiles.

The dependency and income distribution relationship was consistently stronger for female income-receiving units than their male counterparts. For females,

Table 4-4

Age-Related Influences on Income Inequality and Distribution: Elasticities[1]

	Gini Coefficient	Top Quintile	Fourth Quintile	Middle Quintile	Second Quintile	Lowest Quintile
Aggregate[2]	.466****	.336**	.054	-.329	-.816****	-.976****
Total Families	.375***	.389**	-.019	-.347	-.702*****	-.738
Total Individuals	.418*****	.599*****	-.570**	-.136	.052	-5.49****
Husband-Wife Families	.471***	.492**	-.222	-.235	-.765***	-.594***
Wife in Labor Force	.824*****	.838***	-.677	-.490	-.390	-.821***
Wife out of Labor Force	.234*	.366**	-.188	-.326	-.426*	-.451*
Male-Headed Families	.184	.261	.026	-.181	-.656**	-.641**
Male Individuals	.284**	.465***	-.205	-.599***	-.363	-2.43*****
Female-Headed Families	.268	.429	-.113	-.297	-.758**	-1.12**
Female Individuals	.513*****	.549****	-.215	-.094	-.686**	-5.49****

[1]Elasticities reflect the percent change (at the mean) in the Gini coefficient or quintile income share associated with a one-percent change (at the mean) in the dependency ratio (number of individuals under 18 and over 64/number of individuals between 18 and 64), times 100. Computations are based on regression results presented in Appendix Tables A4-1 to A4-6.

[2]Aggregate and totals reflect a weighted average of income-receiving units.

**** p $\leq$ .001
*** p $\leq$ .01
** p $\leq$ .05
* p $\leq$ .10

however, inequality increased with share reductions in the second and bottom quintiles, not the middle quintile.

How Does Increased Dependency Increase Income Inequality?

Dependency is related to income inequality and distribution in three important ways. First, since the nonworking population (young and old) has relatively little income, an increasingly dependent population increases the proportion of the low-income population. This increases inequality by decreasing the income share for individuals at the bottom of the distribution.

Since World War II, however, structural changes have occurred that have altered the income of the elderly. During this period, Social Security increased in both participant coverage and level of benefits. This dramatically increased the income levels and reduced labor force participation for individuals over 65. For (potential) early retirees (45 to 64), this increased income more rapidly and increased labor force participation more slowly than for the general population. These changes reduced income inequality by increasing the income of the (mostly low-income) elderly.[16] These structural changes in Social Security explain the trends in Table 4–3 showing the *general* equalization of postwar individual incomes and reduction in the top-to-bottom income share ratio that were particularly pronounced for older individuals.

For younger dependents, however, no such changes occurred. Table 4–1 shows that both income and labor force participation rates rose less for those aged 16 to 19 than the general population. Thus, the increase in inequality associated with increased dependency stemmed from increases in *youth* dependency associated with fluctuating fertility and decreasing infant mortality.

Second, both earnings and unemployment are correlated with age. With differential earnings across ages, the baby boom altered the composition of high-wage and low-wage workers in the labor market. Since labor market earnings increase with age until about age 55, a population weighted with young workers increases the relative number of low-wage workers. This increased inequality, since the number of low-wage workers increased the proportion of workers at the bottom of the earnings distribution, and decreased inequality as their earnings converged toward the middle.[17]

Since unemployment rates are highest for youth, aggregate unemployment rates increased as the baby boom entered the labor market. This increase intensified when the number of jobs failed to increase with the number of new labor market entrants. This not only increased joblessness rates but also forced college-educated labor market entrants into jobs traditionally performed by high school graduates.[18] Since increased unemployment and the shifting "down" of workers lowers the income share at the bottom of the income distribution, inequality increased until the labor market absorbed the baby boom.

Third, earnings are inversely related to cohort size. This implies that the baby-boom's influence on inequality did not stop with initial labor market entrance, since relative earnings of this particular cohort are decreased. Empirical research generally verifies that a large labor market cohort (formed by increased births) reduces earnings to members; however, disagreement exists as to the magnitude and duration of the effect.[19]

How important were each of these explanations in changing aggregate income inequality? Pyatt (1976) and Paglin (1977, 1975) formally decompose the Gini coefficient into three additive parts:

$$G = G_1 + G_2 + G_3 \qquad\qquad (4\text{--}1)$$

where

G_1 = inequality coming from overlaps[20] between cohorts (e.g., income differentials between "rich" retirees and "poor" workers) (explanation one)

G_2 = the contribution of pure intracohort inequality (explanation two)

G_3 = (the age Gini) inequality from differences in the mean incomes of different cohorts (explanation three).

Because the three measures are interdependent, a rise in G_3, because of the increase in age-income differentials, must reduce the overlap, G_1, holding G_2 constant. This interdependence between G_3 and G_1 causes researchers to incorrectly attribute much of the demographic change in income inequality to changes in the age-income profile, G_3. Most of the change in inequality stems from changes in intracohort dispersion, G_2.[21]

This discussion is particularly germane to over-time changes in U.S. income inequality. Inequality from overlaps between cohorts, G_1, was reduced by expanding Social Security programs, yet inequality from differences between the mean income of different cohorts, G_3, increased as the baby boom entered the labor market. Because of the interdependence between the two, the latter offsets part, if not all, of the overlap reduction. These counteracting effects may have reduced dependency-induced inequality effects to increases in intracohort income dispersion, G_2. This increased dispersion stemmed from both increased unemployment and increased variance in labor market earnings associated with a large influx of workers into the labor market. Since this variance reduced as workers gained labor market experience, inequality lessened as the baby boom entered the labor market (reduced dependency) and gained work experience.[22]

DISCUSSION AND CONCLUSIONS

Although increased Social Security decreased postwar inequality with increased income to the (low-income) elderly population, the major impact of dependency change is increased inequality. This absolute inequality increase will continue since earnings variance is increased with the large (baby boom) labor force cohort.

Increased dependency increased income inequality with income increases in the top quintile and income reductions in the bottom quintile(s) for all income-receiving units. These effects are stronger for unrelated individuals than families, for dual-earning as opposed to single-earning husband-wife families, and for female rather than male income-receiving units.

Since little relative change occurred in the individual income of the young dependent population, fluctuating births (and to a much lesser extent reductions in infant mortality) accounted for much of the alteration in income inequality and share distribution associated with changing dependency. The largest dependency changes during the postwar period were the baby boom, baby bust, and echo boom. The baby boom initially increased dependency and, hence, increased income inequality through income polarization. As the baby boom entered the labor market and the baby bust arrived, dependency and income inequality fell. Although the initial entrance of the baby boom into the labor market intensified inequality as earnings variance between and within cohorts increased, the variance reduced with its absorption.

Earnings variance changes, associated with the baby boom, explain between-unit differences in magnitude between dependency and inequality. Female labor supply response to changing wages is greater than that for males.[23] Since both labor supply and earnings contribute to income variance, increased earnings variance invokes greater labor supply responses from women than men. Dependency changes therefore are stronger for women than men since women alter labor supply with earnings changes. That is, increased earnings variance from decreased dependency affects both male and female wages but also affects female labor supply. Likewise, the dependency-induced income inequality change of dual-earning, husband-wife families is stronger than for nonworking-wife families since dual-earning families have a higher labor supply response (from women) than the single-earning families.

The relationship between dependency and income inequality is stronger for unrelated individuals than families for two reasons. First, many elderly live as unrelated individuals. An increase in the number of (low-income) elderly directly increases unrelated-individual income inequality by increasing the proportion of low-income units. Second, many nonelderly unrelated individuals are young singles who receive a greater proportion of their income from labor market earnings than older family heads. Because baby-boom inequality influences are primarily through alterations in labor market income, this increased income inequality for unrelated individuals more than for families, where earnings are a smaller part of income.

NOTES

1. Von Weizsacker (1988) discusses fertility and mortality influences on income distribution.

2. Russell (1982) and Rindfuss and Sweet (1972) provide much of the material on the baby boom.

3. Total fertility rate is the number of children a woman would bear if she completed her childbearing years and bore children at the prevailing rate of women currently bearing children. Rates cited are from the U.S. Bureau of the Census (1975).

4. The comparable alterations in fertility across subpopulations is important since it negates inequality changes associated with differential fertility across income classes (Lam, 1986).

5. Gibson (1976) and Moore and O'Connell (1978) discuss factors creating the baby bust.

6. Schultz (1974) summarizes the "new home economics." Willis (1973), Becker and Lewis (1973), and DeTray (1973) outline fertility within this paradigm. Westoff (1979) discusses historical declines in fertility rates.

7. Recent studies have incorporated supply-side (biological) fertility determinants into the new home economics paradigm (cf., Easterlin and Crimmins, 1985).

8. The relationship between the opportunity cost of children (female employment) and fertility is not straightforward since both cohort and period effects intervene (Clogg, 1982; Smith, 1981; Pullum, 1980; Duncan, 1979; Fienberg and Mason, 1979; Farkas, 1977; Mason et al., 1973). Estimation of the relative strengths of cohort and period effects on fertility and female employment consistently show predominance in period effects. That is, more variation in fertility is explained by assuming period-specific effects that raise and lower all cohorts in a similar manner (Namboodiri, 1981). These results are more consistent with the new home economics than Easterlin since increased price levels of children, which affect all cohorts, account for lower fertility rates.

9. See Easterlin et al. (1980) for elaboration.

10. The majority of deaths to young adult males is from violence—accidents, homicide, and suicide. Increased mortality from these sources offsets minor improvements in other areas (Weiss, 1976).

11. Increased life expectancy favors women over men (difference of five years in 1947 and slightly over seven years in 1983). Since infant mortality rates differ dramatically by race (nonwhite infant mortality exceeds white infant mortality by over seventy percent—National Center for Health Statistics, 1980; Bouvier and Van Der Tak, 1976) and by socioeconomic status (Cramer, 1987), life expectancy for whites and high-income groups is greater than for nonwhites and poor. With reduced racial (infant) mortality differences, increased gender differences (National Center for Health Statistics, 1979), and stability in socioeconomic status differences (Adamchak and Stockwell, 1978), nonwhite females now have a life expectancy at birth exceeding white males (75.2 to 71.8). Unless stated, all historical mortality statistics are from the U.S. Bureau of the Census (1975) and all post–1970 statistics are from the U.S. Bureau of the Census (1986a).

12. Of course, the inequality-increasing movement of elderly into separate living quarters also increased the psychological well-being of the elderly. These psychological benefits of living alone are not included in the empirical measure of inequality or income level.

13. Danziger and Gottschalk (1986a) present an over-time discussion of income inequality and all income-receiving units with children. Ross and Sawhill (1975) discuss female-headed income-receiving units.

14. Since Bowen and Finegan (1969) first estimated the impact of children on female labor supply, numerous studies have attempted to disentangle the complex fertility-labor

supply relationship. Voydanoff (1987) outlines these issues in a nontechnical manner while Cramer (1980) presents a more technical analysis.

15. Since the same Gini coefficient underlies differing income distributions, the lack of significance between the Gini coefficient and dependency is not inconsistent with significant changes in the share distribution.

16. Parsons (1984, 1982, 1980a) and Haveman and Wolfe (1984) debate the degree to which these changes can be attributed to Social Security and Disability Insurance.

17. Creedy and Hart (1979) empirically support the increase in the age-earnings profile. Empirical evidence also supports the relationship of increased inequality with an increased proportion of low-earning workers. The pattern of increasing and decreasing labor force growth (associated with the baby boom and baby bust) initially increased the variance in labor market earnings but decreased variance as the cohorts aged and gained labor market experience (Dooley and Gottschalk, 1985). Much of this within-cohort variance in labor market earnings stems from variances in level of or returns to education (cf., Connelly, 1986; Dooley and Gottschalk, 1984; Berger, 1984; Plotnick, 1982).

18. Levy and Michel (1985) discuss the failure of the labor market to increase jobs sufficiently to absorb the baby boom. Howe (1988) relates this phenomenon to the "shifting down" in the jobs held by the educated population.

19. Berger (1985), Smith and Welch (1981), and Welch (1979) empirically show the inverse relationship between labor market earnings and cohort size. The disagreement on the magnitude and duration of this effect stems from restrictions placed on the estimation models. Dooley and Gottschalk (1984) assume labor is a single homogeneous factor of production. Freeman (1979) assumes workers are imperfect substitutes across age groups while Welch (1979) assumes workers are imperfect substitutes across experience-schooling groups. Berger (1985) generalizes from Welch's theoretical model and makes endogenous the speed of transition from the learner to worker phase. Connelly (1986) discusses the outcomes of varying specifications. These cohort effects are stronger for college-educated workers (Berger, 1984; Stapleton and Young, 1984), with the returns to college education inversely related to the size of entry cohorts (Berger, 1983; Freeman, 1977).

20. Nelson (1977) and Johnson (1977) elaborate on the overlap component.

21. Morley (1981) supports the large role of intracohort dispersion in increased inequality while Danziger and Smolensky (1977) support the interdependence proposition.

22. Kurien (1977) empirically substantiates increased income dispersion with increased unemployment and variance in labor market earnings from the baby boom cohort while Dooley and Gottschalk (1984) empirically show decreased inequality with increased labor market experience.

23. See Killingsworth (1983) for a summary.

5

Labor Supply Changes: Female Labor Force Participation

Working women do not earn as much as working men. Compared to the average working man, the average working woman works fewer hours, has less tenure on the job, is employed in different occupations, has more home responsibility, and faces wage and employment discrimination. These characteristics produce lower earnings for women and impoverishment for many female-headed income-receiving units.

Table 5–1 highlights many of the male-female earnings differences. To avoid the obvious earnings reduction associated with fewer hours supplied, the table examines only full-time, full-year workers. For all categories of women, female earnings were consistently lower than male earnings from 1970 to 1985. During this time, however, the average earnings of all workers *decreased* by nearly five percent while average female earnings *increased* by six and one-half percent. Thus, female earnings are converging toward the average. Black women, women over 25, and women maintaining their own families had the largest earnings gains over the period.

Much of the earnings gains stemmed from occupational shifts, with little change in the female-male earnings ratio within each occupation between 1970 and 1985 (Table 5–1).[1] With few exceptions, the female-to-male earnings ratio consistently ranged between .5 and .7. Consistency also existed in female occupational employment. While females dominated employment in certain occupations (clerical and service), they were underrepresented in most blue-collar occupations and in management throughout the period.[2] The female-male occupational differences partially accounted for the aggregate female-male earnings differential since women were overrepresented in low-paying areas (e.g., cler-

Table 5–1
Characteristics of Female Workers

	1950	1960	1970	1980	1985	Percent Change[2]
Earnings[1]						
All Workers (Male and Female)	-	-	360	342	343	-4.7
Female	-	-	260	263	277	6.5
16-24	-	-	244	219	210	-13.9
24 and over	-	-	266	278	296	11.3
Wives	-	-	263	267	285	8.4
Women maintaining families[3]	-	-	252	269	278	10.3
White	-	-	263	265	281	6.8
Black	-	-	224	242	252	12.5
Occupation--percent female and (earning ratio)[4]						
All Occupations	27.9	32.5	38.0	44.2	-	58.4
White Collar						
Professional	39.5	38.1 (.61)	39.9 (.64)	46.2 (.66)	-	17.0
Managers	13.7	14.5 (.53)	16.6 (.55)	28.2 (.55)	-	105.8
Clerical	62.3	67.6 (.68)	73.6 (.64)	81.0 (.60)	-	30.0
Sales	34.3	36.7 (.41)	38.6 (.43)	49.1 (.49)	-	43.1
Blue Collar						
Craft	3.0	2.9 *	5.0 (.54)	6.3 (.63)	-	110.0
Operative	27.3	28.1 (.59)	31.5 (.58)	33.6 (.60)	-	75.8
Laborer	3.7	3.5 *	8.4 (.68)	11.2 (.76)	-	202.7
Service						
Private Household	94.8	96.4 *	96.5 *	97.2 *	-	2.5
Other	44.7	52.4 (.57)	55.0 (.56)	60.8 (.61)	-	36.0

[1]Analysis contains only full-time, full-year workers. All earnings are in 1985 dollars and represent median weekly earnings of full-time wage and salary workers. Consistent data prior to 1970 are not available.

[2]Computed as the difference over the period divided by the initial period (times 100). Many of the large percent changes reflect small initial bases.

[3]This category is "other marital status" in 1970.

[4]The earning ratio (in parenthesis) is the ratio of female-to-male earnings for full-time, full-year wage and salary workers. Earning ratios are not available for 1950. Consistent occupational distributions are not available for 1985. Asterisks indicate a data base too small for computations.

Table 5–2
Trends in Female Labor Force Participation[1]

	1950	1960	1970	1980	1985	Percent Change[2]
Total (female)	31.4	34.8	42.6	51.1	54.5	73.2
Single females	50.5	44.1	53.0	61.5	65.2	29.1
Married females (with husband present)	23.8	30.5	40.8	50.1	54.2	127.7
Married with children under 6	11.9	18.6	30.3	45.3	53.7	351.3

[1]Female Labor Force Participation = $\dfrac{\text{number of women employed or unemployed}}{\text{number of noninstitutionalized women}}$

[2]Computed as the difference over the period divided by the initial period (times 100).

ical) and underrepresented in high-paying areas (e.g., management and craft). Some women overcame this occupation segregation. Although nearly eighty percent of all clerical workers are still women, between 1972 and 1984 women increased their percentage in executive ranks from about twenty to thirty-three percent. Within each occupation, however, women were overrepresented in the lower echelons of the hierarchy. This within-occupation segregation accounted for lack of parity in occupational female-male earnings ratios.[3]

TRENDS IN FEMALE LABOR FORCE PARTICIPATION

One of the most dramatic increases in labor supply over the last forty years was increased female labor force participation. Although females had increased their participation since the turn of the century, the rate of increase increased dramatically during the 1960s and 1970s. Because of the social (e.g., increases in women's power) and economic (e.g., women competing with men for jobs) implications of this dramatic labor market influx, increasing attention has been paid to female labor market activities.

From 1950 to 1985, female labor force participation increased from slightly over thirty percent to over fifty percent (Table 5–2). This represents a seventy percent increase in participation over the period, with the major influx occurring during the 1960s and the 1970s.

While all subgroups of women increased their participation over the period, initial participation levels and rates of change varied dramatically. While married women initially had lower participation rates than single women, the gap narrowed considerably by 1985 (Table 5–2). Traditionally, married women with children under six had the lowest participation rates; however, between 1950 and 1985, these women increased their participation by over 350 percent. By

1985, the participation distinction between all married women and women with preschool children was negligible and the differential between married women and single women was much lower. Although the male participation rate still exceeds the female rate (the male rate was 76.3 percent in 1985), convergence occurred as male labor force participation decreased and female participation increased.

Female labor force participation rates also differed among sociodemographic groups. Although black females consistently had higher rates than white females, the racial difference converged as white women increasingly entered the labor market over the period. In 1985, the black female labor force participation rate was 56.5—an increase of only 2.4 percentage points over whites. Female labor force participation also varied positively with years of schooling. In 1983, college graduates had participation rates above seventy-five percent while women not completing high school had participation rates near fifty percent.[4]

Not all women labor market entrants were full-time employees. In 1985, over twenty-five percent of employed women worked part-time (less than 35 hours a week). Only about ten percent of male workers were part-time employees. For women, part-time employment status varies by marital status and with the presence of children. Nearly one-third of employed women with preschool children work part time.[5] Thus, although married female labor force participation increased dramatically over the period (particularly for women with preschool children), female labor supply is still not equivalent to men's since a significant portion of the employment is part-time.

Explanations for the Changes

Changes in female labor market activities occurred for several reasons: economic, social, and institutional. Economic theories posit that women base their participation decision on the relative costs (e.g., loss of home production) and benefits (e.g., wages) of labor market activities. Since World War II, female real wages increased in absolute terms even though they remained a constant fifty-nine percent of male wages.[6] Higher wages increased the benefits from labor market participation and the opportunity cost of home production. Concurrently, fertility reductions reduced the benefits from home production.[7]

Traditionally, within the family, women specialized in home production. They moved in and out of the labor market as the need for home production (primarily child care) fluctuated. This intermittent participation caused women to self-select into occupations where skills were less likely to atrophy during periods out of the labor market (following childbirth) and to decrease human capital investments in post-school training over continual participants. As the benefits to home production decreased with decreased fertility and the benefits to market participation increased with increased female wages, women increasingly entered the labor market and spent less time out of the labor force after childbirth. As a consequence, women increased their levels of education and work experience. This increased human capital led to further wage increases.[8]

Demand-side labor market changes also occurred, with dramatic (occupational) employment growth in areas of traditional female employment (e.g., clerical and service workers). This increased demand for "female" workers was augmented by increased entrance of women into "atypical" occupations. The latter effect was limited since women faced occupational crowding into "female" occupations with statistical discrimination.[9]

Traditionally, employers attributed higher turnover rates to women because of their intermittent labor force participation. To reduce turnover costs, employers hired women only into positions with little training where turnover was not costly. With few labor market opportunities, females were socialized into homemaker roles. This makes the circle complete. Women are socialized into intermittent labor force participation, employers restrict female employment opportunities because of intermittent participation, and female intermittent participation is reinforced because of reduced wages and employment opportunities.[10]

This cycle was broken somewhat with changes in attitudes toward women's roles and antidiscrimination legislation. The 1960s was a period of great social change for women. In 1963, with the publication of Betty Friedan's *The Feminine Mystique*, social attention to the psychological and emotional stress accompanying the role of the unpaid housewife increased. The explicit exposure of the housewife's low status facilitated women's entrance into the labor market. Although immediately following World War II most (married) women worked out of economic necessity, changing societal norms during the late 1960s and early 1970s facilitated women's labor market activities for noneconomic reasons (particularly with intrafamily consensus) and increased acceptance of work in "atypical" (i.e., male) occupations.[11]

Institutional change often reflects attitudinal change. The Equal Pay Act of 1963, Civil Rights Act of 1964 (and 1972 Amendment), and Executive Orders 11246 and 11478 (Affirmative Action) facilitated equal employment opportunities for women (and minorities). Since occupational employment segregation was the major employment obstacle for women, the Civil Rights Act and Affirmative Action facilitated increased female labor force participation with reduced occupational segregation.[12] Legislation was not 100-percent effective, however, since between and within occupational segmentation still exists for females.[13]

FEMALE LABOR FORCE BEHAVIOR AND INCOME DISTRIBUTION

With differences in male and female earnings, the entrance of women into the labor market altered the income distribution in a number of ways. First, all else equal, an increase of (low-paid) women into the labor market increased the number of low-income workers and, therefore, increased the dispersion of aggregate earnings. Second, increased female labor force participation altered the composition of income-receiving units. As wives entered the labor market, the relative number of dual-earning, husband-wife families increased while the relative number of single-earner husband-wife households decreased. Since dual-earning families have more equal income distributions than single-earning families, this reduced inequality. Third, with increased female labor force participation fostering women's economic independence and increasing the relative number of (often impoverished) female-headed income-receiving units, inequality increased. Fourth, with decreased occupational segregation, women increasingly competed with men for wages. This altered the distribution of male earnings. Thus, increased female labor force participation altered the income distribution, though the a priori direction of the net effect is uncertain.

Table 5–3 shows the estimated relationship and elasticity between female labor force participation and income inequality and distribution. While increased female labor force participation results from both demand-side and supply-side changes in the labor market, the estimation technique controls for demand-side changes in industrial and occupational employment.

In the aggregate, female labor force participation did not significantly alter income inequality but did increase the lowest-quintile income share. Inequality decreased for families and unrelated-individual units with increased female labor force participation. For husband-wife families, significant inequality reductions occurred only for dual-earning families. The insignificant aggregate relationship and significant disaggregate relationships indicate that compositional changes (e.g., increases in dual-earning households) associated with increased female labor force participation were less relevant than direct alterations in income-receiving-unit earnings distributions.

For female-headed income-receiving units, increased female labor force participation had little impact on income inequality or share distribution. There was, however some income transferred from the fourth to the middle quintile for female unrelated individuals.

The largest impact of increased female labor force participation on income inequality and distribution was for male income-receiving units. For both male-headed families and male unrelated individuals, increased female labor force participation reduced income inequality. For both groups, the entrance of females into the labor market reduced the top-quintile income share and increased the bottom-quintile income share. These effects were stronger for male unrelated individuals than male-headed families. For male unrelated individuals, increased female labor force participation also increased the fourth-quintile income share. For male-headed families, female labor force participation increased the second-quintile income share.

Why Does Female Labor Force Participation Alter Income Inequality?

For income-receiving units (families and unrelated individuals), labor market income variance (inequality) is a function of the variances and covariances of male and female earnings:[14]

Table 5-3

Female Labor Force Participation Influence on Income Inequality and Distribution: Elasticities[1]

	Gini Coefficient	Top Quintile	Fourth Quintile	Middle Quintile	Second Quintile	Lowest Quintile
Aggregate[2]	-.213	.106	-1.28	.432	.912	1.96**
Total Families	-.640*	-.511	.153	.523	.327	.063
Total Individuals	-.914***	-.662*	.086	.966**	1.03	1.50
Husband-Wife Families	-.517	-.431	.526	-.350	.812	.640
Wife in the Labor Force	-1.06*	-.515	-.813	1.25	.723	1.16
Wife out of the Labor Force	-.302	-.143	-.540	.547	.677	.271
Male-Headed Families	-1.25***	-.864*	-.115	1.14	1.58*	1.82**
Male Individuals	-1.04****	-1.12***	1.21*	.771	.633	3.48***
Female-Headed Families	.023	.119	-.131	-1.09	.617	.398
Female Individuals	-.328	.110	-1.30**	1.68**	.244	.438

[1]Elasticities reflect the percent change (at the mean) in the Gini coefficient or quintile income share associated with a one percent change (at the mean) in female labor force participation. Computations are based on regression results presented in Appendix Tables A4-1 to A4-6.

[2]Aggregate and totals reflect a weighted average of income-receiving-unit components.

**** p < .001
*** p |∨| .01
** p |∨||∨| .05
* p |∨||∨| .10

$$s^2_{ru} = s^2_m + s^2_f + 2\mathrm{Cov}_{mf} \tag{5-1}$$

where:

s^2_{ru} = variance in unit's income distribution

s^2_m = variance in male's earnings

s^2_f = variance in female's earnings

Cov_{mf} = covariance in male-female earnings.

For husband-wife, dual-earning families, changes in income inequality occur with variance changes in male and female earnings distributions and covariance changes between the distributions. Variance change in the male earnings distribution alters inequality with potential alterations in the husband's relative earnings ranking, while variance change in the female earnings distribution alters family income with potential alteration in the wife's relative earnings ranking. Covariance change, associated with the pairing of the husband and wife, increases inequality as covariance increases (e.g., high-earning men and women marry) and decreases inequality as covariance decreases (e.g., high-earning men marry low-earning women and family income converges toward mean levels).

For male income-receiving units and husband-wife families with nonworking wives, income inequality changes only with changes in the male earnings distributions since female earnings (and husband-wife covariance) are not part of the unit's income. For female income-receiving units, income inequality changes occur only with variance changes in the female earnings distribution.

Changing female labor force participation alters the variance of male and female earnings distributions and the covariance of earnings within the family. The degree of male and female earnings alteration depends on the employment of entering women. If females enter only "female" jobs, the level and variance of male earnings remain unaltered but the female level and/or variance of earnings changes with (occupationally different) increased labor supply. If females only enter "male" jobs, the level and variance of female earnings remain unaltered but the level and/or variance of male earnings changes with (occupationally different) increased labor supply.

Neither of these extremes existed. Although female workers were not perfect substitutes for males because of occupational segregation, their entrance altered the male earnings distribution as employment increased in traditionally male-dominated spheres. Thus, the effect of increased female labor force participation on the male earnings distribution depends on the influence of females entering "male" occupations.

Competition theory of occupational assimilation explains the impact on wages of females entering male occupations. As women enter a particular occupation, they increase competition for wages with increased labor supply. Since female wages are sixty percent of male wages, women work for lower wages than the men already employed in the occupation. This increased competition from lower-wage workers causes men's wages to fall. Thus, increased female labor force participation lowered male labor market earnings as women entered male-dominated occupations.[15] Since women selectively entered male-dominated occupations (e.g., women entered professional/management positions more rapidly than skilled craft or laborer positions), the distribution of male earnings altered as females entered occupationally distinct labor markets.

Previous empirical research has shown that entering females increased competition and lowered occupational wages for all but the lowest levels of the male-occupational structure. This explains the finding that increased female labor force participation decreased the top-quintile income share and increased the bottom-quintile income share for male income-receiving units. If females lowered the wages for men at the top of the male earnings distribution (e.g., for professionals and managers), the income share of high-wage men declined. Likewise, if females left unchanged the wages for men at the bottom of the earnings distribution (e.g., laborers), the income share of low-wage men increased relative to the (reduced) top of the distribution. The result is decreased income inequality for male income-receiving units as females entered the labor market.[16]

In contrast, increased female labor force participation had little impact on female income-receiving-unit income inequality and distribution. Since the major source of dispersion in the female earnings distribution is from the large number of zero earners and the low earnings of part-time workers, increased female labor force participation reduced variance in the female earnings distribution. Increased participation had little impact on the female-headed income-receiving unit's distribution, however, since participation probabilities changed little for these units.[17]

Increased female labor force participation altered the income distribution for husband-wife families with changes in both the male and female earnings distribution and the earnings covariance. Consistent with inequality reductions in both the male and female earnings distribution, previous studies consistently found large inequality reductions with increased female labor force participation for husband-wife families.[18] In contrast, our results indicate only a modest impact.

Earlier studies found a low covariance between husband-wife earnings, with female earnings a fraction of male earnings.[19] Since male earnings were the major determinant of the husband-wife income distribution, and increased female labor force participation reduced their dispersion, income inequality for husband-wife families fell. Low levels of husband-wife earnings covariance reinforced this reduction. Early studies showed that although high-earning men married women with high earnings potential, the women were less likely labor force participants than women with low-earning husbands. Thus, early increases in female labor force participation reduced income inequality through increased labor supply of women married to low-earning men.

Over time, the within-family covariance between male and female earnings changed as female labor force participation increased. Since both husband-wife earnings correlation and individual labor supply decisions determine husband-wife earnings covariance, family type (e.g., high-income single-earning or low-income dual-earning families) strongly influences covariance. Within the new home economics paradigm, families form because a production-oriented household can achieve specialization gains over individual endeavors with division of labor. That is, family formation increases the sum of nonmarket (e.g., "housework" or utility) and market (e.g., income) production over individual endeavors.[20]

The family type formed depends on two spousal production characteristics, substitution and complements. When spousal characteristics substitute for each other, specialization results with (in general) the male devoting energy to market production and the female devoting energy to nonmarket production (i.e., nonparticipation in the labor force). This produces single-earner families. When spousal characteristics complement each other, "complementary needs" are fulfilled as the characteristics contribute to the utility of both individuals (e.g., joint labor market participation). This produces dual-earner families. As female labor force participation increased and the marital search increasingly involved complementary labor force skill acquisition, income inequality increased as assortative mating led to high (low) income men marrying high (low) income women.

Prior to 1980, wife labor force participation fell with increases in husband's earnings (Table 5–4). By 1980, however, the relationship between female labor force participation and husband's earnings was shaped like an inverted U. By 1985, the labor force participation of women with husbands who had earnings in the top quintile was greater than that of women with husbands who had earnings in the bottom quintile. There was also differential growth in wives' median earnings over the period. From 1967 to 1980 the median earnings grew faster for women married to men with earnings in the bottom quintile than for women married to men in the top quintile. This equalized inequality with increased female labor force participation. Between 1980 and 1985, however, this trend reversed and the median earnings grew faster for women married to high-income men than women married to low-income men. Thus, from 1980 to 1985 both labor supply and earnings of women married to high-income men increased more than for women married to low-income men. This suggests inequality increases associated with increased female labor force participation after 1980.

These patterns of change explain the smaller reduction in inequality from increased female labor force participation found in this study than in previous research. Prior to 1980, increased female labor force participation and earnings favored low-income households; however, after 1980, increases favored high-income households. The over-time changes in the type of females entering the labor market produced small over-time effects.[21]

Table 5–4
Earnings of Wife by Earnings of Husband, 1967–1985

WIFE

Husband's Earnings	1967[1]		1970		1980		1985		Percent Change[4] 1967–1980		1980–1985	
	Percent With Earnings[2]	Median[3] Earnings	Percent With Earnings	Median Earnings	Percent With Earnings	Median Earnings	Percent With Earnings	Median Earnings	Percent With Earnings	Median Earnings	Percent With Earnings	Median Earnings
Top Quintile	42.6	9074	43.4	9039	60.4	9935	68.7	11800	41.7	9.5	13.7	18.8
Fourth Quintile	52.0	9084	51.1	8953	67.0	10048	70.5	11169	28.8	10.6	5.2	11.2
Middle Quintile	57.8	8678	56.7	9128	69.8	9241	72.5	10002	20.8	6.1	3.9	8.2
Second Quintile	57.4	8153	57.1	8313	66.5	9139	73.1	9147	15.9	12.1	9.9	.1
Bottom Quintile	57.8	5925	55.0	7014	60.9	6763	60.6	7181	5.4	14.1	.5	6.2
Median Top Quintile Median Bottom Quintile		1.53	—	1.29	—	1.47	—	1.65	—	—	—	—

[1]Data are not available for earlier years. Table includes only husband–wife families in which the husband and wife had some earnings.

[2]"Percent with Earnings" is associated with the midpoint of each quintile.

[3]"Median Earnings" (1985 dollars) is the median earnings associated with the midpoint of each quintile.

[4]Computed as the difference over the period divided by the initial period (times 100).

SUMMARY AND CONCLUSIONS

Female labor force participation has increased dramatically since World War II. Although females are still predominately employed in clerical positions to the exclusion of craft and laborer positions, female professional and management employment has increased. This increase decreased income inequality for most income-receiving units.

For males, increased female labor force participation decreased earnings in higher-paying occupations and left unchanged earnings in lower-paying occupations. This reduced income inequality for male income-receiving units with decreased top-quintile income share and increased bottom-quintile income share.

For female income-receiving units, increased female labor force participation had little impact on income inequality or distribution. Since the labor force participation probabilities of this group have changed little since World War II and since much of the aggregate dispersion in female earnings stems from the large number of nonparticipants, overall changes in female labor market activity did not change inequality for this group.

For husband-wife families, increased female labor force participation reduced income inequality somewhat. This reduction was fairly great prior to 1980; however, since 1980 increased female labor force participation has increased both the labor supply and relative (female) earnings of women in high-income households. Thus, although increased female labor force participation prior to 1980 decreased income inequality, it increased inequality after 1980. Over the 1947 to 1985 period, this produced a small equalizing effect.

NOTES

1. Although most research supports an unchanging female-male earnings ratio, there is some debate. See Blau and Beller (1988) and Carlson and Swartz (1988) and the discussions following for a summary of the debate.

2. Because of low initial bases, the percent increase in female employment over the period is most dramatic in blue-collar occupations.

3. Blau and Ferber (1987), Beller (1985), and Davis (1980) discuss changing employment patterns.

4. See Smith and Ward (1984) for statistics and discussion of education and female labor force participation.

5. See Barrett (1979) for a discussion of part-time work.

6. Wages increased for several reasons. In general, real wages rose until 1973 with productivity increases. Additionally, women increasingly undertook education and training (i.e., increased human capital) over the period. For elaboration see Smith and Ward (1985, 1984).

7. Chapter 4 discusses the employment-fertility relationship.

8. Mincer and Polachek (1974) outline the economic rationale for the division of labor in the family and for the specialization for women in nonmarket production. Polachek (1981, 1975) expands on their theory to show that familial divisions of labor influence

women's investment in human capital. Mott and Shapiro (1982) discuss decreasing time spent out of the labor force and increasing investment in human capital.

9. Bergmann (1974) and Chapter 8 discuss both statistical discrimination and occupational crowding.

10. See Groneau (1988) for a similar analysis with respect to wages.

11. Matthews (1987) discusses the historical degradation of the role of the unpaid housewife. Mott (1982), Milkman (1976), and Smuts (1971) discuss the motivation (and employment) changes in women's work. Of course, this study ignores these large social-psychological benefits of women working.

12. The source of occupational segregation is hotly debated, with the source attributed to women's choice (cf., Mincer and Ofek, 1982; or Polachek, 1985, 1981, 1979), lack of mobility ladders for women (Wolf and Rosenfeld, 1978), and discrimination (Beller, 1982; Bergmann, 1974) combined with nonpecuniary motives for specialization in home skills (England, 1985, 1984, 1982).

13. Beller (1982, 1980) examines the impact of the Civil Rights Act on female employment and Leonard (1986, 1985a, b) discusses the impact of Affirmative Action. Results show small impacts of the legislation for white women and larger impacts for black women.

14. See Mincer (1974) for elaboration.

15. See Hodge and Hodge (1965) for theoretical elaboration of competition from assimilating females and Synder and Hudis (1976) for empirical verification.

16. Women's entrance into high-wage occupations lowered wages of men in top-level occupations and hence reduced the top-quintile income share. At the same time, this increased the relative income share of men in high-paying occupations without much women's entrance (e.g., craft). This increased the fourth-quintile income share.

17. Since the mid–1970s women delayed marriage, increased divorce, and increased their propensity to live alone. This increased the number of female unrelated individuals and female-headed families but did not change their labor force probability. Tienda and Glass (1985) discuss the high labor force participation rates of female unrelated individuals. The low (and unchanging) labor force participation rate of female-headed families is a result of the negative supply effects of AFDC (cf., Blau and Robins, 1986; Moffit, 1986; or Robins, 1985), insufficient job opportunities (cf., Levy and Michel, 1986b; Gottschalk and Danziger, 1985), and inadequate quality child care (cf., Moore and Hofferth, 1979). For a good summary of changes over this period, see Bianchi and Spain (1984). Schoen et al. (1985) discuss marriage and divorce and Michael et al. (1980) discuss living alone.

18. Treas (1987) summarizes and synthesizes these studies and other relevant research on working wives and family income inequality. Notable studies include Betson and Van Der Gagg (1984), Groneau (1982), Hovarth (1980), and Sweet (1971).

19. See Harris and Hedderson (1981) and Danziger (1980) for early studies on low covariance in husband-wife earnings while Pfeffer and Ross (1982) and Mincer (1974) show the strong labor supply role of the low covariance.

20. Becker (1981) discusses the "new home economics" while Berk and Berk (1982) provide an excellent critique. England and Farkas (1986) discuss marriage contracting and Glenn and Taylor (1984) empirically support increased assortative mating.

21. These results are also consistent with cross-national studies finding differential inequality impacts of increased female labor force participation for husband-wife families with varying levels of participation (Winegarden, 1987). Cross nationally, increased

female labor force participation starting from low levels of participation *increased* income inequality; however, at participation rates around fifty percent, increased female labor force participation reduced inequality for husband-wife families. Since participation rates were about 50–70 percent between 1967 and 1985, we find equalizing effects. This study indicates that future participation increases (perhaps above 70 percent) may once again increase income inequality.

6

Government Redistribution Efforts: Cash Expenditures on Social Insurance

Although federal and state governments recognized their ability to insure against certain risks prior to the 1930s (e.g., by 1929 all but four states had worker's compensation laws), the Depression increased awareness of the economic risks of unemployment, old age, death, and disability.[1] The severity of the Depression dramatized the individual's inability to insure adequately against economic risk and severe impoverishment resultant from widespread breakdowns in the economic system.

The social programs enacted during the Depression were explicitly redistributory. To alleviate economic hardship associated with not working, many programs redistributed income from the working to the nonworking. With equity as a goal, programs were structured to provide a disproportionately large income share to low-income individuals (or households). Thus, the Depression not only spurred the first widespread government intervention in insuring against economic hardship, it also explicitly established the government's role in creating a more "equitable" income distribution.

The Social Security Act was enacted in 1935 to aid the hardest hit of the Depression. This law established two insurance programs, old-age benefits for eligible retired workers (and their dependents in 1937) and unemployment insurance, and categorical federal-state grant programs to aid the needy aged and blind (1935) and the permanently and totally disabled (1950). Consolidation of these funds under Supplemental Security Income (SSI) occurred in 1972. The original Social Security Act also established Aid to Dependent Children (ADC), a program that evolved into the primary "welfare" program Aid to Families with Dependent Children (AFDC).

The indigent also received aid under specifically targeted programs. Medicaid (medical care for the poor) was established in a 1950 amendment to the Social Security Act. The Food Stamp Act of 1964 established the food stamp program. The Omnibus Reconciliation Act of 1981 established low-income home energy assistance. The Department of Housing and Urban Development provided housing-expense relief with low-rent public housing, rent supplements, and interest reductions. Many states provided general assistance to persons ineligible for unemployment insurance or AFDC.

Targeted nonpoor groups have a long history of receiving government aid. Veterans have received benefits since the 17th century. The Civil Service Retirement System established retirement benefits for federal government employees in 1920. Railroad retirees gained pensions under the Railroad Retirement Act of 1934 (amended in 1937).

These social-redistribution efforts fall into two categories, social insurance and social welfare.[2] Within each category, benefits are paid in cash and in kind. Social-welfare programs provide assistance to the low-income population and are usually asset and income tested. Inadequate income is the primary criterion of eligibility. Benefits are not conditioned on past contribution to the programs but are usually conditioned on present need and circumstance (e.g., children, elderly, blind). Both cash and in-kind benefits of social-welfare programs decrease as income from other sources increases. These programs include SSI, AFDC, Medicaid, food stamps, and housing assistance.

Social-insurance programs replace income lost due to events beyond an individual's control (e.g., unemployment, disability). Both eligibility and benefit level depend on past contribution and present circumstance. Financial need has no bearing on cash or in-kind payment receipt. These programs include OASDI (Old Age Survivors and Disability Insurance—"Social Security"), Railroad Retirement, Public Employee Retirement, Unemployment Insurance, Medicare (medical care for the aged), Worker's Compensation, and Veteran's benefits.

Both social-welfare and social-insurance programs directly alter the income distribution by providing income for certain segments of the population. Social-welfare programs explicitly raise the income share of the poor by providing cash and in-kind benefits to low-income individuals. Social-insurance programs redistribute income from the working to the targeted nonworking individuals. Since, by design, social-welfare programs reduce income inequality, this chapter examines only the distributional impacts associated with increased spending on social insurance.

TRENDS IN SPENDING AND PROGRAMS

While cash expenditure payments for both social-insurance and social-welfare programs increased from 1950 to 1984, the most dramatic increases came from social-insurance programs, primarily Social Security (Table 6–1). The increase in social-welfare payments stemmed from increases in AFDC and the imple-

Table 6-1
Trends in Government Spending (Cash Benefit Payments)

Program	Audience	1950[1]	1960	1970	1980	1984	Percent Change[2]
Social Insurance							
Social Security (OASDI)	Aged (and dependents)	3.5	40.0	102.0	199.3	249.0	7014.3
	Disabled (and dependents)						
Railroad Retirement	Aged and Disabled (and dependents) of railroads	2.0	4.4	4.7	6.5	6.6	230.0
Public Employee Retirement	Aged and Disabled of Public Sector	3.7	9.3	24.0	51.7	61.2	1554.1
Unemployment Insurance	Unemployed	9.8	10.3	10.6	24.0	16.7	70.4
Disability Benefits	Disabled	.3	1.3	2.0	1.8	1.9	533.3
Workers' Compensation	Disabled	2.8	4.8	8.1	17.6	20.5	632.1
Veterans' Pensions/ Compensation	Retired and Disabled Military	9.4	12.4	14.9	14.8	14.5	54.3
Social Welfare							
Public Assistance	Aged	11.1	3.8	40.0	58.8	63.4	471.2
	Children						
	Blind						
Supplemental Security Income	Aged Poor	-	-	-	10.8	11.6	--
GNP	-	1288.7	1870.5	2812.9	3578.9	3988.5	209.5

[1] All numbers are in 1985 dollars (billions) and include federal, state, and local expenditures.

[2] Computed as the difference over the period divided by the initial period (times 100). Large numbers reflect small bases in the initial period relative to expenditure increases.

mentation of SSI.[3] Throughout the entire period, the vast majority of government spending was on social-insurance programs—about seventy-three percent of expenditures in 1950 and eighty-three percent in 1984. Social Security accounted for most of the social-insurance payments (except 1950), although non-Social Security social-insurance payments consistently exceeded social-welfare payments.

From 1950 to 1984, OASDI increases were the most dramatic of all programs, with both increased coverage and benefit levels.[4] Legislation liberalized eligibility standards in 1950, 1954, 1956, 1965, and 1987. The 1961 Social Security Amendment permitted men to retire at age 62. While much of the pre–1970 increase in Social Security payments came from increased coverage, most of the post–1970 increase came from increased benefit levels. In June 1975, Social Security benefits became adjusted annually with changes in the consumer price index. The combination of rapid inflation and the increased elderly population dramatically increased the level of payments during the 1970s and early 1980s.

Since Unemployment Insurance and Worker's Compensation programs are state-run, benefit levels and eligibility criteria differ among states.[5] In general, states liberalized eligibility and benefits for both programs over the period. The federal government directly enters the programs by extending unemployment benefit payments up to twenty-six additional weeks during periods of high unemployment. During the high unemployment years of the 1970s, these federal supplemental benefits were available in many areas.

While all programs had different changes in payment level over the period, Murray (1984) argues that all *patterns* of change were consistent since all programs showed real expenditure increases between 1950 and 1965, steeper increases between 1965 and 1978, and leveling off between 1979 and 1980. Thus, the impact of social programs was strongest during the 1970s, with steeper rates of increased benefit levels.

INDIRECT IMPACTS OF SOCIAL-INSURANCE PROGRAMS

Social-insurance programs directly redistribute income from the working to nonworking (insured) population while indirect redistribution arises with altered labor supply and savings incentives.[6] In theory, social-insurance programs reduce both labor supply and saving by creating public-funded alternatives. Thus, planned redistribution effects from social-insurance programs may be lessened because program benefits serve as a monetary substitute for labor market earnings and interest from savings.[7]

Labor Supply

Intertemporal labor-supply responses result from age-related transfer programs, including retirement programs.[8] Both earlier retirement and/or decreased labor supply in preretirement years result from increased availability of nonmarket (nonprivate) income. The guaranteed income benefit of social-insurance programs produces a pure income effect in the increased consumption of "retirement" (leisure) while the (implicit) tax rate creates income and substitution effects unambiguously reducing preretirement labor supply.

Empirical studies of the retirement incentives accompanying OASDI confirm these preretirement labor supply disincentives.[9] The size of the disincentive, however, is uncertain because of potential increases in labor supply at younger ages and differing empirical specifications in estimation models.[10] Empirical studies also confirm the negative relationship between labor supply and disability insurance (with varying estimated magnitudes)[11] and labor supply and unemployment insurance (increased unemployment duration of about four to five weeks).[12]

Savings

Standard economic life-cycle theories of consumption posit saving during work years to support consumption during retirement. Since compulsory retirement benefits provide alternatives to private savings, aggregate savings may be altered in three ways.[13] First, no reduction in aggregate savings occurs if the savings of the retirement plan offset private savings. Second, private savings increase for consumption in a now larger retirement period or with increased bequests. Third, private savings decrease with an increase in expected retirement transfers that may increase net wealth and consumption ability. Thus, the impact of social-insurance programs on savings is theoretically ambiguous.

Unfortunately, neither time-series nor cross-sectional data analysis provides a consistent answer, although recent studies suggest that Social Security's impact on savings is small.[14] Although empirically unmeasured, other social-insurance programs (e.g., disability and unemployment insurance) may have small reduced savings effects since the precautionary savings motive is removed.

Structural Redistribution

Income redistribution is inherent in the structure of all social-insurance programs. Benefit schedules and eligibility rules determine the magnitude of redistribution. The largest social-insurance program, Social Security disability and retirement, computes benefits on the average monthly earnings in covered employment (AME) prior to retirement, disability, or death. Years of low earnings or disability are dropped. For workers with a history of low wages, a special minimum benefit is computed; however, for most workers, a bracketed, weighted formula applies to AME. The bracketed formula favors individuals with low earnings with a higher replacement of AME at lower earnings. This base figure (the replacement portion of AME) is then adjusted by a family benefit figure.[15] Survivors are eligible for equal benefits as the (sole) beneficiary. When both husbands and wives are independently eligible for transfer payments, wives (with lower labor market earnings) receive the higher payments—usually as a spouse rather than under their own entitlement.

Since unemployment insurance and worker's compensation are state-based programs, benefit levels and eligibility vary. In general, both systems base payments on previous weekly wages (usually above 50-percent replacement) up to a maximum benefit. Many states alter benefits with the worker's marital status and number of dependents. Most states delay benefits following the reporting of unemployment or disability, limit the number of weeks of eligibility, and restrict eligibility by circumstances surrounding unemployment or disability.[16]

In sum, most redistribution impacts of social-insurance programs are deliberate. That is, with the exception of preretirement labor supply reductions, savings and labor supply disincentives appear to be small, while payment schedules and eligibility favor those with low income. These redistribution effects stem from higher earnings replacement of low-income individuals and ceilings on maximum benefits in virtually all programs.

Program Disincentives

Murray (1984) argues that the government, by providing benefits to certain conditions (e.g., unemployment, retirement, out-of-wedlock childbearing) provides incentives for individuals to alter their behavior. The behavior modification occurs because benefits (income) can be obtained without working. Because individuals respond to incentives of social policy and are not inherently hard-working or moral, the expansion of social-policy expenditures during the 1970s had the unintended consequence of increasing inequality by removing work and family-formation incentives. Thus, inequality increased along with social expenditures because the composition of income-receiving units changed—the proportion of female-headed units and low-income, nonworking individuals increased while the proportion of husband-wife units decreased. Aggregate inequality therefore increased with an increasing proportion of low-income units. Within-unit inequality is also increased by prolonged nonworking periods (e.g., extended unemployment, early "retirement" with disability).

RELATIONSHIP OF SOCIAL-INSURANCE EXPENDITURE TO INEQUALITY

Increased gross national product (GNP) accompanied increased social-insurance expenditures during the postwar period. While increased social-insurance expenditures reflect the government's increased redistribution attempts, real GNP increases reflect economic growth. Since some of the growth in social-insurance expenditures stemmed from economic growth and not increased redistribution efforts, the more accurate measure of government redistribution is the ratio of social insurance spending to GNP.

Table 6–2 shows the estimated relationship between the percentage of GNP

Table 6-2

Government Influences on Income Inequality and Distribution: Elasticities[1]

	Gini Coefficient	Top Quintile	Fourth Quintile	Middle Quintile	Second Quintile	Lowest Quintile
Aggregate[2]	**-.135**	**-.188**	**.275**	**-.006**	**.091**	**.384**
Total Families	.141*	.359****	-.615***	-.181	.070	.237
Total Individuals	-.020	.051	-.097	-.151	.263	.765*
Husband-Wife Families	.196**	.345**	-.452	-.293	-.057	.104
Wife in Labor Force	.168	.214	-.214	-.138	-.175	.102
Wife out of Labor Force	.200**	.280**	-.375	-.160	-.157	-.004
Male-Headed Families	-.030	.195*	-.559**	.004	.138	.468****
Male Individuals	-.006	.121	-.288*	-.066	.180	.194
Female-Headed Families	-.222*	-.127	-.036	.110	.326	.648**
Female Individuals	-.176***	-.067	-.051	.017	.236	.998***

[1]Elasticities reflect the percent change (at the mean) in the Gini coefficient or quintile income share associated with a one-percent change (at the mean) in the ratio of government spending on social insurance to GNP. Computations are based on regression results presented in Appendix Tables A4-1 to A1-6.

[2]Aggregate and totals reflect a weighted average of income-receiving unit components.

**** $p \leq .001$
*** $p \leq .01$
** $p \leq .05$
* $p \leq .10$

as social-insurance expenditures and income inequality and distribution. In the aggregate, relative increases in social insurance decreased income inequality by reducing the top-quintile income share and increasing the bottom-quintile share.[17] These results were not consistent across income-receiving units. For families, income inequality increased as income shifted from the fourth to the top quintile. Although the estimated inequality relationship was insignificant for unrelated individuals, the lowest-quintile income share increased with social-insurance expenditures. For husband-wife families, relative social-insurance expenditures increased income inequality only for families with a nonworking wife by increasing the top-quintile income share.

Increased social-insurance expenditures did not significantly alter income inequality for male-headed units, although the income distribution changed. For both male-headed families and unrelated individuals, the fourth-quintile income share fell and, for male-headed families, the top and lowest quintile income share increased. Income inequality declined for female-headed units with an increased bottom-quintile income share.

Why Do Differences Exist in the Influence of Social Insurance on Income Inequality?

While the totality of transfer programs (i.e., both social insurance and social welfare) unambiguously reduced income inequality during the postwar period, the impact of social insurance alone is somewhat ambiguous. This study finds few between-unit effects and many within-unit effects.[18] The within-unit changes were particularly strong for female unrelated individuals. Other studies confirm this finding by showing differing impacts of government transfers among income-receiving units, with most of the income inequality reductions stemming from reduced poverty among the elderly because of Social Security expenditures.[19]

These within-unit changes reduced aggregate income inequality (counter to Murray's argument). Increased benefits for the retired, widows, unemployed, and disabled altered the income distribution of existing income-receiving units and encouraged the formation of certain types of units. Much of the increase in unrelated-individual units (particularly female) stemmed from Social Security-induced income increases. Although increased unemployment and disability payments also permitted maintenance of certain units, these increases were smaller than retirement benefit increases. With increased weight on the now more equally distributed (female) retired income-receiving units, aggregate income inequality fell with increased social-insurance expenditures.

Within-unit changes were not consistent among all income-receiving units. All female-headed income-receiving units had more equally distributed incomes (due to an increased lowest-quintile income share) with increased government expenditures on social insurance. This confirms poverty reductions for the elderly (unrelated individuals) with increased Social Security benefits and for female-headed families with AFDC.

Male-headed income-receiving units had decreasing upper middle-class income (the fourth-quintile share) with increased social-insurance expenditures. While part of this decrease may result from "financing" transfers to low-income groups, it may also result from ceilings placed on benefits. Since unemployment, disability, and Social Security payments are a percentage of past wages with minimum and maximum levels, the income distribution remains unaltered with the exception of those at the maximum and minimum level. Since highest-paid workers have lower program participation rates (less unemployment and disability) and higher "other" income, those in the top quintile are unaffected by the benefit structure. Thus, the ceiling lowers relative earnings of the upper middle class (i.e., fourth quintile). Since program benefits have a floor and increase with dependents, male-headed families in the lowest quintile have an increased income share.

For single-earner, husband-wife families, income inequality increased with social-insurance expenditures. This increase stemmed from increases in the top-quintile income share. These families may be the recipients of the increased early retirement benefits associated with Social Security. While low-income families may not be able to "afford" retirement (inadequate pensions, savings, etc.), those in the top-quintile of earnings are economically able to retire early. Thus, income is redistributed toward upper-income individuals. Dual-earning families had no distributional change with increased social-insurance expenditures, primarily because this group contains few retirees. Retirees usually do not have a spouse in the labor force.

SUMMARY AND DISCUSSION

Virtually all government policy has redistribution effects. Since social-insurance programs link income benefits to past and present behaviors, income is redistributed from workers to specific groups of nonworkers. Since social-insurance programs have little impact on savings and the majority of their labor-supply effects stem from reductions in retirement and preretirement labor (universal across income-receiving units), within-unit income redistribution stemmed from structural aspects of the benefits schedules.

This study finds that increased social-insurance expenditures reduced aggregate income inequality slightly, although differences vary by income-receiving unit. Since most distributional alteration stemmed from program structure, alterations in benefit payments and eligibility differentially alter within-unit income distribution.

The significant aggregate reduction in income inequality and the differences across units suggest that the program benefit structure altered the composition of income-receiving units. Counter to Murray's argument, however, the compositional changes reduced aggregate inequality. The apparent increase in (low-income) elderly unrelated individuals and early retirees in single-earning families associated with increased Social Security benefits is consistent with Murray's thesis of program incentives increasing the proportion of nonworking individuals with government transfers (e.g., retired, unemployed, nonfamily units). Although Murray presents the compositional changes as negative, these compositional changes may be positive. The increased psychological benefits the elderly gained from living alone or early retirement is the explicit goal of Social Security and may outweigh program costs. Because of the size of Social Security, compositional effects from increased elderly households outweigh other potential compositional effects (e.g., increased female-headed families). Thus, aggregate income inequality is decreased with decreased poverty among the (low-income) elderly and not increased, as Murray suggests, with increased nonworking units.

NOTES

1. This chapter focuses solely on social programs and does not discuss education or employment programs (Chapter 7) or general "quality of life" programs. Much of the initial discussion of social programs comes from *Social Security Bulletin* (1987), which provides an outstanding history and summary of most social programs.

2. Social-insurance and social-welfare programs are not the totality of government redistribution efforts. Danziger and Portney (1988) delineate and discuss four categories of redistribution: income, occupation opportunity/status, health or quality of life, and political power. Social insurance and social welfare encompass only one area of redistribution. Since the other areas do not directly transfer income, discussion of these programs is limited or nonexistent. Because social-psychological benefits, noncash economic benefits, and taxation from these programs are not included in the analysis, our discussion of the effect of government may understate the extent of redistribution.

3. In-kind benefits also increased over the period. In 1965, Medicare and Medicaid became available and had expenditures of about sixty billion dollars. Food stamps became available in 1964 and had about a ten billion dollar expenditure. Housing assistance for the poor began in 1937 and had an expenditure of about seven billion dollars. All dollar amounts are from the early 1980s. See Danziger et al. (1981) for a discussion.

4. Derthick (1979) discusses over-time changes in Social Security.

5. For historic evolutions see Baily (1977) or U.S. Department of Labor (1976) (Unemployment Insurance System), National Commission of State Workmen's Compensation Laws (1973) (Worker's Compensation), or Hamermesh (1977).

6. Danziger et al. (1981) review both social-insurance and social-welfare programs and their direct and indirect redistribution effects.

7. While taxes also altered the income distribution, this study focuses on pretax income, hence, taxation is not discussed here. Betson et al. (1988), Sammartino and Kasten (1988), and Pechman (1985) provide discussion.

8. See Feldstein (1974). "Real world" additions to Feldstein's model confirm work disincentive effects (e.g., Hamermesh, 1979; Hanoch and Honig, 1978; Killingsworth, 1976).

9. For a review, see Aaron (1982).

10. Estimated Social Security labor force disincentive effects range from 100 percent (Pellechio, 1978) to negligible impacts (cf., Gordon and Blinder, 1980 or Blinder et al., 1980). Burkhauser and Turner (1978) show increased labor supply at younger ages partially offsetting later disincentive effects.

11. Haveman and Wolfe (1984) and Parsons (1984) debate the disincentive magnitude of disability insurance.

12. See Moffitt and Nicholson (1982) or Hamermesh (1979, 1977).

13. Sheshinski (1978) argues that no reduction in aggregate savings occurs. Feldstein (1974) and Barro (1978, 1974) argue that savings increased. Ando and Modigliani (1963) argue that savings decreased.

14. See Williamson and Jones (1983) or Munnell (1982).

15. For example, using a retiree at age 65 without a spouse as the base, the benefit is increased with a spouse and decreased with early retirement.

16. Disability claims may be limited by aggregate dollar amounts rather than time.

17. These results are understated since the government further equalized income with social-welfare programs (Chapter 2 and Danziger et al., 1981), taxes (Pechman, 1985), and direct employment of workers (Durden and Schwarz-Miller, 1982).

18. Results contradict Butler and McDonald's (1986) findings of large interdistributional effects (e.g., between units) but few intradistributional inequality changes (e.g., within units) associated with government variables.

19. Baum and Sjogren (1988) specifically link decreased inequality to Social Security effects of decreased poverty among the elderly while Danziger and Plotnick (1977) show differential impacts of government transfers for income-receiving units.

7

White-Nonwhite Differences: Labor Demand, Labor Supply, Government, and Income-Receiving Unit Structure

Whites have much higher incomes than nonwhites. Because of discrimination in labor, education, capital, and housing markets, and racially different labor market behavior, the structure of the nonwhite income distribution differs dramatically from the white distribution.[1] From 1950 to 1985, white median income levels consistently exceeded those of nonwhites, irrespective of whether the income-receiving unit was families, unrelated individuals, or workers (Table 7–1). For families, nonwhite income was about half of white income from 1950 to 1960, with relative increases between 1960 and 1970 and little relative change thereafter. Nonwhite families received slightly under two-thirds of the income of white families from 1970 to 1985. Racial disparities in unrelated-individual income show that, with the exception of 1960, nonwhites consistently received between two-thirds and three-fourths of white income. Nonwhite full-time, full-year workers consistently received about three-fourths of white workers' income.

Lower relative income of nonwhites lead to higher relative poverty levels (Table 7–1). In 1960, over one-half of all blacks were impoverished—over three times the rate of white poverty. With both absolute and relative poverty falling between 1960 and 1985, slightly over 30 percent of all blacks lived in poverty in 1985—2.75 times the white poverty rate.

These racial discrepancies in median incomes and poverty rates created differing white-nonwhite income distributions. By all measures—Gini coefficient, top-to-bottom share ratio, and middle-quintile income share—nonwhites consistently had more unequally distributed incomes from a greater positive skew than whites. Part of this larger variance in nonwhite income stemmed from the larger

Table 7-1
Racial Differences in Income and Inequality

	1950			1960			1970			1980			1985		
	Nonwhite[1]	White[2]	Ratio	Nonwhite	White	Ratio	Nonwhite	White	Ratio	Nonwhite	White	Ratio	Nonwhite	White	Ratio
Income[3]															
Median Family Income	8352	15395	.54	1173	21195	.55	18052	28358	.64	18072	28596	.63	18635	29152	.64
Median Unrelated-Individual Income	3651	4983	.73	387	6756	.57	6214	9095	.68	7552	11440	.66	8782	12249	.72
Median Weekly Earnings[4]	–	–	–	–	–	–	274	371	.74	278	351	.79	277	355	.76
Persons in Poverty (Percent)[5]	–	–	–	56.2	18.1	3.10	33.5	10.0	3.35	32.5	10.2	3.1	31.3	11.4	2.75
Inequality															
Gini Coefficient	.420	.389	1.08	.446	.381	1.17	.397	.340	1.17	.407	.343	1.19	.402	.344	1.17
Top Quintile Income Share															
Bottom Quintile Income Share	16.0	13.2	1.12	19.0	12.1	1.57	12.5	8.9	1.51	12.5	8.5	1.47	13.0	8.7	1.50
Middle Quintile Income Share	.165	.173	.95	.152	.174	.87	.169	.198	.85	.161	.196	.82	.168	.197	.85

[1] Nonwhites are not confined to blacks.

[2] "Ratio" reflects the ratio of the nonwhite value over the white value.

[3] All income and earnings are in 1985 dollars.

[4] Full-time, full-year workers.

[5] Poverty statistics reflect white-black comparisons and are based on individuals not receiving units.

Figure 7–1
Racial Differences in Income Inequality over Time: Gini Coefficients

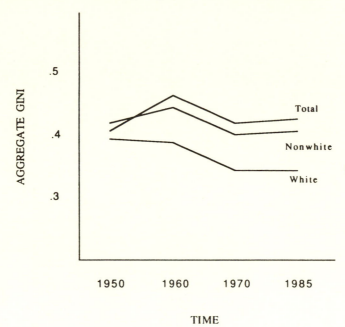

TIME

within-race differences in socioeconomic class, experience (or age variance), weeks worked, schooling, and spatial location.[2]

Over time, the nonwhite income distribution, in comparison to the white distribution, became increasingly more unequal. That is, the nonwhite and white income distributions were more similar in 1950 than in 1985. Between 1950 and 1985, the nonwhite-to-white ratios of Gini coefficients increased, top-to-bottom share ratios increased, and middle-quintile shares declined. This *between*-race discrepancy increased concern about the bifurcation of income *within* the nonwhite population.

Almost all between-race distributional change occurred between 1950 and 1960. Between 1960 and 1985, the relative ratios of the Gini coefficients and share distribution did not alter. Figures 7–1 and 7–2 illustrate these parallel post–1960 changes by showing within-race and aggregate income inequality and share distribution. The increasing disparity between nonwhite and white income inequality from 1950 to 1960 increased aggregate income inequality sharply enough to exceed the (relatively unequal) nonwhite distribution after 1960 (Figure 7–1). The same pattern existed in share distributions (Figure 7–2). Because ag-

Figure 7–2
Racial Differences in Income Share Distribution over Time

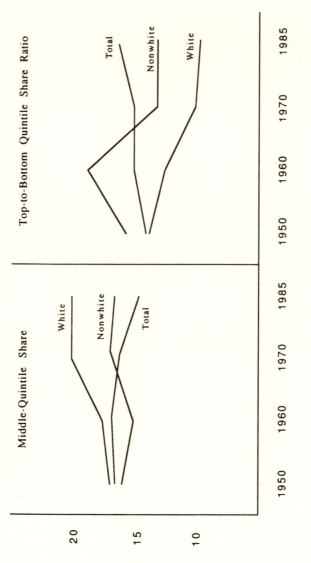

gregate shares became more unequal than within-race shares between 1960 and 1970, by 1985, the aggregate middle-quintile share was smaller than the within-race shares and the aggregate top-to-bottom share ratio was greater than the within-race ratio. Since both whites and nonwhites showed similar patterns in distributional change, the over-time between-race divergence in income inequality and share distribution directly increased aggregate income inequality.

In sum, although nonwhite-white income *levels* converged slightly during the postwar period (primarily between 1960 and 1970), between-race income distribution diverged. Although within-race income distributions became more equal from 1950 to 1985, the equalization within the white income distribution was greater. The apparent conflict between converging income levels and diverging income distributions arises because over-time distributional changes take two forms, between-race and within-race changes. Most studies examining white-nonwhite income differentials focus on between-race inequality. Current concern over potential bifurcation of black income, however, has heightened interest in within-race inequality. Since changes in aggregate income inequality result from both within- and between-race changes, this chapter examines both. Analysis initially examines between- and within-race charcteristics and income differences and then examines between- and within-race distributional differences.

WHITE-NONWHITE CHARACTERISTIC CHANGES

From 1950 to 1985, the demographic charcteristics of both whites and non-whites changed (Table 7–2). In 1950, nonwhites were 95-percent black, had a median education level of the sixth grade, a fertility rate of 3.6 children per woman, and a dependency ratio of nearly three-fourths. By 1985, only 83 percent were black, fertility fell to a near-replacement level of 2.2, median educational levels increased (particularly between 1970 and 1985) to high-school graduation, and dependency fell slightly. From 1970 to 1985, the proportion of nonwhite husband-wife families decreased from nearly one-half to one-third of all income-receiving units while the proportion of female-headed units and unrelated individuals increased.

The same general over-time changes occurred in the white subpopulation. In 1950, the median education level for whites was the ninth grade, fertility was 3.2 children per woman, and dependency was 63 percent. By 1985, median education exceeded high-school graduation and fertility fell to a below-replacement level of 1.7. From 1970 to 1985, the proportion of husband-wife families decreased from nearly two-thirds to slightly over one-half of all income-receiving units while the proportion of female-headed units and unrelated individuals increased.

Some of these within-race changes brought near racial parity in demographic characteristics (Table 7–2). By 1985, little racial difference existed in the proportion of unrelated individuals and levels of education. Racial disparities increased, however, in the proportion of husband-wife families and in fertility rates. Nonwhites had higher fertility and were much more likely than whites to

Table 7-2
Racial Differences in Demographic Characteristics, 1950–1985

	1950			1960			1970			1980			1985		
	Nonwhite[1]	White	Ratio[2]	Nonwhite	White	Ratio	Nonwhite	White	Ratio	Nonwhite	White	Ratio	Nonwhite	White	Ratio
Income-Receiving Unit (Percent)															
Husband-Wife Families	–	–	–	–	–	–	53.3	72.5	.74	40.0	63.2	.63	36.6	60.6	.60
Female-Headed Families and Female Unrelated Individuals	–	–	–	–	–	–	34.7	19.6	1.77	43.7	24.2	1.81	46.7	25.6	1.82
Unrelated Individuals	–	–	–	–	–	–	22.0	18.4	1.20	28.0	26.2	1.07	28.5	27.8	1.03
Demographic Characteristics															
Percent Black	95.5	–	–	94.3	–	–	89.6	–	–	83.8	–	–	80.3	–	–
Dependency[3]	73.7	63.6	1.16	94.4	79.6	1.19	96.0	77.0	1.25	74.0	63.7	1.16	70.5	61.1	1.15
Total Fertility Rate[4]	3575	3230	1.11	4522	3533	1.28	3067	2385	1.29	2323	1749	1.33	2224	1719	1.29
Median Education Completed	6.6	9.0	.73	8.0	10.9	.73	9.8	12.1	.81	12.0	12.5	.96	12.3	12.7	.97

[1]Nonwhites are not confined to blacks. For 1970 through 1985, race comparisons for income-receiving units and education are for blacks and whites.

[2]"Ratio" represents the nonwhite value over the white value.

[3]The dependency ratio is the summation of individuals under 18 and over 64 divided by those between 18 and 64 (times 100).

[4]The total fertility rate is the number of children 1,000 women would have if they lived through childbearing years and gave birth at prevailing age-specific fertility rates.

live outside husband-wife families. Little change occurred over time in the relative levels of female-headed income-receiving units or dependency.

Within- and between-race labor market changes also occurred from 1950 to 1980 (Table 7–3). While both whites and nonwhites showed the same trends in labor force behavior (with different rates of change), employment patterns differed dramatically.[3]

The different over-time movements in employment caused convergence in industrial and occupational employment, primarily because nonwhite employment shifts ran counter to the aggregate trends. A higher proportion of nonwhites were employed in both the service and manufacturing sectors in 1985 than in 1950. Because of initially high employment levels in the service sector and increasing manufacturing employment, the nonwhite service-to-manufacturing employment ratio *decreased* between 1950 and 1980. For whites, the service-to-manufacturing employment ratio doubled over the period. These within-race changes caused ultimate convergence in between-race industrial employment. Convergence was not absolute, however. By 1980, in comparison to whites, nonwhites were overrepresented in government, service (with decreased representation over time), and transportation/communications, were near parity in manufacturing, and were underrepresented in other sectors.

Nonwhite workers had large increases in both professional/managerial and craft employment (albeit in the lower echelons) and dramatic decreases in service and farm/operative/laborer positions. Whites had little change in professional, farm/operative/laborer, and service employment, slight increases in clerical and sales employment, and slight decreases in craft employment. These within-race occupational employment shifts caused some convergence in between-race occupational employment; however, occupational employment patterns were still diverse in 1980. Nonwhite employment in low-skill (and low-wage) service or farm/operative/laborer positions was consistently higher than for whites.

While between-race employment converged with racial differences in over-time patterns of change, between-race labor force behavior diverged with similar over-time patterns of change (Table 7–3). From 1950 to 1980, both white and nonwhite unemployment and female labor force participation increased while male labor force participation decreased; however, levels of change between the races differed dramatically. Rapid increases in nonwhite unemployment caused nonwhite unemployment to more than double white unemployment by 1980 and male labor force participation rates decreased more rapidly for nonwhites than whites over the period. The combination of increased unemployment and decreased labor force participation for nonwhite men caused large relative and absolute increases in nonwhite male joblessness. The same was not true for women. The more rapid entrance of white women into the labor force converged female labor force participation rates to near parity by 1980.

This portrait of change in white-nonwhite income, demographic, and labor market characteristics masks several important over-time interrelationships. Prior to 1960, discrimination played a large role in nonwhite earnings capacity irre-

Table 7–3
Racial Characteristics of Workers[1]

	1950			1960			1970			1980		
	Nonwhite[2]	White	Ratio[3]	Nonwhite	White	Ratio	Black	White	Ratio	Black	White	Ratio
Labor Force Characteristics												
Unemployment Rate	9.0	5.7	1.58	10.2	4.9	2.08	8.2	4.5	1.82	14.3	6.3	2.27
Female Labor Force Participation Rate	46.1	33.3	1.38	48.2	36.5	1.32	49.5	42.6	1.16	53.2	51.2	1.04
Male Labor Force Participation Rate	85.2	85.6	1.00	83.0	83.4	1.00	76.5	80.0	.96	70.6	78.2	.90
Industry												
Agriculture	19.8	11.9	1.66	10.0	6.7	1.49	3.6	3.7	.97	1.7	3.0	.57
Mining	.8	1.8	.44	.4	1.1	.36	.3	.8	.38	.5	1.1	.45
Construction	5.5	6.3	.87	5.8	6.2	.94	5.3	6.1	.87	4.3	6.1	.70
Manufacturing	18.8	27.2	.69	20.2	29.2	.69	24.3	26.2	.93	23.2	22.3	1.04
Transportation/ Communications/ Public Utilities	6.3	8.1	.78	5.7	7.4	.77	8.7	7.7	1.13	8.9	7.1	1.25
Trade	11.7	19.7	.59	13.9	19.6	.71	–	–	–	13.9	21.2	.66
Finance/Insurance/ Real Estate	1.6	3.6	.44	1.8	4.6	.39	3.0	5.2	.58	4.8	6.2	.77
Service	32.2	16.9	1.91	36.8	20.2	1.82	36.0	24.9	1.45	35.1	28.0	1.25
Government	3.4	4.6	.74	5.4	5.1	1.06	4.9	4.6	1.07	7.5	5.0	1.50
Service Manufacturing	1.71	.62	2.76	1.82	.69	2.64	1.48	.95	1.58	1.51	1.25	1.21

Occupation

Professional/Managerial	6.1	25.5	.24	9.1	20.0	.46	14.1	23.9	.59
Clerical/Sales	9.4	24.2	.39	18.2	30.4	.60	25.2	31.1	.81
Craft	7.4	16.6	.45	9.6	14.6	.66	8.9	13.4	.66
Operatives/Laborers/									
Farm	42.2	24.3	1.74	35.2	23.9	1.47	28.7	20.0	1.44
Service	35.0	9.3	3.76	27.8	11.0	2.53	23.1	11.6	1.99
Blue Collar[4]/White Collar	3.20	.82	3.90	1.64	.76	2.16	.95	.60	1.60

[1]Table includes only employed persons with 1970 and 1980 restricted to those 16 and over. Incomplete or incompatible data prevent 1985 comparisons on industry and occupation. Labor force characteristics in 1985 do not differ dramatically from 1980.

[2]Nonwhites are not restricted to blacks.

[3]The ratio represents the sector employment of nonwhite (black) over white.

[4]This definition differs slightly from the independent variable since farm workers are included as blue-collar workers.

spective of (noted) human capital differences (e.g., education) or levels of impoverishment. Because occupational segregation (observed in Table 7–3) produced the greater income disparities for highly educated nonwhites, traditional paths to economic success were weakened for nonwhites. Throughout the 1960s, however, earnings converged as the labor market tightened, labor market discrimination declined, the relative positioning of nonwhite workers improved (e.g., converging industry and occupational employment), and human capital characteristics converged.[4] The earnings convergence was particularly strong for younger, more educated workers,[5] females, and those in the South.[6] By the 1970s, racial income differentials narrowed with increased nonwhite occupational mobility[7] and nearly equivalent white-nonwhite returns to education.[8] The remaining racial income differentials were constant after 1970.

While postwar convergence of white-nonwhite income is well established, three unresolved issues remain. First, the remaining racial income discrepancies may no longer represent the "inheritance of race" but the "inheritance of poverty." That is, as the significance of race in earnings differentials declined, the significance of background increased. Since nonwhites are more likely than whites to have a low socioeconomic background, reduced earnings now result from their background, not their race.

Second, single-year convergence in white-nonwhite earnings mask differences in the stability of middle-class status. That is, at any point in time, aggregate white and nonwhite income converges; however, unlike their white counterparts, middle-class nonwhites do not retain their relatively high earnings for long periods and, hence, move in and out of the middle class.[9]

Third, levels of white-nonwhite employment diverged after the early 1970s. Increased nonwhite unemployment[10] and decreased male labor force participation[11] increased nonwhite joblessness over whites and reversed the convergence in educational returns and income.[12] Using both joblessness and earnings as labor market outcomes, men showed little over-time racial convergence in income or educational returns while women show near complete convergence.[13] The combination of earnings convergence and employment divergence for men accounted for the parallel white-nonwhite movement in income inequality since 1960.

Why Did Some Racial Characteristics Converge and Others Diverge?

After 1950, white-nonwhite differences in income, education, female labor force participation, and employment converged while differences in joblessness and income-receiving-unit structure diverged. Even with convergence, dramatic racial differences still exist in occupational employment and poverty. Both reduced discrimination and institutional change explain these over-time patterns of change and resultant outcomes.[14]

Discrimination. Although several models explain the rationale underlying discrimination,[15] the dominant economic model is Becker's (1971) "taste for discrimination.''[16] Within this model, individuals act as if they would (directly or indirectly) pay to associate with some persons instead of others. In the labor market, the discriminator can be an employer, employee, consumer, government, or the entire white community. Market discrimination exists with a difference between the actual ratio of white-nonwhite wages and the ratio as it would exist without discriminating individuals. With equal between-race productivities, market discrimination exists when the white-nonwhite wage ratio does not equal one. Market segregation exists if the physical contact of whites and nonwhites is minimized (i.e., employment segregation). Competitive forces erode segregation/discrimination slowly, however, because differing racial productivities, abilities, work habits, and skills are often production complements. Since continued segregation/discrimination results in the ''crowding'' of nonwhites into certain occupations, unemployment is increased and wages (and marginal productivity) are decreased in ''nonwhite'' occupations.[17]

Other models of discrimination more explicitly model its source. Statistical discrimination results from employer cost minimization with use of signals.[18] Since data on individual productivity differentials are unavailable, race serves as one of the signals indicating an individual with low productivity. Discrimination also results from the use of nonracial signals (e.g., educational quality) since nonwhites may have difficulty obtaining the signals and employers may use different signals for nonwhites than whites.

A monopoly model of race discrimination posits that whites act as a (hiring) monopoly sanctioned by the government.[19] Using the monopoly of economic power, whites maximize social (as opposed to Becker's physical) distance from nonwhites and increase the wage disparities between the groups. Allocation of white and nonwhite laborers is efficient (i.e., there is no ''crowding'') but nonwhite wages are lower than marginal productivity and, preferably, near subsistence. White power over nonwhites also causes lower skill levels in nonwhites, as white employers, workers, unions, and communities maintain their superior power position.

Segmented labor market theories extend monopoly-power models and posit racial barriers truncating competition for employment by confining nonwhites to low-paying employment structures.[20] Racial barriers preventing nonwhite movement into higher-paying positions result from (employer and union) discrimination and are strengthened by labor market segregation in employment and confinement to ghettos. In contrast to white employment structures, employers create nonwhite employment structures that elicit unstable work patterns and high rates of absenteeism from workers. These characteristics confirm discriminatory employer and union practices (e.g., nonwhites are unstable, therefore it pays to discriminate). Ghettos, containing massive poverty and an integral part of industrial capitalism, produce cultural barriers for nonwhites by providing an environment conducive to the development of unstable work patterns.[21]

Converging racial employment, education, and income differentials indicate a reduction in racial discrimination and segregation over the period. Discrimination/segregation has not vanished, however. Differentials in occupational employment patterns, poverty, and income still exist and racial differences in joblessness and income-receiving unit structure are increasing. This suggests continued use of white employment power with resultant statistical discrimination and occupational crowding from segregation.

Institutional Changes. The 1960s produced dramatic changes in legislation and judicial decisions affecting nonwhite access to the labor market and education and altering racial disparities in income, poverty, and training levels.[22] In the labor market, the Equal Pay Act of 1963 outlawed differential payment for identical jobs. The more extensive Title VII of the Civil Rights Act of 1964 (with the 1972 amendment) outlawed discrimination in hiring, promotion, firing, transferring, training, and pay and established the Equal Employment Opportunity Commission (EEOC) for enforcement. Executive Order 11246 (1965— President Johnson) mandated "Affirmative Action" in the hiring of blacks and other minorities for all businesses with government contracts or funding. Section 8A of the Small Business Act designed a portion of all government contracts for minority-owned firms. Court cases reinforced legislative antidiscriminatory action. *Quarles v. Phillip Morris* (1968)[23] and *United States v. Local 189 United Papermakers and Paperworkers* (1969)[24] ruled against seniority systems perpetuating discrimination. *Griggs v. Duke Power* (1971)[25] increased the breadth of Affirmative Action and the enforcement possibilities of the EEOC by restricting the use of credentials unrelated to successful job performance.

Judicial decisions also altered human capital markets. Education quality converged as *Brown v. Board of Education* (1954)[26] struck down the separate but equal doctrine and *Green v. County School Board (1968)*[27] ruled that freedom-of-choice schooling decisions were inadequate unless mixed classrooms resulted.

The government directly entered the human capital and labor markets during the 1960s and 1970s by sponsoring employment and training programs. Employment in economically depressed areas was provided under the Area Redevelopment Act (1961) and training was provided to displaced workers under the 1962 Manpower Development and Training Act. A plethora of programs (e.g., Job Corps, Neighborhood Youth Corps) provided skills, training, and/or general antidelinquency and socialization education for youths during the 1960s. The Emergency Employment Act (1971) moved away from skill training toward countercyclic employment by providing employment to disadvantaged youth. In 1973, the Comprehensive Employment and Training Act (CETA) consolidated all employment and training programs. CETA saw its replacement in the Jobs Training and Partnership Act (1982), which, with a more restricted budget, lessened the government's role in employment and training and more actively recruited private business in the process.[28]

Resultant Changes in Racial Characteristics. Increased nonwhite human capital investment and decreased discrimination and occupational segregation (although slight) reduced racial income disparities over time. Simultaneously, increased nonwhite income and changes in poverty programs (Chapter 2) altered economic incentives (for nonwhites) in the areas of human capital, employment, and receiving-unit structure.[29] If education (and occupation and earnings) differentials resulted from individual rational behavior, nonwhites invested less in education because of lower returns.[30] Since nonwhite educational benefits fell with lower (discriminatory) earnings and higher rates of time preference and educational costs increased with capital market imperfections and a poverty background not conducive to learning, reductions in labor market discrimination and capital market imperfections (at a minimum) increased educational benefits, reduced educational costs, and increased educational returns for nonwhites. This caused the racial convergence in educational differentials.

Converging educational returns created vintage effects—increased nonwhite education (and wages) only for young workers. Thus, aggregate nonwhite wage convergence was slow because young nonwhite workers had increased education (and wages) over their older counterparts. These vintage effects lessened the role of population age structure on the nonwhite income distribution since young nonwhite workers were not low-wage workers (as compared to older workers).

While reduced discrimination and increased education explain racial convergence of education and income, changing industrial and occupational employment and/or government poverty programs explain divergence in white-nonwhite employment and income-receiving unit structure and the halt in income convergence.

Murray (1984) argues that the Great Society programs, however well-intentioned, exacerbated the poverty and joblessness problems of nonwhites by creating work disincentives. This is illustrated by increased expenditures for poverty and labor market programs during the 1970s producing stagnant (nonwhite) poverty and joblessness rates. Government programs, by providing work disincentives and a social safety net, encouraged joblessness rather than employment at menial jobs. Nonwhites, with lower wages, are closer to the (marginal) level where government programs enter the labor market decision. Since many labor market programs also created disincentives to form husband-wife families (Chapter 2), nonwhites (low-income) as a group were further hindered by an increased proportion of female-headed families and poverty backgrounds (increasingly used as a labor market signal indicating an individual with low productivity).

In contrast, Wilson (1987) argues that increased black joblessness and decreased husband-wife families resulted from shifts in industrial and occupational employment. Employment changes were particularly severe for central-city, low-skilled black males. Since the manufacturing-to-service shift decreased the number of unskilled and semiskilled positions located in central cities (where most blacks live), the shifting economic base removed job opportunities for nonwhites and caused their unemployment rates to soar. Decreased male labor force participation rates resulted as a discouraged-worker response to high unemployment levels. With increased joblessness among black males and convergence in female employment and wages, the marriageability of black males decreased. That is, single black woman and black men had equivalent labor market opportunities, hence, marriage rates decreased. This increased the proportion of female-headed income-receiving units and decreased the proportion of husband-wife families.

Summary.   Dramatic changes occurred within and between the nonwhite and white subpopulations between 1950 and 1985, although the reasons underlying the changes are not straightforward. Some between-race change resulted in convergence of labor-market activity consistent with reduced discrimination and occupational segregation (e.g., industrial and occupational employment, female labor force participation, income, education). Some change resulted in divergence of labor market activity, consistent with both increased government spending and shifting employment (e.g., unemployment, socioeconomic status (poverty), male labor force participation, and female-headed income-receiving units). These changes in nonwhite and white characteristics, which underlie earnings determination, directly led to changes in the within-race and between-race income distributions.

RACIAL DIFFERENCES IN INCOME INEQUALITY AND SHARE DISTRIBUTION

Table 7–4 shows the estimated influence of dependency, industrial and occupational employment, income-receiving unit, and social-insurance expenditures on income inequality and share distribution for whites and nonwhites and in the aggregate.

The dependent variable of the racially stratified equations is income inequality or share distribution for either the white or nonwhite income distribution.[31] Aggregate equations reflect results of aggregate analysis presented earlier. The comparison of racially stratified estimates (within-race influences) to aggregate estimates allows inference about between-race inequality and distribution movements. If within-race estimates (sign and significance) are similar to aggregate estimates, the economic, demographic, and government influences have the same impact on within-race and aggregate distributions. If aggregate estimates are significant and stratified estimates are not, economic and demographic changes in aggregate income inequality stemmed from between-race income distributions and did not alter within-race distributions. If aggregate estimates are insignificant and stratified estimates are significant, aggregate inequality changes resulted from compositional change. In this case, the compositional change reflected within-race change.

The income-receiving unit independent variable measures the change in the ratio of female-headed income-receiving units to husband-wife families. It provides a measure of relative increases in (low-income) female-headed units or relative decreases in husband-wife units. Income-receiving-unit changes were significant influences on within-race income inequality and share distribution for both races. Since receiving-unit changes were not significant influences on the aggregate distribution, the increasing proportion of female-headed units increased within-race income inequality but did not alter the aggregate distribution. This

Table 7-4
Racial Differences in Influences on Inequality: Elasticities[1]

	Gini Coefficient	Top Quintile	Fourth Quintile	Middle Quintile	Second Quintile	Lowest Quintile
Aggregate						
Occupation	.283	.088	.190	-.338	-.435	-.025
Industry	.490****	.466**	-.175	-.406	-.656***	-.988***
Dependency Ratio	.466*****	.336**	.054	-.326	-.816****	-.976****
Female Labor Force Participation	-.213	.106	-1.28	.432	.912	1.96**
Government	-.135**	-.188**	.275	-.006	.091	.384**
Income-Receiving Unit	-.014	-.252	.738	-.052	-.399	-.571
Nonwhites						
Occupation[2]	-.399***	-.342**	.068	.250*	1.70****	1.01***
Industry	-.050	-.093	.114*	.038	.167	-.331
Dependency Ratio	.021	-.029	.103**	-.050	.708***	-.513***
Female Labor Force Participation	-1.30****	-1.20****	.303*	1.23****	.096	3.49****
Government	.023	.055	-.050	-.101**	-.052	.319**
Income-Receiving Unit	.586****	.528****	-.133	-.504****	-.802***	-1.62****

Table 7-4 (continued)

	Gini Coefficient	Top Quintile	Fourth Quintile	Middle Quintile	Second Quintile	Lowest Quintile
Whites						
Occupation	-4.08***	-.143	-.439**	.420***	.526***	.805***
Industry	-.003	-.098	.052	.068	.009	-.246
Dependency Ratio	-.244*****	-.164**	-.039	.323*****	.034***	-.029
Female Labor Force Participation	-.982*****	-.080	-1.44*****	.752***	1.60*****	2.60*****
Government	-.082*	-.046	-.074	.074	.015	.322*****
Income-Receiving Unit	.352**	.110	.594***	-.248*	-.590***	-1.00*****

[1]Elasticities reflect the percent change (at the mean) in the Gini coefficient or quintile income share associated with a one-percent change (at the mean) in the influence's value. Computations are based on regression results presented in Appendix Tables A4-7 to A4-12 for race and A4-1 to A4-6 for the aggregate.

[2]All influences represent their construct as independent variables (ratios times 100). Occupation reflects blue-collar to white-collar employment. Industry reflects service to manufacturing employment. Dependency ratio reflects the population aged under 18 and over 64 to the population 18 to 64. Female labor force participation reflects the number of employed and unemployed females 16 and over to the total number of like-aged females. Government reflects spending on social insurance relative to GNP. Income-receiving unit reflects female-headed to husband-wife units.

**** p $\leq$ .001
 *** p $\leq$ .01
  ** p $\leq$ .05
   * p $\leq$ .10

supports the Chapter 2 conclusion that, in the aggregate, race rather than income-receiving unit dominated changes in the income distribution.

For both whites and nonwhites, relative increases in female-headed units increased within-race inequality by reducing the income share of the lowest three quintiles and increasing the income shares at the top. This is consistent with high levels of poverty for both white and nonwhite female-headed units. Since nonwhites had greater share increases at the top than whites, the overlap between the bottom of the white income distribution and the top of the nonwhite distribution increased. Thus, increases in the relative number of female income-receiving units had no discernible impact on aggregate income inequality.

Changing employment had different within-race inequality and aggregate inequality influences. Occupational shifts, an insignificant influence on aggregate income inequality, increased within-race income inequality. For both racial groups, as relative blue-collar employment decreased, within-race inequality increased, with the bottom two quintiles losing income share and the top quintile gaining income share. Thus, occupational shifts increased within-race income inequality with increasing income polarization. Although the direction of the impact was similar for both races, the magnitude (on inequality) was stronger for nonwhites than whites.

Figure 7–3 graphically portrays these phenomena by showing white and nonwhite Lorenz curves developed from the average quintile shares between 1947 and 1985. The aggregate Lorenz curves show the deviation from "perfect equality" for the white and nonwhite income distributions. "Perfect equality" is defined as each quintile of the population receiving 20 percent of the income share and is illustrated by the 45-degree line. Any movement toward the 45-degree line indicates reduced inequality. Figure 7–3 also shows changes in the white and nonwhite Lorenz curves associated with a one-percent increase in dependency and a one-percent decrease in relative blue-collar employment.

Figure 7–3 shows a dramatic inequality reduction for both whites and nonwhites with a one-percent increase in occupational shifts (i.e., relative increases in blue-collar employment). The movement toward equality is particularly pronounced at the top of the distribution for nonwhites and in the middle of the distribution for both races. Increased income inequality and income polarization (stronger for nonwhites than whites) associated with occupational shifts are consistent with Wilson's (1987) contention of the bifurcation of black income with employment changes.

Although industrial employment shifts significantly increased aggregate income inequality and share distribution, there was no significant impact on within-race distributions. That is, relative increases in service-sector employment did not alter the income distribution of either whites or nonwhites, but it polarized aggregate income. This results from increased divergence in the white and nonwhite income distributions (i.e., increased between-race inequality) with increased joblessness for nonwhites as employment shifts.

Changing population age structures differentially influenced within-race in-

Figure 7–3
Lorenz Curves for Whites and Nonwhites: Dependency and Occupational Changes

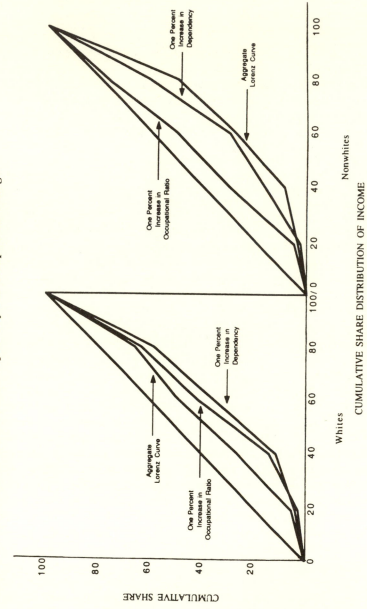

come inequality and distribution, with the magnitude of the inequality impact about 10 times higher for whites than nonwhites and often of a different sign. For whites, increased dependency *decreased* inequality by increasing middle-class income (via the income share of the middle and lowest quintiles) and reducing the top-quintile income share. This is seen graphically in Figure 7–3. For nonwhites, increased dependency reduced the lowest-quintile share and polarized middle-class income (by increasing the second and fourth quintile income share). Thus, dependency reductions associated with the aging baby boom reduced white middle-class income. For nonwhites, decreased dependency increased the top-quintile share, reduced the variance in nonwhite middle-class income, and increased the bottom-quintile share. For nonwhites, this reflects the ''vintage effects'' of increased education quality and quantity of younger nonwhite cohorts offsetting traditionally lower earnings of younger workers.

Within-race distributional changes associated with dependency can explain aggregate changes of reduced dependency decreasing inequality. Current increases in the (aggregate) bottom-quintile income share resulted from increases in the top-quintile share of the nonwhite distribution. Current reductions in the (aggregate) top-quintile income share resulted from offsetting within-race distributional changes.

The influence of increased female labor force participation and social-insurance expenditure on within-race inequality generally followed aggregate patterns. Increased female labor force participation reduced within-race income inequality by increasing the lowest-quintile income share for both races. In addition, within-race middle-class income increased. Although inequality changes were slightly stronger for nonwhites, distributional impacts (i.e., share movements) were slightly stronger for whites. The similarity in aggregate and within-race income inequality and distribution changes with social-insurance expenditures does not support Murray's contention of increased inequality associated with government-induced compositional change.

Why Do Racial Discrepancies Exist?

This study uncovered three discrepancies in between- and within-race influences on income inequality and distribution. First, income-receiving unit changes were significant influences on within-race inequality but were not significant influences on aggregate inequality. The strong interaction between race and income-receiving unit produced this discrepancy.[32] From 1947 to 1985, racial income converged, irrespective of unit, while income disparities between husband-wife and female-headed units increased, irrespective of race. The large and growing disparity between the structure of white and nonwhite income-receiving units (nonwhites increasingly have a much lower percentage of husband-wife units) and the between-race convergence of income were offsetting in the aggregate and produced insignificant influences on aggregate inequality. Upon racial disaggregation, however, the offsetting influences of race and income-receiving unit were separated and income-receiving unit significantly influenced within-race income inequality. For both racial groups, increased female-headed units increased income inequality via reductions in the lowest-quintile income share.

Second, differences existed in the influences of changing employment patterns on aggregate and within-race inequality. Consistent with employment increases in jobs located in the top and bottom thirds of the income distribution, shifting occupational employment increased within-race income inequality for both racial groups.[33] Because of racial occupational segregation, expanding employment opportunities at the top and bottom of the income distribution did not alter the aggregate income distribution. Although nonwhites moved into higher-salary professional/managerial and blue-collar positions (Table 7–3), occupational segregation within these positions confined nonwhites to the lower-paid ranks.[34] The bifurcation of occupational employment polarized within-race income as both whites and nonwhites increased employment in top and bottom income positions within their own occupational distribution. Continued occupational segregation, however, left the aggregate income distribution unaltered with occupational employment changes. In the aggregate, compositional exchange occurred as high-income nonwhites (e.g., those in lower echelon professional/managerial positions) replaced whites.

Shifts in industrial employment, a significant influence on aggregate income inequality, did not influence within-race income inequality. With discrimination more prevalent in concentrated sectors of the economy[35] and enforcement of antidiscrimination legislation more prevalent in larger firms, an industrial convergence in discrimination occurred.[36] The increasing similarity of discrimination in the manufacturing and service sectors and the movement of nonwhites into manufacturing left within-race inequality unaltered since less racial stratification existed in both sectors.

Third, population dependency had different influences on aggregate and within-race income inequality. Increased dependency, while increasing aggregate inequality, decreased white income inequality, and had little influence on nonwhite inequality. Thus, the aggregate change resulted from within-race changes. For nonwhites, "vintage effects" of the increased education quality of young nonwhite cohorts offset the traditional age-related increases in the wage structure. This increased income of the bottom of the aggregate distribution and decreased inequality as nonwhite youth reduced dependency and entered the labor market.

Increased female labor force participation and social-insurance expenditures had similar influences on within-race and aggregate inequality.[37] The similar equalizing role of government on aggregate, white, and nonwhite income distributions shows the nondiscriminatory impact of increased indigents' income. For nonwhites, however, the increased lowest-quintile income share accompanied a reduced middle-quintile share. Thus, middle-class nonwhites provided support for impoverished nonwhites.

SUMMARY

In many areas nonwhites made tremendous gains after World War II. Racial discrimination decreased and racial discrepancies in education and in intraoccupational and interindustrial earnings lessened. In other areas, nonwhites did not fare well. While all races increased the proportion of (often impoverished) female-headed units, nonwhites witnessed a greater than average growth. Nonwhite joblessness increased as relative (and absolute) unemployment rates increased and relative (and absolute) male labor force participation rates decreased. Although racial occupational employment converged, segregation still exists since nonwhites are still confined to employment in lower-paying positions.

Between 1947 and 1985, white and nonwhite income distributions diverged while income distributions within each race narrowed. From 1950 to 1960, nonwhite income inequality increased, causing increased aggregate inequality with increased between-race distributional disparity. Income inequality fell in both white and nonwhite distributions during the 1960s and stabilized from 1970 to 1985.

Changes in occupational employment and income-receiving unit composition played a major role in these within-race distribution changes. Changes in industrial employment, female labor force participation, and social-insurance expenditure had greater (or equivalent) effects on aggregate distributional changes than within-race distributional changes. Changes in population dependency had similar impacts on the white and aggregate income distributions, but had no systematic influence on the nonwhite distribution since traditional age-related earnings patterns do not hold in time-series analysis for nonwhites.

Results support dramatic influences of occupational employment and income-receiving-unit structure on increased within-race income inequality; however, the exact mechanisms producing these changes is unknown. Nonwhites were unduly harmed by shifting occupational employment, consistent with Wilson's thesis of structural mechanisms creating economic hardships for nonwhites. Nonwhites were also unduly harmed by an increasing proportion of female-headed units, consistent with Murray's thesis of AFDC-induced breakdowns in the family creating economic hardships for nonwhites. Murray's argument is weakened considerably, however, since factors altering within-race income distribution are stronger than income-receiving-unit factors in altering income inequality. Neither Murray nor Wilson stress the role of race in recent economic hardships for nonwhites, yet results of this study clearly indicate strong interactions of race and economic and demographic forces on income inequality. Economic and demographic forces had different influences on within-race income distributions and between-race differences in characteristics and income distribution influences on aggregate inequality. Thus, race is still a key factor in U.S. income inequality.

NOTES

1. Conceptually, this chapter focuses on the human capital and labor markets—the primary income source for most income-receiving units. Brimmer (1988) discusses racial differences in capital markets while Leigh (1988) discusses differences in housing markets.

2. See Smith and Welch (1979) for elaboration.

3. Labor force data on nonwhites are not available after 1967, hence, the racial comparisons for 1970 and 1980 are black and white.

4. See Gwartney (1970) or Duncan (1969) for an analysis of pre–1960 discrimination and Welch (1973), Thurow (1969), Butler (1983), Freeman (1972), Duncan and Hoffman (1983), and Smith and Welch (1977) for analysis of white-nonwhite earnings convergence during the 1960s. Wilson (1980), Farley (1977), Leigh (1976), and Freeman (1973) discuss the "inheritance of poverty."

5. Since human capital convergence began with younger cohorts, young workers fared better than older workers in relative earnings. If the convergence also increased the quality of education for younger nonwhites—the "vintage effect" (Hoffman, 1979; Link et al., 1976; Welch, 1973)—white-nonwhite earnings differentials will continue to narrow as higher-educated young cohorts replace lesser-educated older cohorts in the labor market. If convergence is confined to entry-level positions with differences in on-the-job training favoring whites after hiring (Murray, 1984; Lazear, 1979; Freeman, 1973), earnings differentials will increase as cohorts age.

6. The South was slower than the rest of the country in showing income inequality alterations favoring blacks (Fossett et al., 1986).

7. Freeman (1978, 1973) finds that during the 1964–1975 period, the ratio of nonwhite-to-white income fell with ascending levels of skill (with the exception of craft workers). Because of increased earnings convergence with skill, much of the improvement stemmed from convergence in relative occupational status.

8. Wilson (1980) discusses stability differences in middle-class income. Gottfredson (1981) discusses research on educational convergence.

9. Datcher-Loury (1986) argues that state dependence and heterogeneity account for observed disparities in black-white stability differences.

10. Particularly problematic is the high absolute and relative unemployment levels of black teenagers. The causes of teenage unemployment increases include increased spatial differentiation between jobs and nonwhites, increased teen-cohort growth outstripping the labor demand, and changed quality or type of nonwhite education (Cogan, 1982; Gilman, 1965).

11. Parsons (1980b) argues that larger labor force withdrawals of black men results from increased Social Security and disability benefits favoring those with the least favorable labor market opportunities (i.e., nonwhites).

12. When nonwhite-white returns to education and income levels are compared without accounting for employment differentials, sample selectivity problems arise since the lowest-productivity nonwhite workers are removed from the sample. Jud and Walker (1982) discuss biases in educational returns and Butler and Heckman (1977) discuss biases in income.

13. Darity and Myers (1980) show the parity in nonwhite-white female income resulting from lower labor force participation rates of white women.

14. Disagreement exists over the extent of reduction in discrimination. Bergmann and Lyle (1971) and Ashenfelter (1970) find evidence of substantial discrimination during the 1960s (particularly for women) while Freeman (1973) proclaims the "collapse of discriminatory patterns" during the same period.

15. For reviews see Masters (1975), Darity (1975), Marshall (1974), or Gordon (1972).

16. For a critical survey see D'Amico (1987). Chiswick (1973) performed an empirical test on employee taste for discrimination and Kruger (1963), Welch (1967), and Arrow (1972) expanded and modified the basic theory.

17. Bergmann (1971) details occupational crowding.

18. For a critical review see Aigner and Cain (1977). Arrow (1972) and Phelps (1972) initiated these theories and Spence (1973) detailed the outcomes.

19. Thurow (1969) developed this model. Model expansion occurred in Darity and Williams (1985) to encompass cultural differences and Marshall (1974) to show employers, communities, and unions maintaining the monopoly.

20. Chapter 3 discusses segmented labor market theories (i.e., structural theories) and Flanagan (1973) provides a critical review of their application to racial discrimination. Harrison (1972) discusses the role of segmentation and culture and Beck et al. (1978) discuss the outcomes.

21. More radical theories posit that the employer gains from playing one race of laborers against another (Baron and Sweezy, 1966) to weaken unions (e.g., using blacks as strikebreakers—Bonacich, 1972) and to reduce the political power of labor. Racism also allows white laborers the psychological benefit of scapegoats (Bonacich, 1976). The result is capitalists' gain and laborers'—white and nonwhite—loss (Reich, 1982) and a prevalence of class discrimination mediating race discrimination—and lowered nonwhite returns to education (Wright, 1978; Schiller, 1971; Brofenbrenner, 1970). See Cloutier (1987) for a critique.

22. For an excellent overview see Haveman (1977).

23. See 279 F. Supp. 505 (E. D. Va. 1968).

24. See 301 F. Supp. 906 (E. D. La. 1969).

25. See 401 U.S. 424 (1971).

26. See 347 U.S. 483 (1954).

27. See 391 U.S. 430 (1968).

28. Expansion and contraction of poverty programs were outlined in Chapter 6 and, therefore, are not discussed here.

29. This is the classic chicken-and-egg problem. Did increased human capital (e.g., quality or quantity of education) reduce discrimination (e.g., Bergmann and Lyle, 1971) or did reduced discrimination increase human capital (e.g., Smith and Welch, 1977)?

30. For a critical review, see Darity (1982) or Harrison (1971).

31. Racial stratification of data by income-receiving units only exists for families and unrelated individuals. Consistent with previous studies showing dramatically different effects within family type and for male and female unrelated individuals (cf., Opitz and Bean, 1988; Bianchi, 1980; Bianchi and Farley, 1979; Farley, 1977), income-unit stratification within the races did not produce meaningful results.

32. Farley (1984) shows significant per capita income alteration within races while Wojtkiewicz (1988) shows insignificant between-race alterations. Bianchi (1980) shows convergence of racial income irrespective of unit and Bianchi and Farley (1979) show increasing disparity between husband-wife and female-headed units.

33. As a whole, growth into relatively high-paying professional and managerial occupations offset growth in low-paying clerical and sales positions (Table 7–3 and Westcott, 1982).

34. Blue-collar occupational segregation is also consistent with a white-protectionist analysis of unions (Beck, 1980). Unions maintain the favorable economic status of whites to the detriment of nonwhites. Thus, as unions lose strength, within-race inequality increases. (Beck's analysis showed the converse.) For a full discussion on assimilating minorities into the workplace and the extent of segregation of minorities see Snyder and Hudis (1976), Taeuber et al. (1966), and Hodge and Hodge (1965). These studies do not

explore the extent that racial occupational segregation results from race or class discrimination.

35. See Hessel and Palmer (1978).

36. See Leonard (1985) and Daymont (1980).

37. Similarities in the racial effects of increased female labor force participation is consistent with research showing similar impacts of increased labor market activities of women with reductions in both racial group's family income inequality (Lehrer and Nerlove, 1984b). The larger reduction for nonwhites can be explained with larger black husband-wife earnings covariance (Lehrer and Nerlove, 1984a; Smith, 1979) and convergence of white-nonwhite earnings (Albelda, 1986; Quester and Greene, 1985).

8

Summary of the Past and Predictions of the Future

The preceding chapters described estimated past relationships between income inequality and share distribution and income-receiving-unit composition, industrial and occupational employment, population dependency, female labor force participation, and government spending on social insurance.

The conclusion from this analysis is twofold. First, although aggregate income inequality was less in 1985 than in 1947, income inequality had increased since the 1970s as the income distribution became more polarized (i.e., bottom-to-top income movement). This polarization stemmed from a decreased proportion of manufacturing employment, an increased proportion of female-headed units, and, to a lesser extent, increased population dependency. While most distributional change came from bottom-to-top income movements, the "lower middle class" (i.e., second quintile) also lost income share. The inequality increase would have been greater, but both increased female labor force participation and increased social-insurance expenditures equalized the income distribution. The equalizing impact from increased female labor force participation weakened after 1980, however, and the equalizing impact from social-insurance was weaker than other forces.

Second, these aggregate trends varied dramatically within individual income-receiving unit income distributions and within white and nonwhite income distributions. This implies that the economic and demographic forces under study influenced income inequality in three ways. First, postwar changes altered the composition of income-receiving units. Because income-receiving units had different income distributions, changes in the proportion of units altered the aggregate income distribution. Second, postwar changes differentially altered the income distribution *within* each income-receiving unit type or each race. Demographic and economic changes did not affect all income-receiving units in the same manner. Distinct differences occurred by race and/or gender of head and by family or unrelated-individual living arrangements. The (differential) alteration of within-unit income distributions then altered the aggregate distribution. Third, postwar changes altered the income distribution *between* each group. Over the period there was increasing income disparity by gender (feminization of poverty) and race (differential employment and demographic impacts). The changing relationship of income between groups then altered aggregate inequality. Thus, changes in aggregate income inequality since World War II resulted from income distributional shifts *within* income-receiving units, distributional shifts *between* units, and changing composition of income-receiving units.

The preceding chapters focused on the estimated influence of a single influence on aggregate and disaggregate income distributions. This chapter summarizes these relationships for individual income-receiving units by discussing the relative impact of economic and demographic change on each income-receiving unit's income distribution. These past relationships are then used to estimate future income distributions.

INCOME INEQUALITY DIFFERENCES BY INCOME-RECEIVING UNIT

Table 8-1 shows the income inequality elasticities (i.e., elasticity associated with the Gini coefficient) for each economic, demographic, and government influence by income-receiving unit and race and shows the maximum percent change in the influence between 1947 and 1985. Increased government spending on social insurance had the largest change—a 438 percent increase. Employment changes were next largest, with relative manufacturing employment decreasing by 235 percent and relative employment in blue-collar occupations decreasing by 50 percent. The relative composition of income-receiving units changed by 90 percent as the proportion of female-headed units increased and husband-wife units decreased. Female labor force participation increased by over 70 percent. Population dependency increased by 32 percent with the birth of the baby boom. Each of these changes differentially impacted the aggregate income distribution, individual income-receiving unit income distributions, and white and nonwhite distribution.

Aggregates, Families, and Unrelated Individuals

In the aggregate, both industrial employment change and population dependency had about equal impacts on income inequality changes over the period (Table 8-1). That is, both industrial employment shifts and increased population dependency increased income inequality with nearly the same magnitude (i.e.,

Table 8–1
Inequality Influences and Numeric Changes: Elasticities and Percentage Change

	Industry[1]	Occupation	Dependency	Female Labor Force Participation	Government	Income-Receiving Unit
Maximum Percent Change	235.3[2]	51.9	32.7	72.0	438.9	90.7
Aggregate[3]	.490****	.283	.466****	-.213	-.135**	-.018
Families	.315**	.452*	.375***	-.640*	.141*	–
Unrelated Individuals	.368***	.211	.418****	-.914***	-.020	–
Husband–Wife Family	.276*	.663*	.471***	-.517	.196**	–
Wife in the Labor Force	.434*	.589	.824***	-1.06*	.168	–
Wife out of the Labor Force	.189	.513**	.234*	-.302	.200**	–
Male–Headed Units						
Families	.358**	-.194	.184	-1.25***	.195*	–
Unrelated Individuals	.258**	-.146	.284**	-1.04****	.121	–
Female–Headed Units						
Families	.231	.025	.268	.023	-.127	–
Unrelated Individuals	.363***	.271	.513***	-.328	-.067	–
Race						
White	-.003	-.408***	-.244****	-.982****	-.082*	.383**
Nonwhite	-.050	-.399***	-.021	-1.30****	.023	.738***

[1] All influences represent their construct as independent variables (ratios times 100). Occupation reflects blue-collar to white-collar employment. Industry reflects service to manufacturing employment. Dependency ratio reflects the population aged under 18 and over 64 to the population 18 to 64. Female labor force participation reflects the number of employed and unemployed females 16 and over to the total number of like-aged females. Government reflects spending on social insurance relative to GNP. Income-receiving unit reflects female-headed to husband-wife units. Maximum percent change values were computed as the difference between 1947 and 1985 divided by the 1947 value for all variables except dependency. The maximum change for dependency occurred between 1947 and 1964.

[2] The boldfaced numbers represent the maximum percent change over the 1947-1985 period. This was computed as the maximum difference over the period divided by the initial period (times 100). Elasticities, not in boldface, represent the percent change (at the mean) in the Gini coefficient associated with a one-percent change in the influence. Elasticity computations were computed on regression results presented in Appendix Tables A4-1 to A4-6.

[3] Aggregate and totals reflect a weighted average of income-receiving unit components.

**** $p \leq .001$
*** $p \leq .01$
** $p \leq .05$
* $p \leq .10$

equivalent elasticities). Government spending, the other significant influence on aggregate income inequality, had only about one-third the influence of industrial and dependency changes. Changes in occupational employment, female labor force participation, and income-receiving-unit composition did not significantly alter aggregate income inequality.[1]

For families, all influences significantly altered income inequality. Neither social-insurance expenditures nor changing occupational employment significantly influenced income inequality for unrelated individuals, however. Increased female labor force participation dominated the income inequality change for both families and unrelated individuals with a one-percent increase decreasing inequality by .64 and .9 percent. Changes in industrial and occupational employment and relative increases in population dependency equally impacted family and unrelated-individual income inequality. For families, changing occupational employment had a slightly greater impact. Increased social-insurance expenditures increased family income inequality (husband-wife families with nonworking wives only) and had no impact for unrelated individuals.

Race

With economic and demographic changes altering between-race income distributions, differences exist in the impact on within-race and aggregate income distribution. For whites, all economic and demographic influences, except industrial employment, altered the income distribution. The strongest influence was female labor force participation, with a one-percent increase in female labor force participation decreasing income inequality by one percent. Changing occupational employment and income-receiving-unit composition were the next strongest influences, with an impact less than half the size of female labor force participation. Relative increases in population dependency decreased income inequality for whites (a reversal from aggregate trends), with a magnitude slightly less than that for occupational and income-receiving-unit changes. Increased social-insurance expenditures decreased income inequality slightly, a one-percent increase in government spending reducing inequality by only .08 percent.

For nonwhites, only occupational employment, female labor force participation, and income-receiving-unit composition significantly altered the income distribution. Female labor force participation had a very strong equalizing impact, a one-percent increase reducing income inequality by 1.3 percent. Changes in income-receiving-unit composition were also fairly strong—a one-percent increase in the relative proportion of female-headed units increased income inequality by .74 percent. Occupational employment shifts increased income inequality, but the impact was only about half as great as the income-receiving-unit impact.

Husband-Wife Families

For husband-wife families, all influences significantly altered income inequality except female labor force participation. A one-percent decrease in relative blue-collar employment decreased husband-wife family income inequality by .7 percent, while a one-percent increase in population dependency increased inequality by about .5 percent. Industrial employment shifts and government spending both increased income inequality with one-third the impact of relative decreases in blue-collar employment.

Within husband-wife families, economic and demographic influences differed for those with working and nonworking wives. Because the composition of the dual-earning families changed, female labor force participation, the strongest influence on aggregate income inequality, was an insignificant influence for single-earning families. Increased population dependency increased income inequality for both working and nonworking-wife families with a stronger impact for dual-earner families. Occupational employment shifts altered inequality for nonworking-wife families and industrial employment shifts altered inequality for dual-earning families. Government spending increased income inequality for the nonworking-wife families and had no impact for dual-earning families.

Male and Female-Headed Units

Economic and demographic influences differentially altered male-headed and female-headed units. For all male-headed units, a one-percent increase in female labor force participation led to a greater than one-percent decrease in income inequality. This resulted from increased occupational wage competition from females that reduced the relative earnings of high-wage men. Industrial employment shifted income inequality for both male-headed families and unrelated individuals, with a greater impact for families. Increased social-insurance expenditures increased income inequality slightly for male-headed families. For male unrelated individuals, relative increases in population dependency increased inequality with the same magnitude as industrial employment changes.

None of the economic, demographic, and government changes altered income inequality for female-headed families. For female unrelated individuals, however, increased population dependency and industrial employment shifts increased income inequality. No other changes significantly altered income inequality.

TOTAL ECONOMIC, DEMOGRAPHIC, AND GOVERNMENT IMPACTS

The income inequality elasticities reflect the percent change in income inequality associated with a one percent change in the independent variable construct. With different magnitude of over-time change in each variable, equal elasticities did not have equivalent impacts on inequality. With similar elasticities, the greater total impact on inequality is determined by the greater percent change in each variable over the period.

When significant, female labor force participation had the greatest impact (elasticity) on income-receiving-unit income inequality, followed by changes in industrial employment and population dependency. The latter two usually had equivalent elasticities. The government spending elasticity usually lagged far behind, indicating a weak influence on income inequality. For whites and non-whites, changes in income-receiving-unit composition altered income inequality less than female labor force participation but more than most other influences.

The total impact of each economic, demographic, and government influence is the interaction of the inequality elasticity and the percent change of each influence. Because changes are predicted to continue, the past estimated impact (elasticity) can be interacted with future changes. Thus, the total impact of economic, demographic, and government changes on income inequality can be estimated for 1947 to 1985, 1985 to 1995, and 1995 to 2000 (Table 8–2). Between 1947 and 1985, shifting industrial employment had the largest total impact on income inequality change because of large relative reductions in manufacturing employment. The impact of shifting industrial employment on inequality was twice as large as any other influence. With continued large projected employment changes, this strong impact on increasing inequality will continue through 2000. Increased social-insurance expenditures had the next largest total impact on income inequality from 1947 to 1985. Although the government influence (elasticity) was always small, the large percent change over the period (438 percent) decreased income inequality with an impact about half the size of shifting industrial employment. Future changes in government spending are unknown.

From 1947 to 1985, population dependency, female labor force participation, and shifting occupational employment had equivalent total impacts on inequality changes, each with about one-fourth the impact of social-insurance expenditure. Increases in dependency and occupational employment shifts increased inequality while increases in female labor force participation decreased inequality. Since increased female labor force participation offset occupational employment shifts over the period, the cyclic change from changing population dependency was apparent.

Between 1985 and 2000, both *reduced* dependency (aging baby boom) and increased female labor force participation will reduce inequality. By 2000, however, the reduced inequality associated with reduced dependency and increased female labor force participation will not outweigh the increased inequality associated with occupational employment changes.

Within both white and nonwhite income distributions, changes in income-receiving-unit composition played a major role in altering income inequality. For nonwhites, the total impact of relative increases in female-headed units was nearly as great as changes in government spending. These forces offset each

Table 8–2

Total Economic and Demographic Influences on Income Inequality, 1947–2000[1]

	1947–1985	1985–1995[2]	1995–2000
Industry	115.36	20.73	8.77
Occupation	14.69	1.71	2.62
Dependency ratio	15.24[3]	-1.26	-1.49
Female labor force participation	-15.34	-1.64	-.92
Income-receiving units	-1.63	-.17	-.09
Whites	31.95	3.33	1.69
Nonwhites	53.15	5.55	2.82
Government	-59.25	–	–

[1]Total change is the result of the aggregate inequality elasticity times the maximum percent change over the period. Both values (and definitions) are presented in Table 8-1.

[2]Projections are based on projected changes in the influences times the elasticity estimated on the 1947 to 1985 period.

[3]The net impact over the 1947 to 1985 period for the dependency ratio falls to .455. This change results from the maximum change in the dependency ratio occurring when the largest segment of the baby boom was still under 18. Since the baby boom was over 18 by 1985, dependency remained close to 1947 levels and the net change is far less than the maximum impact.

other since increasing female-headed units increased income inequality while government spending decreased it. For whites, the relative increase in female-headed units increased inequality, with a total impact about two-thirds that of government spending.

FUTURE

Future economic and demographic changes are expected. Projections suggest that employment shifts, population aging, and increased female labor force participation will continue, although the rate of change may differ from postwar trends. Using projected changes and past associations between economic, demographic, and government changes and income inequality and distribution, future income distributions were simulated. This section presents results of simulated income inequality and distribution for 1995 and 2000.

Table 8–3
Predicted Population and Economic Characteristics: 1995, 2000

	1985	1995	2000	Percent Change[1] 1985– 1995	Percent Change[1] 1995– 2000
Income-Receiving Units					
Percent husband-wife families	58.0	54.7	53.1	-5.7	-2.9
Percent female-headed income-receiving units	27.8	28.7	29.2	3.2	1.7
Percent unrelated individuals	27.7	30.4	31.8	9.7	4.6
Demographic Characteristics					
Median age	31.0	34.7	36.3	11.9	4.6
Dependency ratio	62.0	63.7	61.7	2.7	-3.1
Economic Characteristics					
Female labor force participation	54.7	58.9	61.5	7.7	4.4
Percent employed as blue-collar workers	28.1	26.3	24.3	-6.4	-7.6
Percent employed as white-collar workers	55.1	54.9	55.9	-.4	1.8
Percent employed in manufacturing	19.9	17.2	15.2	-13.6	-11.6
Percent employed in the service industry	21.3	26.2	27.3	23.0	4.2

[1]Computed as the difference over the specified period divided by the initial period.

Economic and Population Predictions

Table 8–3 summarizes predicted changes in economic and demographic characteristics and income-receiving-unit structures.[2] In general, a continuation of past trends is projected through the year 2000. The proportion of husband-wife families will continue to decrease as the proportions of unrelated individuals and female-headed units increase. The population's median age will rise as the baby boom ages and the dependency ratio will rise and fall with the birth and aging of the echo boom. The proportion of blue-collar workers will continue to fall, but the proportion of white-collar workers will remain fairly stable. Employment shifts from manufacturing to service will continue and female labor force participation will continue its increase.

Many of the projected supply-side changes in the labor market and income-receiving-unit structure are explained by the changing population age structure—the aging baby boom, baby bust, and the arrival and aging of the echo boom.[3]

Aggregate population growth will increase the labor force by about 18 percent between 1986 and 2000—a slowdown of the rapid growth generated by the baby boom during the 1970s and 1980s.[4] As the baby bust enters the labor market and women slow their growth in participation rates, labor force growth will slow. Continuing current trends, the labor force will become increasingly nonwhite and female until the year 2000.[5] While the white labor force will grow by about 15 percent, the black, Hispanic, and Asian (and other races) labor force will grow by 29, 74, and 70 percent, respectively.

The increase in the nonwhite portion of the labor force will stem from increased immigration. Although blacks currently have higher fertility rates than other nonwhite groups, their relative number in the nonwhite ranks will decrease as immigration of other groups (particularly Hispanics and Asians) continues. The increase in the proportion of women in the labor force stems from continued increases in female labor force participation and decreases in male labor force participation. While men's projected labor force growth is about 12 percent, women's labor force growth is about 25 percent. As female labor force experience increases from past participation increases, female wages will move closer to parity with male wages. Thus, future increased participation will continue to lessen the gender gap in wages.

The age composition of the labor force will follow the aging of the baby boom and echo boom. The 16 to 24 year-old age group will decline into the mid–1990s with the baby boom and baby bust aging, and will increase by the mid–1990s as the echo boom reaches adulthood. Through the early 1990s, the aging baby boom will increase the population aged 25 to 34; however, by the mid–1990s this group will decline as the baby bust enters "early career" stage. The population aged 55 to 64 will decline through the mid–1990s and then increase rapidly as the baby boom enters this "later career" stage.

Population age changes will also alter the composition of income-receiving units. Since youth initiate most new income-receiving units, income-receiving-unit formation will slow as the baby bust reaches adulthood. With decreased youth income-receiving units and increases in the elderly population (increased life expectancy), the elderly will be a higher proportion of unrelated individuals.

On the demand side of the labor market, employment will grow about 19 percent between 1986 and 2000. This is a slowdown of about .2 percent a year over the rate in the 1980s.[6] Projected productivity increases (due to a more mature, educated, and experienced labor force, greater stability in energy prices, and favorable growth in the capital-labor ratio) will continue GNP growth of about 2.4 percent per year. Nearly all the growth in industrial employment will occur in the service-producing industries. With the exception of the construction industry, goods-producing industries will have virtually no employment change through 2000. Manufacturing output will continue to increase between 1986 and 2000 as productivity increases offset employment declines. Agricultural employment declines will continue as will large employment growth in both the trade industry and the finance, insurance, and real estate industries. Most service-sector employment growth will stem from growth in health care (increased number of elderly) and business services. Most growth in government-sector employment will stem from state and local growth (including increased educational services).[7] The fastest-growing occupational employment will be service-oriented or white-collar: technicians, service workers, professionals, sales, executives, and managers. Blue-collar occupations and clerical positions will have below-average employment growth.

Income Implications of Projections

These employment and population projections have implications for the level of future earnings. Occupational employment shifts will most likely harm those with low levels of education since the fast-growing occupations require at least one year of college. Most occupations requiring only a high-school diploma or less will have declining employment. Blacks, Hispanics, and, to a lesser extent, women will face decreased demand for their services since growth in their traditional occupational employment will be slow. These negative outcomes (e.g., decreased wages or unemployment) from slowing demand will be intensified by projected supply increases. That is, while jobs traditionally held by nonwhites and women will increase at below-average rates, their number will increase at above-average rates.

While women and nonwhites potentially face a deteriorating labor market, youth will have a greatly improved market. As the supply of youth workers decreases with the baby-bust labor market entrance, jobs traditionally held by youth will increase at above-average rates. With service-sector growth and above-average employment increases in food service, retail sales, and construction (areas of traditional youth employment), the (accelerated) demand for youth workers could exceed (limited) supply without wage increases.

The projected tight youth labor market may offset the deteriorating nonwhite and female labor markets if women and nonwhites move into employment traditionally held by youth. Two forces may prohibit this movement.[8] First, low-wage workers—youth, women, and nonwhites—have different characteristics and levels of productivity. This makes substitution difficult. Second, for the same gender, youth and older workers are complements, not substitutes, while cross-gender substitution occurs only for older workers. This suggests that neither older and younger workers nor women and youth are substitutes in employment.

In sum, while aggregate employment is predicted to continue along past trends, the labor market for youth, female, and nonwhite workers may change. The deteriorating labor market for women and nonwhites may erode their wages and/or increase their joblessness. Increasing productivity of these groups (e.g., increased experience for women and increased education for nonwhites) could offset wage deterioration, especially if accompanied by movement into atypical occupations. At best, this suggests a continuation of the stagnant female and nonwhite relative earnings witnessed in the past decade. Youth, however, may have increased wages and decreased unemployment in the future. This could alter projected income distributions as traditionally low-income youth workers have increased wages.

Predicted Income Inequality and Share Distribution

Predicted employment, population, and female labor force participation changes can be linked with their past estimated relationships with income inequality and share distribution to simulate income inequality and share distribution for the years 1995 and 2000 (Table 8–4).[9] Predicted Gini coefficients and income share distributions are based on the 1980 demographic and economic income distributions (or labor force participation rates) and predicted changes. Appendix 2 details the prediction procedure. These projected income inequality and distribution changes show distribution change with only a single economic or demographic change and constant income distributions within each industry, occupation, age group, and income-receiving unit type. These projections are based on the entire 1980 income distribution (of employed workers, individuals, or income-receiving units) and not just on changes in the independent variable construct.

As the proportion of youth decreases in the future, income inequality will be reduced, at least through 1995. Inequality reductions will stem from reductions in the top- and fourth-quintile income shares and increases in the middle, second, and bottom quintile shares. Between 1995 and 2000, rearrangement of middle-class income will occur as the second-quintile income share falls and the middle-quintile share increases. This age-related income inequality reduction results from a reduced proportion of young. This age-related inequality reduction trend may be intensified if the tight youth labor market reduces income variance among youth.

Increased female-headed and decreased husband-wife income-receiving units will increase income inequality through 1995 with slight increases thereafter. Inequality increases stem from increases in the top-quintile income share and reductions in middle-class income (the second and fourth quintiles). The slight inequality reduction after 1995 will stem from a slight reduction in the top-quintile income share. Of course, improvements in the youth labor market (for unrelated individuals) and a deterioration in the female labor market (for female-headed units) may alter these calculations.

Employment shifts from blue collar to white collar and from manufacturing to service will have virtually no effect on income inequality through 1995, although the shift from manufacturing to service will increase inequality slightly. Both industry and occupation changes will reduce income inequality from 1995 to 2000 by decreasing the top-quintile income share. Changing occupational employment will increase the middle-quintile income share while changing industrial employment will rearrange middle-class income (fourth, middle, and

Table 8–4

Predicted Economic and Demographic Effects on Income Inequality and Distribution

Demographic and Economic Changes

Prediction[1]	Dependency			Income-Receiving Unit			Occupation ·			Industry		
	1980	1995	2000	1980	1995	2000	1980	1995	2000	1980	1995	2000
Gini Coefficient	.517	.506	.508	.413	.435	.430	.481	.481	.477	.481	.485	.479
Top Quintile	.566	.560	.559	.469	.498	.493	.530	.528	.525	.536	.532	.527
Fourth Quintile	.235	.229	.231	.242	.228	.228	.243	.249	.245	.233	.242	.245
Middle Quintile	.131	.134	.141	.158	.155	.157	.135	.129	.135	.137	.139	.135
Second Quintile	.056	.065	.057	.094	.085	.089	.075	.076	.077	.076	.069	.075
Lowest Quintile	.012	.013	.013	.037	.034	.033	.077	.018	.018	.018	.017	.018

Female Labor Force Participation

	1980	No Change[2]		5% Increase		10% Increase		15% Increase		20% Increase	
		1995	2000	1995	2000	1995	2000	1995	2000	1995	2000
Gini Coefficient	.365	.368	.368	.367	.368	.360	.365	.356	.357	.348	.349
Top Quintile	.426	.429	.428	.430	.429	.424	.422	.427	.426	.410	.409
Fourth Quintile	.243	.244	.246	.251	.243	.247	.246	.229	.230	.245	.245
Middle Quintile	.172	.169	.167	.169	.173	.162	.176	.175	.179	.175	.179
Second Quintile	.107	.113	.114	.108	.104	.120	.106	.119	.115	.118	.117
Lowest Quintile	.051	.045	.046	.051	.051	.049	.049	.050	.051	.051	.050

[1]Predicted Gini Coefficient and quintile share distributions reflect predicted income distributions with changes only in one factor. For example, the 1995 and 2000 dependency columns reflect the predicted income distribution associated with predicted changes in the age composition of the population assuming constancy in other factors. The predictions reflect predicted distributions of age (for example) and the 1980 distribution of income. The 1980 distribution is the aggregate income distribution. All predictions are based on "moderate" projections, although computations made on differing projection series show the same trend. Female labor force participation projections are based on family income-receiving unit distributions. For a more complete discussion of procedures, see Appendix 2.

[2]No growth: married women participate at 1980 rate (50.213) in 1995 and 2000
  Increase of 5%:   married women participate at 55.213 in 1995 and 2000
  Increase of 10%:   married women participate at 60.213 in 1995 and 2000
  Increase of 15%:   married women participate at 65.213 in 1995 and 2000
  Increase of 20%:   married women participate at 70.213 in 1995 and 2000

Table 8–5
Predicted Aggregate Income Inequality and Share Distribution

	1980	1985	1995[1]	2000
Gini Coefficient	.413	.433	.441	.491
Top Quintile Income Share	.469	.504	.549	.533
Fourth Quintile Income Share	.242	.229	.214	.289
Middle Quintile Income Share	.158	.147	.110	.089
Second Quintile Income Share	.093	.086	.086	.075
Lowest Quintile Income Share	.037	.033	.042	.019

[1]Predictions reflect all predicted changes in population age and income-receiving-unit structures, industry and occupation employment, and female labor force participation with constant (1985) proportion of government spending on social insurance. Computations were based on results of the "aggregate" regression equations presented in Appendix Tables A4-1 to A4-6. Predictions are the solution to the equation using 1995 and 2000 independent variable values.

second quintiles). Since these predictions are based only on employed individuals, the impact of joblessness is not included. This may dramatically alter predicted outcomes if joblessness among nonwhites continues to increase.

While increased female labor force participation reduced income inequality prior to 1980, future increases in female employment will not have the same effect without increases of at least 15 percentage points. If the rate of female labor force participation increase slows (i.e., increases of five percentage points or less between 1985 and 2000), the post–1980 trend will continue and income inequality will increase. Since a slowing rate of increase is predicted, future inequality increases with increased female labor force participation are likely. This increase may be intensified as the composition of entering females becomes more high-income.

When all economic and demographic predicted changes are considered, aggregate income inequality is predicted to increase through 2000 (Table 8–5).[10] The inequality increase will stem from increases in the top two quintiles' income share and decreases in the bottom three quintiles' income share—continued income polarization combined with a reduction in middle-class income. This inequality increase may intensify with increased unemployment associated with a deteriorating labor market for nonwhites and females or may lessen with a tight labor market for youth.[11]

NOTES

1. Significant distributional changes may accompany an insignificant Gini coefficient change.

2. Tschetter (1988) evaluates the validity of economic projections.

3. Future changes are summarized in Kutscher (1987) and Hudson Institute (1987) (labor market), U.S. Bureau of the Census (1984) (population), and U.S. Bureau of the Census (1986c) (income-receiving units). Russell (1982) outlines the influence of the aging baby boom on consumption in various markets. More recent and in-depth responses of different markets to the baby boom can be found in Shipp (1988), Edmondson (1987), or Lazer and Shaw (1987).

4. The section on the predicted economic growth is drawn from Saunders (1987) and the section on predicted labor force growth is drawn from Fullerton (1987). All statistics reported are based on "moderate" growth scenarios. Smith and Ward (1984) discuss the impact of future female labor force participation increases.

5. Schwartz (1988) and Bouvier and Agresta (1985) discuss population increases of Hispanics and Asians.

6. The section on occupational projections is drawn largely from Silvestri and Lukasiewicz (1987). The section on industrial projections is drawn largely from Personick (1987). All statistics reported are based on "moderate" growth scenarios.

7. The number of elementary-school aged children will soon increase, with new record-high enrollments in the late 1990s (echo boom). The number of high-school aged youth will decline until about 1990 (the baby bust) and then increase. These population changes account for the current increasing focus (and future worries) in educational employment. The number of college-age youth 18 to 24 will decline through the year 2000.

8. See Burggraf (1984) and Levine and Mitchell (1988).

9. Numerous implicit and explicit assumptions are made for these predictions. Explicitly, predictions assume constant within-component income distributions. That is, the distribution of income within each age category (for example) remains as it was in 1980. Changes result only from the relative size of each category. Within-component distributional changes (Maxwell, 1989b) would alter these estimates.

10. Aggregate predictions (Table 8–5) are based on a fixed relationship between a unit change in the economic and demographic independent variable construct and a constant unit change in inequality and income distribution. Predictions also assume that future changes mirror past changes in impact (e.g., Bergmann et al., 1980). For example, future increases in female labor force participation and nonwhite immigration come from individuals with characteristics identical to past entrants. These assumptions may bias predictions. See Treas (1987) for discussion with respect to female labor force participation.

11. Other unknown influences may also affect future inequality. Changes in governmental policy between 1985 and 2000 are more than likely; however, the direction of policy change cannot be ascertained with any degree of certainty. Likewise, economic "shocks" such as the oil shocks in the 1970s or the Vietnam war in the 1960s cannot be anticipated, yet their economic impact on the income distribution is substantial.

9

Conclusions and Policy Implications

The preceding chapters outlined past aggregate and disaggregate trends in income inequality and distribution from 1947 to 1985 and simulated future income distributions through 2000. The goals were to describe inequality and distributional changes, to determine which economic and demographic factors were associated with the changes, and to determine whether inequality changes resulted from a declining middle class or increasing distinctions between the haves and have nots (i.e., income polarization).

In general, this study documented demographic and economic determinants of the recent upturn in inequality associated with increased income polarization. That is, most shifts in the income distribution came from changes in the top and bottom quintile shares. The decline in "middle-class income" usually stemmed from reduction of "lower middle-class income"—the second quintile—and was usually part of income polarization. Although both demographic and economic factors increased income inequality and income polarization, shifting industrial employment dominated movement because of its greater percent change over the period. These general trends, however, differed dramatically within individual income-receiving units and within the white and nonwhite income populations.

CONCLUSIONS

Chapter 1 raised five empirical questions surrounding the changing income distribution that this study answered.

1.   Is middle-class income declining? If so, is the decline due to the transitory aging of the baby boom or to permanent changes in industrial-occupational employment?

Distributional shifts were greater at the top and bottom of the income distribution than at the middle. This held true in the aggregate and within most income-receiving units. When middle-class income decreased, most of the decline came from the "lower middle class." That is, the second quintile lost income share. While shifting industrial employment and increased population dependency had the same influence on changing inequality, the larger percent change in employment meant the total inequality change from employment shifts outweighed the change from dependency. Changes in the population age structure directly reduced middle-class income (the middle quintile) for male unrelated individuals—the only reduction in the "middle" middle-class income found in this study. Thus, from 1947 to 1985 the more permanent changes in employment structures accounted for most of the change in income inequality, and most of the reduction in middle-class income came from the *lower* middle class.

The finding that most of the recent inequality increase came from income polarization rather than reduced middle-class income appears to conflict with reports of the declining middle class. This conflict is illusory. Most studies examining declining middle-class income do not simultaneously examine income polarization nor do they partition middle-class income (i.e., they examine the totality of the middle of the income distribution rather than each third within the middle). This study does find reductions in *lower* middle-class income. By examining income polarization with shifts in the middle, however, the stronger trend of income polarization can be seen. By partitioning middle-class income into thirds and examining middle-class shifts with income polarization, the declining middle class appears as part of a bottom-to-top income movement rather than a reduction in the middle.

2.   Has increased female labor force participation created a society of high-income, dual-earning families at the expense of low-income units or has it reduced distributional dispersion and equalized income?

Prior to 1980, increased female labor force participation reduced inequality through two mechanisms. First, the income distribution of husband-wife families reduced inequality through increases in the relative income of wives in low-income families. This impact lessened over time, however. Between 1980 and 1985, increased female labor force participation increased both the labor supply and relative female earnings in high-income families. A continuation of the post–1980 trend would increase future inequality with continued increases in female labor force participation, and may produce a larger proportion of high-income, dual-earning families. Second, increased female labor force participation reduced inequality for male-headed income-receiving units. With increased labor supplied, females increased wage competition for high-income males and, hence, decreased the income share of the top quintile of male-headed units. This trend of reduced inequality may intensify as women continue to train as labor force participants and offset the increase in high-income, dual-earning families by reducing wages of high-income men.

3. Does government spending on social-insurance programs increase the income share of the bottom fifth of the income distribution while other fifths lose a significant share?

In the aggregate, increased spending on social insurance decreased inequality by increasing the income share of those at the bottom of the distribution and reducing the income share of those at the top. This result did not hold within all income-receiving-unit distributions, however. Specifically, nonmarried, male-headed families and all female-headed income-receiving units showed gains at the bottom while nonmarried, male-headed units showed reductions in upper middle-class income (fourth quintile). Some income-receiving units (male-headed families and nonworking-wife husband-wife families) showed increased inequality with income share gains at the top as spending on social insurance increased. This is due to increased income of early retirees associated with increased Social Security.

4. Do employment, dependency, female labor force participation, and government spending changes influence income inequality and distribution uniformly among income-receiving units and between the races?

No. Aggregate trends were not consistent among income-receiving units. In some cases (e.g., spending on social insurance), some income-receiving units had contradictory influences when compared to aggregate trends. In other cases (e.g., changes in occupational employment and the composition of income-receiving units) significant alteration in inequality existed only when examining within-race distributions. Thus, the effects of economic, demographic, and government influences on income inequality are extremely complex. They altered the aggregate income distribution through alteration of both within-group inequality, between-group inequality, and composition of income-receiving units.

5. What are likely future income inequality and distributions, given projected changes in the population age structure and industrial-occupational employment?

Employment shift from manufacturing to service was the primary determinant of the post–1970 inequality increase. Changes in the composition of income-receiving units (i.e., increased female-headed units) exerted a strong demographic influence on increased income inequality within both white and nonwhite income distributions. Transitory changes in population dependency played a relatively minor role. Currently, decreased dependency associated with the aging baby boom offsets some of the inequality increase from employment changes; however, with the birth of the echo boom, all demographic and economic structures will again work to increase inequality. Thus, our aggregate inequality predictions show inequality increases through 2000. Inequality increases may be intensified with a deteriorating labor market for nonwhites and women. However, inequality increases may be offset for two reasons. First, future *employed* workers may have more equally distributed income due to employment shifts. If workers can make the transition to new employment patterns through (re)training, inequality may stabilize. Second, the youth labor market may tighten, with increased demand in jobs traditionally held by youth and decreased supply with the baby bust. This will raise income of traditionally low-income workers and, therefore, may stabilize income inequality.

POLICY IMPLICATIONS

This book has minimized normative judgments in describing income inequality and distribution. Interpretations of demographic and economic associations with income inequality changes and projected distributions have had minimal value-laden analysis. This section is a divergence from that path. It sets the goals of reversing the post–1970 trend of increased income inequality and income polarization and reducing race and gender-based receiving-unit differences in income levels and distributions. It then sets out a policy agenda that will alter labor demand and supply forces to achieve the goals.

Labor Demand

The employment shift from the manufacturing to service sectors and blue-collar to white-collar jobs has been the primary determinant of recent increases in income inequality and income polarization. The shift has displaced skilled workers from jobs without reemployment opportunities at equivalent wage levels. Concurrent slowdowns in productivity increases and declines in union strength have further eroded wage growth. New job creation has expanded job opportunities at the high and low end of the earnings distribution. These labor market changes maintained differences in between-race and between-gender income levels and distributions.

Increasing inequality and income polarization, resultant from employment shifts, could be alleviated with better integration of workers into the labor market. Currently, workers are estranged from management policies with a one way (top-down) flow of communication. This prevents productivity-enhancing suggestions from employees and informed worker decisionmaking regarding impending layoffs. Hoerr (1988) has shown productivity decreases associated with top-down information flows in the steel industry and the potential productivity gains with better integration of workers in the firm's decisionmaking process. With improved communication between workers and management, via worker ownership or intensive management-union communication, productivity increases would increase wages. Improved communication would also decrease unemployment and wage loss upon plant shutdowns or layoffs since workers would receive advance notification of impending company crises. Their response may aid management decisionmaking by providing voluntary reduction of the labor force (i.e., workers would quit) or wage cuts. This would reduce the antagonism created with current policies of short-notice involuntary layoffs or plant shut-downs and relocation.

A broad industrial policy, cornerstoned by the recently enacted plant-closing legislation, could ease the short-run transition of displaced workers with training and placement aid. Expansion of training programs for displaced workers could reduce unemployment and increase the supply of skilled workers to bottlenecked industries by exchanging obsolete skills with marketable skills. Wage subsidies to growth industries would facilitate competitiveness in sunrise industries by reducing production costs and providing firms with financial incentives to provide on-the-job training to workers.

Women and nonwhite workers should be better integrated into the labor market. Current employment shifts intensify between-race inequality and post–1980 trends in increased income inequality with increasing labor force participation of high-wage women. Since inequality between races and the sexes exist, in large part, because of occupational segregation, employment projections for women and nonwhites are dismal. While below-average growth in jobs tradi-tionally held by women and nonwhites is expected, above-average labor supply growth is expected. This suggests future increases in between-race and between-gender inequality unless barriers preventing women and nonwhites from enjoying occupational mobility are broken. This integration of women and minorities into the workplace can increase the supply of labor to occupations with bottlenecks and can improve their economic status.

This integration can be accomplished only with changes in both the demand and supply side of the labor market. Enforcement of affirmative action-type programs can break down labor market and educational barriers facing women and nonwhites but cannot, in the short run, change stereotypic beliefs and actions of those in the labor force. That is, women socialized from birth into a primary role as a homemaker and a secondary role as a worker in a stereotypic job cannot be expected to perform adequately as top-management officials. Likewise a nonwhite from a ghetto-type environment cannot be expected, without adequate preparation, to succeed in higher education. Long-range policies need to free individuals from stereotypic beliefs and attitudes by providing labor market role models and educational support from birth.

Labor Supply: Income-Receiving Units, Female Labor Force Participation, and Dependency

Prior to 1980, concurrent increases in female-headed income-receiving units and female labor force participation acted as counteracting forces on aggregate income inequality. After 1980, both increased income inequality, although this must be cautiously interpreted. The impact of increased female-headed units (and decreased husband-wife units) on increased inequality is strongly interacted with race. Race is the dominant influence. Current increases in female labor force participation increase inequality with increased assortative mating in husband-wife families, but decrease inequality through reductions in male earnings in high-earning occupations. Given these associations, the most effective inequality-reduction policies should facilitate the labor supply of low-income and nonwhite female-headed units. This necessitates increasing the benefits (wages) from working and reducing the cost (child care). Women's wages have remained a constant two-thirds of men's for decades primarily because occupational segregation prohibits accumulation of on-the-job training and mobility into higher-paying positions. These barriers must be broken for female wages to reach parity with male wages.

Lower wages are devastating to female labor supply since the opportunity cost of working—child care—is high. Many women, particularly those heading families, are excluded from labor market activities because their wages cannot cover the cost of child care. This necessitates providing affordable, quality child care to facilitate the entrance of (low-income) women into the labor market. The provision of quality child care is also an investment in our future resources—children. By providing children with a nonracist, nonsexist learning environment early in life, future workers will be more educated and will carry fewer productivity-reducing discriminatory attitudes into the labor market. Of course, child-care concerns should not be confined to women. Many female-headed families are impoverished upon divorce and are confined to poverty because of inadequate (or nonexistent) child support from the father. Men must be made responsible for their children. This will free women for labor market activity and, hopefully, provide children with economic and emotional support from both parents. These issues are particularly germane to nonwhite women who face racial as well as gender constraints in employment and economic status.

Increased labor force participation of (low-income) women and of (jobless) nonwhites with the reduction of occupational barriers is essential for future inequality reductions and for efficient labor market operation. As the baby bust ages and enters the labor market during the 1990s there will be a shortage of traditional new labor market entrants. While this labor shortage can be reduced with increased supply of women and nonwhites, current occupational segregation prevents substitution of youthful entrants and women and nonwhites. A more efficient use of our current human resources with the breakdown of occupational segregation could replace labor "lost" from declining fertility rates.

Race

Because nonwhites had proportionate increases in manufacturing employment during the industry's relative employment decline, nonwhites have been unduly harmed by current employment shifts. The combination of employment shifts and occupational segregation has resulted in their low wages and high rates of joblessness. Current government policies have increased the income of low-income nonwhites but have harmed middle-income nonwhites. Future policies need to be cognizant of unintended racial consequences. Industrial policies need to focus on nonwhite employment problems as well as the general problems created by employment shifts. For example, wage subsidies will not help non-whites if they are targeted to occupations traditionally not opened to nonwhites or if they are targeted to employers located outside the central city. Policies also need to focus on the high, and increasing, joblessness rates of nonwhites. The lack of job opportunities in areas where nonwhites live suggests a discouraged-worker response to unemployment. Increased availability of jobs, both spatially and occupationally, would ease the problem. The strong interactions of race with employment and income-receiving-unit type found in this study suggest that race is still an important factor in economic success and policies should specifically address nonwhite problems as well as aggregate labor market and social problems.

Government

Government policies have met with mixed success in the past. The most effective policies have reduced within-group income inequality. Within income-receiving units, poverty was reduced primarily because of government programs. Poverty reductions were particularly dramatic for unrelated individuals as Social Security benefits to the elderly increased. Policies were less successful at reducing inequality between units. Nonwhite and white income inequality was more divergent in 1985 than in 1950 and female-headed units have increasingly become a larger proportion of the impoverished. Because of the increasing economic disparity between groups, inequality has increased due to compositional changes. That is, the increasing divergence of white-nonwhite inequality is magnified as nonwhites become an increasing proportion of the population. Likewise, the increasing feminization of poverty is important because of the increasing proportion of female-headed units in the population. Future policies should therefore expand beyond the emphasis on within-group inequality and focus on between-group inequalities. This necessitates general programs that better integrate all workers into the labor market process and specific programs that target efforts at the integration of nonwhites and women.

Appendix 1

Computation of Income Inequality and Distribution

Prior to 1958, individual income data were not available from the Current Population Survey, hence, Gini coefficients were computed on the basis of quintiles of income. For consistency, we continued this practice following the methodology outlined in Miller (1963). The example of the procedure presented here uses a single year and income-receiving units; however, the same procedure was used yearly and for industries, occupations, and ages.

A discrete, numeric income distribution for each family type and male and female unrelated individuals was obtained. Total families and total unrelated individuals were obtained from the summation of components. The aggregate was obtained from the summation of total families and total unrelated individuals. Income categories were converted to 1985 dollars using annual consumer price indices (CPI) (Table A1–1).

Aggregate income levels (for all levels of income-receiving units) were computed by summing the product of the number of units falling within each income interval by the interval mean. If the interval was a closed range, the midpoint was used as the mean. If the interval was open ended, a Pareto distribution was fitted using:

$$\overline{X} = X \, (V/V - 1) \qquad\qquad \text{(A1–1)}$$

where

X = lower income limit of open-end interval

V = $c - d/b - a$

Table A1–1
Dollar Adjustments to Nominal Income and Earnings

	CPI (all items)	1985 Adjustment		CPI (all items)	1985 Adjustment
1947	66.9	4.82	1973	133.7	2.41
1948	72.1	4.47	1974	147.7	2.18
1949	71.4	4.51	1975	161.2	2.00
1950	72.1	4.47	1976	170.5	1.89
1951	77.8	4.14	1977	181.5	1.78
1952	79.5	4.05	1978	195.4	1.65
1953	80.1	4.02	1979	217.4	1.48
1954	80.5	4.00	1980	246.6	1.31
1955	80.2	4.02	1981	272.4	1.18
1956	81.4	3.96	1982	289.1	1.11
1957	84.3	3.82	1983	296.4	1.09
1958	86.6	3.72	1984	311.1	1.04
1959	87.3	3.69	1985	322.2	1.00
1960	88.7	3.63			
1961	89.6	3.60			
1962	90.6	3.56			
1963	91.7	3.51			
1964	92.9	3.47			
1965	94.5	3.41			
1966	97.2	3.32			
1967	100.0	3.22			
1968	104.2	3.09			
1969	109.8	2.93			
1970	116.3	2.77			
1971	121.3	2.66			
1972	125.3	2.57			

a = log of lower income limit of interval preceding open-end

b = log of lower income limit of open-end interval

c = log of the sum of frequencies in open-end interval and one preceding it

d = log of frequencies in open-end interval

A cumulative percentage income distribution was obtained based on the numeric distributions. Quintile income limits were then obtained using linear interpolation. The quintile limit was inserted into the original income distribution and the limit was averaged with the original preceding limit. Using linear interpolation, the number of individuals falling below the quintile limit and above the lower limit was found.

Using the quintile limits as bounds, income for each quintile was computed. Aggregate quintile income for the lowest quintile was computed by summing the product of the number of individuals in each category and the category's mean (using the procedure outlined above). For aggregate income of additional quintiles, quintile income was computed as a residual by subtracting the quintile income of all preceding incomes. Each quintile's share was computed by dividing the quintile's income by aggregate income.

Mathematically:

$$s^j = \frac{\sum\limits_{i=1}^{l} N_i \overline{Y}_i - \sum\limits_{i=1}^{l-1} N_i \overline{Y}_i}{\sum\limits_{i=1}^{x} N_i \overline{Y}_i} \tag{A1-2}$$

where

s^j = quintile share for receiving unit j

N_i = number of income-receiving units in the i interval

$\overline{Y}_i$ = the midpoint of a closed income interval (i) or the mean approximated with a Pareto distribution (A1–1) of an open-ended income interval (i)

l = number of income intervals using the quintile limit as the top limit

x = total number of income intervals

The Gini coefficient was computed using the cumulative shares of each quintile:

$$G^j = 1 - [.2(s^{top20} + s^{four\ 20}) + .2(s^{four20} + s^{mid20}) \tag{A1-3}$$
$$+ .2(s^{mid20} + s^{sec20}) + .2(s^{sec20} + s^{low20})\,]$$

where

G^j = the Gini coefficient for receiving unit j

s^{top20} = cumulative income share through the highest quintile

s^{four20} = cumulative income share through the fourth quintile

s^{mid20} = cumulative income share through the third quintile

s^{sec20} = cumulative income share through the second quintile

s^{low20} = income share of the lowest quintile

Appendix 2

Procedure to Calculate Projections

The procedure to project future income distributions is similar to the one used by the U.S. Bureau of the Census (1980) for projecting trends in median household income. Although Census projections maintain a constant Pareto income distribution, this procedure allows the Pareto distribution (hence, Gini coefficient and share distributions) to alter. The example of the procedure presented here uses income-receiving units as the example; however, the same procedure was used for industrial, occupational, and age structures.

Based on the projected income-receiving-unit distribution (i.e., the projected number of families and unrelated individuals), the numeric income distribution was computed by applying the proportion of individuals in 1980 in each income interval:

$$\hat{P}_i = \hat{P}_T \times \frac{P_i^{1980}}{P_T^{1980}} \qquad \text{(A2–1)}$$

where:

$\hat{P}_i$ = projected number of units in income category i

$\hat{P}_T$ = projected number of income-receiving units (from published data)

P_i^{1980} = actual number of units in income category i in 1980 (from published data)

P_T^{1980} = actual number of income-receiving units in 1980 (from published data)

Total families and unrelated individuals were computed by summing across income-receiving units in each income interval. The aggregate income distribution was obtained by summing total families and total unrelated individuals. Income inequality and share distribution measures were computed as outlined in Appendix 1.

Projections for differing levels of married women's labor force participation were based on separating husband-wife families into varying proportions of working/nonworking-wife families. Variations were based on the 1980 percentage of working wives (50.213 percent). Thus:

$$\hat{P}_{ilf} = \hat{P}_{HW} \times X \qquad \qquad (A2\text{--}2)$$
$$\hat{P}_{olf} = \hat{P}_{HW} \times (1-X) \qquad (A2\text{--}3)$$

where

$\hat{P}_{ilf}$ = projected husband-wife families with the wife in the labor force

$\hat{P}_{olf}$ = projected husband-wife families with the wife out of the labor force

$\hat{P}_{HW}$ = projected husband-wife families (from published data)

X = a participation ratio of either

   no change: .50213

   5 percentage point increase: .55213

   10 percentage point increase: .60213

   15 percentage point increase: .65213

   20 percentage point increase: .70213

Aggregate income inequality and share distribution changes for varying proportions of husband-wife, dual-earning families were then projected.

Appendix 3

Data and Data Sources

INCOME

Distributions (in Aggregate, by Income-Receiving Unit, by Race)

1947–1960   Miller, Herman. 1963. *Trends in the Income of Families and Persons in the United States: 1947–1960.* Washington, DC: USGPO.

1961–1985   U.S. Bureau of the Census. Money Income of Households, Families, and Persons in the United States. *Current Population Reports,* Series P–60, various numbers. Washington, DC: USGPO.

Annual Earnings or Income

1950–1960   Miller, Herman. 1963. *Trends in the Income of Families and Persons in the United States: 1947–1960.* Washington, DC: USGPO.

1960–1980   U.S. Bureau of the Census. Money Income of Households, Families, and Persons in the United States. *Current Population Reports,* Series P–60, various numbers. Washington, DC: USGPO.

1985   U.S. Bureau of the Census. 1986. *Statistical Abstract of the United States* (107th ed.). Washington, DC: USGPO.

Husband by Wife Earnings

1967   U.S. Bureau of the Census. Supplementary Report on Income in 1967 of Families and Persons in the United States. *Current Population Reports,* Series P–60, Number 64, Table 4. Washington, DC: USGPO.

1970–1985   U.S. Bureau of the Census. Money Income of Households, Families and Persons in the United States. *Current Population Reports,* Series P–60. Washington, DC: USGPO.

Female Weekly Earnings

1970   U.S. Bureau of the Census. *Statistical Abstract of the United States* (103d ed.). Washington, DC: USGPO.

1980–1985   U.S. Bureau of the Census. *Statistical Abstract of the United States* (107th ed.). Washington, DC: USGPO.

Female Occupation and Relative Earnings

1950–1980   U.S. Bureau of the Census. *American Women: Three Decades of Change.* Special Demographic Analyses, CDS–80–8. Washington, DC: USGPO.

Poverty

1960–1970   U.S. Bureau of the Census. Characteristics of the Low-Income Population, 1970. *Current Population Reports,* Series P–60, Number 81, Table 1. Washington, DC: USGPO.

1980–1985   U.S. Bureau of the Census. Money Income and Poverty Status of Families and Persons in the United States (Advance Report). *Current Population Reports,* Series P–60, Numbers 127 and 154. Washington, DC: USGPO.

LABOR MARKET

Female Labor Force Participation

1947–1970   U.S. Bureau of the Census. 1975. *Historical Statistics of the United States, Colonial Times to 1970.* Washington, DC: USGPO.

1971–1982   U.S. Department of Labor. 1982. *Labor Force Statistics Derived from the Current Population Surveys: A Databook.* Washington, DC: USGPO.

1983–1985   U.S. Department of Labor, Bureau of Labor Statistics. *Monthly Labor Review,* various issues. Washington, DC: USGPO.

By Marital   U.S. Bureau of the Census. *Statistical Abstract of the United States,*
Status   various editions. Washington, DC: USGPO.

Labor Force Participation by Age

1950–1970   U.S. Bureau of the Census. 1975. *Historical Statistics of the United States, Colonial Times to 1970.* Washington, DC: USGPO.

1980–1985   U.S. Bureau of the Census. 1986. *Statistical Abstract of the United States* (107th ed.). Washington, DC: USGPO.

Occupation

1947–1960   Miller, Herman. 1963. *Trends in the Income of Families and Persons in the United States: 1947–1960*. Washington, DC: USGPO.

1961–1982   U.S. Department of Labor, Bureau of Labor Statistics. 1983. *Handbook of Labor Statistics*. Washington, DC: USGPO.

1983–1985   U.S. Bureau of the Census. *Statistical Abstract of the United States*, various editions. Washington, DC: USGPO.

Industry

1947–1970   U.S. Bureau of the Census. 1975. *Historical Statistics of the United States, Colonial Times to 1970*. Washington, DC: USGPO.

1971–1983   U.S. Department of Labor, Bureau of Labor Statistics. 1985. *Handbook of Labor Statistics*. Washington, DC: USGPO.

1983–1985   U.S. Department of Labor, Bureau of Labor Statistics. *Monthly Labor Review*, various issues. Washington, DC: USGPO.

Industry Unemployment

1950–1970   U.S. Bureau of the Census. 1975. *Historical Statistics of the United States, Colonial Times to 1970*. Washington, DC: USGPO.

1980–1985   U.S. Bureau of the Census. 1986. *Statistical Abstract of the United States* (107th ed.). Washington, DC: USGPO.

Occupational Unemployment

1960–1980   U.S. Department of Labor, Bureau of Labor Statistics. 1982. *Labor Force Statistics Derived from the Current Population Survey*. Washington, DC: USGPO.

1985   U.S. Bureau of the Census. 1986. *Statistical Abstract of the United States* (107th ed.). Washington, DC: USGPO.

Unionization

1959   Fuchs, Victor. 1968. *The Service Economy*. New York: National Bureau of Economic Research.

1970   Freeman, Richard B., and James L. Medoff. 1979. New Estimates of Private Sector Unionism in the United States. *Industrial and Labor Relations Review* 32 (January): 143–174.

1980   Kokkelenberg, Edward C., and Donna R. Sockell. 1985.Union Membership in the United States. *Industrial and Labor Relations Review* 38 (January): 497–543.

GROSS NATIONAL PRODUCT AND SOCIAL SERVICES

1947–1970   U.S. Bureau of the Census. 1975. *Historical Statistics of the United States, Colonial Times to 1970.* Washington, DC: USGPO.

1971–1985   U.S. Bureau of the Census. *Statistical Abstract of the United States,* various editions. Washington, DC: USGPO.

DEMOGRAPHIC CHARACTERISTICS

Income-Receiving Units

1947–1970   U.S. Bureau of the Census. 1975. *Historical Statistics of the United States, Colonial Times to 1970.* Washington, DC: USGPO.

1971–1984   U.S. Bureau of the Census, Department of Commerce. Population Profile of the United States. *Current Population Reports,* Special Studies, Series P–23, Number 145. Washington, DC: USGPO.

1985   U.S. Bureau of the Census, Department of Commerce. Projections of the Number of Households and Families: 1986–2000. *Current Population Reports,* Population Estimates and Projections, Series P–23, Number 986. Washington, DC: USGPO.

Median Population Age

1947–1959   U.S. Bureau of the Census. *Statistical Abstract of the United States,* various editions. Washington, DC: USGPO.

1960–1984   U.S. Bureau of the Census. Estimates of the Population of the United States by Age, Sex, and Race: 1980–1985. *Current Population Reports,* Series P–25, Number 985. Washington, DC: USGPO.

1985   U.S. Bureau of the Census. 1986. *Statistical Abstract of the United States* (107th ed.). Washington, DC: USGPO.

Total Fertility Rate

1947–1984   U.S. Bureau of the Census. Population Estimates and Projections. *Current Population Reports,* Series P–25, Number 971. Washington, DC: USGPO.

1985   U.S. Bureau of the Census. 1986. *Statistical Abstract of the United States* (107th ed.). Washington, DC: USGPO.

Dependency Ratio

1947–1949   U.S. Bureau of the Census. *Statistical Abstract of the United States,* various editions. Washington, DC: USGPO.

1950–1970   U.S. Bureau of the Census. Estimates of the Population of the United States by Age, Race, and Sex: July 1, 1967 to July 1, 1969. *Current Population Reports,* Series P–25, Number 441. Washington, DC: USGPO.

1971–1983   U.S. Bureau of the Census, Department of Commerce. Population Profile of the United States. *Current Population Reports,* Special Studies, Series P–23, Number 145. Washington, DC: USGPO.

1984–1985   U.S. Bureau of the Census. *Statistical Abstract of the United States,* various editions. Washington, DC: USGPO.

RACE

Demographic Characteristics (Except Poverty)

1950–1960   U.S. Bureau of the Census. 1975. *Historical Statistics of the United States, Colonial Times to 1970.* Washington, DC: USGPO.

1970–1985   U.S. Bureau of the Census. 1986. *Statistical Abstract of the United States* (107th ed.). Washington, DC: USGPO.

Income-Receiving Units

1970–1985   U.S. Bureau of the Census. Money Income of Households, Families and Persons in the United States. *Current Population Reports,* Series P–60. Washington, DC: USGPO.

Economic Characteristics

1960–1970   U.S. Bureau of the Census. *Statistical Abstract of the United States,* various editions. Washington, DC: USGPO.

1985   U.S. Department of Labor, Bureau of Labor Statistics. 1985. *Employment and Earnings* 32 (August). Washington, DC: USGPO.

Industry and Occupation (1 Digit)

1950   U.S. Bureau of the Census. 1952. *U.S. Census of the Population, 1950: Industrial Characteristics.* Washington, DC: USGPO.

1960   U.S. Bureau of the Census. 1962. *U.S. Census of the Population, 1960: Occupational Characteristics.* Washington, DC: USGPO.

1970–1980   U.S. Bureau of the Census. 1983. *U.S. Census of the Population, 1980: General Social and Economic Characteristics.* Washington, DC: USGPO.

PROJECTIONS

Age

U.S. Bureau of the Census. Projections of the Population of the United States by Age, Sex, and Race: 1983 to 2080. *Current Population Reports,* Series P–25, Number 952. Washington, DC: USGPO.

Income-Receiving Unit

U.S. Bureau of the Census. Projections of the Number of Households and Families: 1986 to 2000. *Current Population Reports,* Series P–25, Number 986. Washington, DC: USGPO.

Industry

Personick, Valerie A. 1985. A Second Look at Industry Output and Employment Trends through 1995. *Monthly Labor Review* 108 (November): 26–41.

———. 1987. Industry Output and Employment through the End of the Century. *Monthly Labor Review* 110 (September): 30–45.

Median Income

U.S. Bureau of the Census. Illustrative Projections of Money Income Size Distributions for Households: 1980 to 1995. *Current Population Reports,* Series P–60, Number 122. Washington, DC: USGPO.

Occupation

Silvestri, George T., and John M. Lukasiewicz. 1985. Occupational Employment Projections: The 1984–1995 Outlook. *Monthly Labor Review* 108 (November): 42–57.

———. 1987. A Look at Occupational Employment Trends to the Year 2000. *Monthly Labor Review* 110 (September): 46–63.

DATA TABLES

Table A3–1
Gini Coefficients for Each Income-Receiving Unit, 1947–1985

	Aggregate	Total Family	Husband-Wife Family Total	Wife in Labor Force	Wife out of Labor Force	Male-Headed Family	Female-Headed Family	Unrelated Individual Total	Male	Female
1947[1]	.401	.378	.369	--	--	.438	.418	.568	.514	.522
1948	.393	.369	.358	--	--	.411	.450	.479	.479	.477
1949	.393	.379	.365	.307	.377	.451	.456	.476	.463	.466
1950	.396	.375	.363	.300	.386	.411	.454	.483	.451	.496
1951	.383	.361	.347	.289	.365	.391	.447	.477	.442	.473
1952	.393	.374	.353	.312	.362	.398	.477	.479	.439	.485
1953	.377	.360	.343	.283	.361	.419	.464	.518	.489	.510
1954	.398	.373	.357	.289	.374	.393	.467	.506	.501	.491
1955	.392	.366	.350	.280	.377	.402	.454	.498	.470	.517
1956	.386	.355	.345	.280	.367	.389	.437	.487	.461	.484
1957	.386	.351	.337	.283	.358	.393	.441	.490	.470	.480
1958	.397	.354	.335	.281	.357	.403	.442	.502	.496	.490
1959	.397	.366	.345	.285	.368	.438	.437	.512	.496	.514
1960	.405	.369	.355	.294	.378	.395	.434	.491	.469	.479
1961	.453	.419	.418	.333	.404	.458	.477	.520	.506	.496
1962	.433	.427	.408	.365	.416	.443	.463	.496	.497	.500
1963	.428	.387	.371	.372	.395	.433	.468	.535	.517	.520
1964	.436	.387	.396	.342	.391	.434	.452	.540	.481	.495
1965	.410	.412	.376	.332	.393	.417	.451	.493	.481	.514
1966	.426	.400	.411	.331	.379	.415	.438	.491	.501	.512
1967	.418	.356	.354	.357	.400	.398	.433	.506	.469	.512
1968	.404	.371	.361	.313	.351	.369	.422	.466	.446	.454
1969	.406	.394	.342	.305	.371	.403	.430	.483	.451	.475
1970	.424	.355	.367	.334	.396	.400	.475	.464	.468	.480
1971	.421	.371	.337	.353	.354	.373	.404	.471	.453	.458
1972	.402	.370	.365	.323	.350	.350	.413	.471	.445	.452
1973	.418	.379	.389	.356	.378	.379	.418	.453	.446	.441
1974	.398	.390	.367	.365	.380	.376	.417	.436	.439	.437
1975	.387	.384	.375	.325	.385	.374	.408	.431	.423	.418
1976	.385	.398	.361	.333	.395	.386	.418	.446	.438	.426
1977	.386	.363	.367	.352	.396	.376	.382	.430	.419	.414
1978	.380	.393	.384	.349	.395	.386	.417	.432	.432	.421
1979	.417	.365	.348	.297	.386	.379	.407	.422	.414	.420
1980	.413	.365	.341	.290	.380	.373	.405	.427	.413	.407
1981	.417	.366	.342	.295	.372	.356	.406	.429	.426	.405
1982	.421	.373	.342	.310	.381	.369	.418	.425	.419	.411
1983	.434	.373	.349	.310	.378	.364	.419	.429	.425	.414
1984	.437	.376	.350	.312	.381	.383	.418	.427	.426	.433
1985	.433	.376	.352	.314	.383	.383	.423	.431	.423	.420

[1]From 1947 to 1960 all data, except aggregates, were drawn from Miller (1966). All aggregates and post-1960 data were computed using the procedure outlined in Appendix 1. The aggregate and totals were computed as a weighted average of the income-receiving-unit components.

Table A3–2
Top-Quintile Share Distribution by Income-Receiving Unit, 1947–1985

	Aggregate	Total Family	Husband-Wife Family			Male-Headed Family	Female-Headed Family	Unrelated Individual		
			Total	Wife in Labor Force	Wife out of Labor Force			Total	Male	Female
1947[1]	.462	.433	.428	--	--	.480	.455	.589	.533	.551
1948	.451	.425	.418	--	--	.461	.482	.509	.504	.501
1949	.453	.428	.420	.371	.435	.474	.488	.502	.487	.491
1950	.437	.427	.420	.368	.441	.461	.486	.503	.465	.523
1951	.438	.418	.413	.364	.427	.432	.471	.494	.455	.498
1952	.438	.422	.413	.382	.425	.439	.503	.500	.464	.516
1953	.433	.410	.402	.358	.414	.457	.485	.530	.513	.529
1954	.451	.419	.411	.361	.426	.433	.490	.530	.516	.526
1955	.443	.418	.408	.355	.430	.442	.482	.520	.488	.546
1956	.439	.411	.405	.355	.425	.426	.462	.513	.476	.523
1957	.439	.405	.398	.357	.414	.435	.467	.510	.490	.514
1958	.454	.410	.403	.360	.419	.440	.472	.525	.514	.514
1959	.452	.414	.406	.359	.424	.479	.470	.538	.516	.540
1960	.462	.421	.412	.365	.433	.443	.466	.510	.487	.506
1961	.488	.501	.510	.424	.484	.537	.551	.572	.579	.554
1962	.514	.527	.536	.448	.503	.539	.506	.527	.566	.546
1963	.458	.469	.420	.457	.449	.497	.505	.593	.587	.566
1964	.480	.442	.447	.480	.476	.467	.520	.616	.528	.532
1965	.451	.466	.472	.397	.449	.489	.521	.539	.533	.560
1966	.485	.500	.510	.437	.479	.470	.475	.552	.577	.552
1967	.503	.417	.428	.462	.497	.474	.502	.572	.511	.577
1968	.437	.448	.457	.347	.429	.417	.465	.526	.478	.508
1969	.474	.489	.380	.399	.467	.475	.486	.549	.488	.537
1970	.496	.401	.409	.426	.495	.498	.710	.513	.525	.546
1971	.510	.418	.425	.448	.407	.467	.468	.489	.489	.509
1972	.445	.456	.462	.483	.438	.418	.458	.509	.509	.533
1973	.470	.482	.493	.519	.470	.460	.465	.524	.517	.526
1974	.481	.489	.501	.524	.483	.468	.498	.483	.507	.499
1975	.437	.473	.480	.399	.465	.440	.473	.489	.488	.487
1976	.435	.501	.431	.429	.492	.459	.477	.512	.504	.480
1977	.434	.459	.459	.450	.531	.509	.437	.485	.467	.490
1978	.426	.477	.476	.472	.475	.463	.473	.504	.491	.488
1979	.467	.432	.415	.379	.456	.447	.456	.475	.463	.494
1980	.469	.426	.409	.374	.450	.438	.466	.492	.468	.472
1981	.475	.429	.413	.379	.438	.420	.463	.487	.484	.464
1982	.480	.437	.411	.389	.454	.427	.472	.481	.478	.478
1983	.496	.435	.421	.391	.448	.424	.472	.488	.480	.476
1984	.500	.439	.421	.391	.453	.446	.474	.487	.483	.504
1985	.504	.439	.422	.394	.454	.447	.477	.484	.473	.477

[1]From 1947 to 1960 all data, except aggregates, were drawn from Miller (1966). All aggregates and post-1960 data were computed using the procedure outlined in Appendix 1. The aggregate and totals were computed as a weighted average of the income-receiving-unit components.

Table A3–3
Fourth-Quintile Share Distribution by Income-Receiving Unit, 1947–1985

			Husband-Wife Family					Unrelated Individual		
	Aggregate	Total Family	Total	Wife in Labor Force	Wife out of Labor Force	Male-Headed Family	Female-Headed Family	Total	Male	Female
1947[1]	.235	.232	.227	--	--	.230	.247	.213	.231	.233
1948	.239	.232	.230	--	--	.232	.242	.249	.248	.255
1949	.230	.235	.233	.244	.229	.252	.239	.259	.253	.263
1950	.256	.236	.234	.240	.224	.228	.247	.266	.268	.254
1951	.243	.233	.229	.235	.224	.249	.257	.267	.274	.264
1952	.244	.235	.231	.231	.225	.243	.235	.254	.254	.252
1953	.243	.240	.236	.240	.233	.236	.254	.244	.227	.248
1954	.245	.240	.237	.239	.232	.246	.248	.245	.249	.243
1955	.246	.234	.232	.237	.228	.242	.245	.248	.255	.234
1956	.245	.236	.233	.239	.226	.248	.258	.253	.267	.241
1957	.245	.237	.235	.239	.228	.238	.252	.253	.258	.247
1958	.238	.237	.231	.239	.228	.248	.249	.249	.250	.252
1959	.242	.236	.231	.238	.227	.227	.253	.239	.249	.236
1960	.238	.234	.233	.241	.225	.234	.249	.257	.261	.258
1961	.277	.210	.209	.201	.213	.194	.200	.236	.191	.244
1962	.197	.197	.129	.215	.203	.187	.249	.267	.205	.257
1963	.265	.204	.259	.204	.274	.231	.258	.214	.200	.249
1964	.259	.251	.257	.137	.199	.283	.256	.174	.255	.248
1965	.249	.250	.189	.250	.247	.200	.215	.250	.246	.231
1966	.239	.181	.182	.188	.182	.249	.285	.217	.193	.240
1967	.181	.232	.231	.191	.185	.195	.211	.208	.268	.188
1968	.271	.228	.181	.330	.228	.270	.259	.232	.266	.236
1969	.219	.177	.297	.221	.177	.214	.253	.223	.261	.219
1970	.214	.287	.287	.219	.175	.178	.111	.241	.238	.209
1971	.178	.283	.209	.217	.280	.186	.256	.272	.272	.257
1972	.263	.199	.198	.100	.199	.214	.258	.225	.225	.224
1973	.256	.198	.197	.100	.200	.205	.266	.215	.209	.198
1974	.202	.198	.117	.110	.198	.199	.214	.261	.216	.235
1975	.253	.195	.174	.249	.209	.231	.230	.240	.229	.225
1976	.256	.176	.233	.210	.187	.219	.242	.233	.228	.250
1977	.257	.190	.228	.239	.126	.127	.250	.247	.260	.217
1978	.260	.206	.207	.154	.219	.224	.242	.223	.232	.239
1979	.231	.230	.246	.225	.225	.229	.263	.246	.265	.218
1980	.242	.243	.239	.228	.235	.237	.235	.230	.244	.237
1981	.240	.241	.236	.227	.240	.242	.244	.243	.240	.244
1982	.237	.237	.237	.234	.228	.246	.245	.247	.238	.235
1983	.232	.241	.235	.231	.233	.244	.247	.238	.243	.241
1984	.230	.239	.236	.232	.230	.236	.245	.237	.240	.225
1985	.229	.240	.236	.232	.231	.238	.245	.240	.243	.239

[1]From 1947 to 1960 all data, except aggregates, were drawn from Miller (1966). All aggregates and post-1960 data were computed using the procedure outlined in Appendix 1. The aggregate and totals were computed as a weighted average of the income-receiving-unit components.

Table A3–4
Middle-Quintile Share Distribution by Income-Receiving Unit, 1947–1985

	Aggregate	Total Family	Husband-Wife Family			Male-Headed Family	Female-Headed Family	Unrelated Individual		
			Total	Wife in Labor Force	Wife out of Labor Force			Total	Male	Female
1947[1]	.166	.167	.169	--	--	.158	.162	.115	.142	.130
1948	.170	.172	.173	--	--	.159	.153	.134	.142	.135
1949	.181	.173	.173	.185	.169	.157	.155	.134	.154	.137
1950	.166	.174	.171	.188	.169	.165	.157	.131	.160	.123
1951	.175	.176	.174	.188	.171	.177	.161	.141	.169	.131
1952	.174	.171	.174	.188	.170	.170	.150	.147	.161	.127
1953	.177	.178	.180	.185	.177	.166	.155	.135	.157	.120
1954	.172	.176	.175	.188	.175	.174	.149	.127	.140	.120
1955	.173	.177	.179	.193	.171	.172	.157	.134	.150	.118
1956	.175	.179	.178	.189	.175	.176	.160	.137	.153	.128
1957	.176	.181	.181	.186	.179	.181	.159	.136	.150	.135
1958	.173	.178	.179	.185	.175	.170	.156	.130	.141	.133
1959	.171	.178	.179	.190	.174	.155	.154	.128	.138	.130
1960	.168	.177	.174	.185	.172	.170	.158	.133	.149	.133
1961	.125	.144	.119	.188	.153	.162	.149	.120	.151	.101
1962	.161	.110	.177	.166	.145	.134	.151	.134	.139	.107
1963	.157	.175	.177	.176	.117	.150	.149	.129	.133	.104
1964	.146	.163	.160	.178	.174	.135	.148	.151	.121	.145
1965	.190	.151	.170	.172	.162	.195	.152	.114	.124	.141
1966	.144	.162	.161	.167	.174	.146	.113	.138	.145	.145
1967	.191	.202	.163	.161	.160	.200	.168	.133	.114	.173
1968	.174	.153	.201	.113	.160	.152	.162	.132	.157	.156
1969	.173	.183	.147	.159	.196	.179	.129	.125	.157	.153
1970	.161	.139	.141	.153	.177	.172	.095	.148	.134	.158
1971	.186	.133	.181	.145	.136	.181	.153	.135	.135	.116
1972	.151	.167	.140	.182	.173	.200	.143	.150	.150	.151
1973	.142	.136	.133	.174	.159	.181	.140	.141	.161	.145
1974	.170	.138	.213	.165	.135	.161	.142	.137	.160	.143
1975	.169	.175	.179	.149	.174	.178	.160	.146	.153	.155
1976	.170	.166	.170	.163	.166	.172	.151	.128	.149	.147
1977	.169	.176	.117	.090	.173	.185	.163	.147	.142	.157
1978	.172	.163	.145	.187	.150	.154	.156	.144	.151	.137
1979	.158	.178	.162	.194	.168	.172	.142	.155	.135	.157
1980	.158	.172	.175	.185	.155	.170	.162	.149	.156	.150
1981	.156	.170	.173	.183	.164	.173	.159	.146	.149	.154
1982	.155	.171	.176	.176	.160	.173	.155	.146	.156	.148
1983	.150	.168	.170	.176	.161	.174	.155	.149	.154	.150
1984	.149	.167	.170	.176	.160	.169	.155	.149	.153	.141
1985	.147	.167	.170	.175	.159	.164	.154	.149	.156	.148

[1]From 1947 to 1960 all data, except aggregates, were drawn from Miller (1966). All aggregates and post-1960 data were computed using the procedure outlined in Appendix 1. The aggregate and totals were computed as a weighted average of the income-receiving-unit components.

Table A3–5
Second-Quintile Share Distribution by Income-Receiving Unit, 1947–1985

	Aggregate	Total Family	Husband-Wife Family Total	Wife in Labor Force	Wife out of Labor Force	Male-Headed Family	Female-Headed Family	Unrelated Individual Total	Male	Female
1947[1]	.103	.118	.121	--	--	.095	.100	.054	.068	.046
1948	.105	.121	.124	--	--	.105	.090	.075	.079	.069
1949	.103	.119	.123	.133	.120	.091	.086	.074	.080	.068
1950	.104	.119	.124	.138	.118	.108	.061	.069	.082	.062
1951	.110	.125	.127	.142	.124	.105	.085	.077	.077	.071
1952	.109	.122	.126	.136	.125	.110	.084	.075	.084	.074
1953	.112	.124	.129	.143	.126	.105	.082	.068	.075	.073
1954	.102	.120	.126	.141	.120	.109	.086	.072	.070	.080
1955	.104	.122	.127	.141	.122	.106	.087	.073	.076	.074
1956	.107	.124	.128	.143	.124	.109	.093	.069	.072	.081
1957	.107	.126	.129	.144	.127	.107	.092	.072	.072	.077
1958	.101	.124	.129	.144	.124	.101	.091	.070	.068	.076
1959	.102	.121	.126	.140	.122	.099	.091	.069	.070	.071
1960	.100	.120	.126	.138	.119	.108	.093	.070	.074	.072
1961	.086	.105	.115	.126	.109	.075	.075	.056	.067	.078
1962	.104	.127	.112	.114	.109	.107	.072	.056	.076	.071
1963	.088	.106	.088	.112	.111	.080	.066	.064	.080	.081
1964	.085	.100	.084	.131	.104	.085	.097	.058	.072	.075
1965	.081	.092	.121	.118	.097	.076	.078	.097	.074	.067
1966	.105	.111	.097	.152	.116	.099	.098	.093	.065	.064
1967	.091	.097	.131	.114	.111	.097	.092	.087	.088	.061
1968	.079	.123	.101	.146	.133	.123	.074	.087	.081	.071
1969	.098	.107	.122	.147	.113	.089	.095	.081	.063	.065
1970	.095	.118	.111	.133	.109	.110	.064	.077	.076	.062
1971	.092	.113	.120	.107	.120	.119	.109	.078	.078	.094
1972	.100	.126	.139	.157	.132	.111	.093	.082	.082	.084
1973	.096	.126	.112	.128	.122	.103	.089	.091	.082	.094
1974	.108	.120	.108	.113	.126	.124	.102	.080	.088	.092
1975	.100	.113	.109	.136	.103	.103	.096	.091	.096	.091
1976	.100	.109	.113	.122	.102	.105	.092	.096	.082	.086
1977	.100	.125	.135	.142	.116	.128	.112	.083	.096	.087
1978	.101	.107	.116	.114	.104	.109	.094	.088	.086	.095
1979	.095	.115	.123	.127	.103	.107	.108	.086	.099	.085
1980	.093	.107	.115	.138	.111	.106	.101	.091	.095	.097
1981	.092	.111	.119	.136	.105	.111	.097	.085	.093	.095
1982	.093	.109	.119	.130	.107	.111	.095	.088	.094	.093
1983	.088	.110	.118	.131	.107	.112	.090	.088	.090	.091
1984	.087	.108	.117	.130	.105	.105	.090	.088	.090	.087
1985	.086	.108	.116	.129	.104	.108	.088	.088	.092	.092

[1]From 1947 to 1960 all data, except aggregates, were drawn from Miller (1966). All aggregates and post-1960 data were computed using the procedure outlined in Appendix 1. The aggregate and totals were computed as a weighted average of the income-receiving-unit components.

Table A3–6
Lowest-Quintile Share Distribution by Income-Receiving Unit, 1947–1985

	Aggregate	Total Family	Husband-Wife Family			Male-Headed Family	Female-Headed Family	Unrelated Individual		
			Total	Wife in Labor Force	Wife out of Labor Force			Total	Male	Female
1947[1]	.035	.051	.055	--	--	.038	.037	.029	.025	.040
1948	.035	.051	.054	--	--	.042	.032	.033	.028	.039
1949	.033	.045	.051	.066	.047	.026	.033	.032	.027	.040
1950	.032	.045	.051	.066	.048	.037	.029	.031	.026	.037
1951	.034	.049	.057	.071	.054	.037	.026	.029	.025	.036
1952	.036	.049	.056	.063	.054	.038	.028	.025	.036	.031
1953	.036	.047	.053	.074	.049	.036	.025	.023	.028	.030
1954	.031	.045	.051	.071	.047	.038	.026	.025	.025	.031
1955	.033	.048	.054	.074	.050	.038	.029	.024	.031	.028
1956	.034	.049	.056	.073	.051	.041	.027	.029	.031	.027
1957	.034	.050	.057	.073	.052	.039	.030	.029	.030	.028
1958	.034	.051	.058	.073	.054	.041	.032	.026	.027	.025
1959	.033	.051	.057	.073	.053	.040	.032	.025	.026	.023
1960	.033	.049	.055	.070	.050	.040	.032	.030	.028	.031
1961	.024	.040	.047	.061	.042	.033	.024	.016	.012	.023
1962	.024	.039	.046	.057	.040	.033	.022	.016	.013	.019
1963	.032	.046	.056	.051	.049	.042	.022	.000	.000	.000
1964	.030	.044	.052	.074	.047	.031	.019	.000	.023	.000
1965	.029	.041	.048	.063	.045	.040	.035	.000	.023	.000
1966	.027	.047	.051	.056	.050	.035	.029	.000	.020	.000
1967	.035	.052	.047	.073	.047	.035	.027	.000	.019	.000
1968	.038	.049	.060	.063	.051	.038	.039	.023	.018	.029
1969	.035	.043	.054	.073	.046	.048	.037	.022	.031	.027
1970	.035	.056	.051	.069	.044	.043	.020	.021	.027	.025
1971	.035	.053	.065	.083	.058	.047	.035	.026	.026	.024
1972	.038	.048	.057	.074	.053	.052	.042	.033	.033	.024
1973	.036	.058	.065	.080	.049	.050	.040	.028	.030	.036
1974	.040	.055	.062	.088	.058	.048	.044	.039	.029	.032
1975	.040	.045	.058	.067	.049	.048	.040	.033	.034	.041
1976	.040	.049	.053	.076	.053	.044	.039	.031	.038	.038
1977	.040	.050	.062	.078	.055	.051	.038	.038	.034	.049
1978	.041	.047	.056	.074	.051	.050	.035	.041	.037	.042
1979	.037	.045	.055	.076	.048	.046	.032	.038	.038	.047
1980	.037	.051	.061	.075	.049	.050	.036	.037	.036	.045
1981	.036	.049	.059	.075	.053	.054	.037	.040	.034	.044
1982	.034	.047	.057	.071	.051	.044	.032	.038	.034	.046
1983	.034	.046	.057	.071	.052	.046	.036	.037	.033	.043
1984	.034	.041	.057	.071	.052	.044	.037	.039	.034	.043
1985	.033	.046	.057	.071	.052	.044	.036	.035	.031	.041

[1]From 1947 to 1960 all data, except aggregates, were drawn from Miller (1966). All aggregates and post-1960 data were computed using the procedure outlined in Appendix 1. The aggregate and totals were computed as a weighted average of the income-receiving-unit components.

Table A3–7
Gini Coefficients by Race, 1947–1985

	White			Nonwhite[2]		
	Total White	Families	Unrelated Individuals	Total Nonwhite	Families	Unrelated Individuals
1947[1]	.382	.366	.555	.428	.406	.466
1948	.384	.360	.488	.421	.406	.468
1949	.389	.367	.483	.418	.417	.439
1950	.389	.369	.489	.420	.404	.486
1951	.383	.351	.480	.413	.404	.460
1952	.375	.357	.477	.394	.369	.457
1953	.380	.350	.521	.414	.394	.428
1954	.388	.360	.494	.432	.404	.526
1955	.380	.353	.504	.418	.388	.464
1956	.377	.346	.495	.416	.395	.464
1957	.374	.340	.489	.430	.399	.458
1958	.378	.341	.503	.434	.412	.476
1959	.380	.348	.520	.437	.410	.494
1960	.381	.353	.500	.446	.417	.511
1961	.359	.363	.504	.431	.418	.516
1962	.354	.350	.497	.426	.398	.489
1963	.354	.350	.497	.428	.401	.481
1964	.356	.351	.512	.420	.404	.477
1965	.337	.346	.485	.412	.388	.468
1966	.343	.340	.480	.407	.377	.474
1967	.341	.339	.489	.398	.387	.472
1968	.337	.340	.479	.424	.387	.461
1969	.338	.341	.479	.394	.382	.463
1970	.340	.346	.475	.397	.392	.470
1971	.340	.347	.470	.395	.393	.474
1972	.338	.351	.476	.395	.400	.480
1973	.332	.347	.456	.391	.398	.478
1974	.335	.347	.440	.391	.399	.454
1975	.340	.350	.437	.395	.392	.460
1976	.339	.349	.443	.398	.398	.458
1977	.340	.354	.439	.396	.411	.458
1978	.339	.354	.437	.399	.410	.469
1979	.332	.354	.428	.409	.416	.468
1980	.343	.355	.429	.407	.411	.458
1981	.341	.359	.437	.409	.418	.469
1982	.346	.369	.436	.410	.431	.474
1983	.345	.370	.444	.416	.438	.476
1984	.346	.371	.439	.394	.439	.474
1985	.344	.379	.437	.402	.432	.469

[1]All total white and nonwhite data were computed as a weighted average of family and unrelated-individual components from the procedure outlined in Appendix 1. Family and unrelated-individual data were drawn from Miller (1966) for 1947 to 1960 and from the U.S. Bureau of the Census (1988) for 1960 to 1985.

[2]Nonwhites are not confined to blacks.

Table A3-8
Top-Quintile Share by Race, 1947–1985

	White			Nonwhite[2]		
	Total White	Families	Unrelated Individuals	Total Nonwhite	Families	Unrelated Individuals
1947[1]	.444	.425	.568	.487	.453	.488
1948	.444	.419	.506	.472	.444	.496
1949	.447	.420	.496	.465	.450	.462
1950	.447	.422	.499	.463	.434	.504
1951	.444	.419	.486	.459	.437	.467
1952	.433	.413	.492	.446	.419	.484
1953	.435	.404	.533	.463	.431	.447
1954	.442	.412	.511	.473	.434	.548
1955	.435	.408	.520	.459	.422	.486
1956	.432	.404	.513	.461	.429	.484
1957	.430	.392	.508	.471	.428	.486
1958	.435	.401	.519	.481	.446	.500
1959	.436	.405	.529	.482	.444	.512
1960	.436	.407	.507	.493	.449	.533
1961	.413	.416	.522	.472	.456	.537
1962	.412	.406	.519	.473	.439	.527
1963	.414	.406	.519	.471	.443	.509
1964	.417	.405	.531	.461	.447	.507
1965	.404	.403	.508	.454	.432	.493
1966	.414	.401	.509	.448	.423	.502
1967	.413	.399	.514	.439	.432	.497
1968	.434	.401	.508	.472	.432	.493
1969	.462	.401	.508	.436	.427	.492
1970	.416	.405	.505	.438	.434	.494
1971	.416	.406	.500	.438	.437	.507
1972	.417	.409	.507	.438	.441	.502
1973	.414	.405	.493	.435	.441	.501
1974	.415	.406	.481	.436	.439	.486
1975	.415	.407	.476	.438	.433	.496
1976	.415	.406	.481	.442	.437	.489
1977	.417	.409	.479	.441	.449	.491
1978	.417	.410	.477	.440	.447	.506
1979	.407	.411	.468	.455	.452	.494
1980	.416	.409	.468	.449	.453	.491
1981	.412	.412	.473	.450	.451	.500
1982	.416	.421	.473	.449	.462	.496
1983	.416	.421	.478	.453	.468	.510
1984	.417	.422	.476	.428	.471	.503
1985	.417	.429	.473	.443	.464	.494

[1] All total white and nonwhite data were computed as a weighted average of family and unrelated-individual components from the procedure outlined in Appendix 1. Family and unrelated-individual data were drawn from Miller (1966) for 1947 to 1960 and from the U.S. Bureau of the Census (1988) for 1960 to 1985.

[2] Nonwhites are not confined to blacks.

Table A3–9
Fourth-Quintile Share by Race, 1947–1985

	White			Nonwhite[2]		
	Total White	Families	Unrelated Individuals	Total Nonwhite	Families	Unrelated Individuals
1947[1]	.238	.229	.225	.237	.238	.250
1948	.237	.230	.252	.245	.244	.245
1949	.239	.233	.261	.251	.246	.265
1950	.239	.232	.266	.255	.252	.259
1951	.235	.232	.275	.252	.251	.276
1952	.241	.231	.256	.247	.239	.246
1953	.243	.236	.242	.247	.250	.275
1954	.244	.237	.256	.257	.255	.234
1955	.244	.235	.249	.259	.256	.258
1956	.244	.234	.253	.254	.254	.264
1957	.243	.235	.255	.256	.261	.259
1958	.242	.234	.253	.250	.250	.255
1959	.243	.236	.251	.253	.253	.251
1960	.244	.237	.261	.248	.252	.249
1961	.244	.236	.249	.259	.245	.243
1962	.240	.238	.249	.251	.245	.226
1963	.237	.238	.251	.256	.246	.246
1964	.232	.238	.244	.259	.242	.247
1965	.227	.237	.251	.259	.247	.255
1966	.220	.235	.242	.262	.250	.249
1967	.218	.237	.246	.264	.246	.254
1968	.213	.235	.242	.251	.248	.251
1969	.211	.235	.242	.263	.247	.250
1970	.213	.236	.244	.263	.248	.252
1971	.213	.236	.243	.263	.247	.244
1972	.209	.236	.238	.262	.251	.252
1973	.209	.238	.238	.261	.248	.252
1974	.210	.238	.239	.261	.250	.252
1975	.216	.239	.242	.263	.251	.247
1976	.214	.239	.240	.262	.253	.250
1977	.214	.239	.239	.262	.252	.243
1978	.213	.239	.238	.264	.251	.240
1979	.216	.238	.241	.257	.253	.250
1980	.219	.240	.242	.263	.252	.246
1981	.223	.242	.242	.266	.255	.244
1982	.224	.241	.243	.267	.253	.251
1983	.222	.241	.240	.268	.253	.247
1984	.220	.241	.240	.275	.251	.242
1985	.218	.239	.243	.263	.251	.250

[1]All total white and nonwhite data were computed as a weighted average of family and unrelated-individual components from the procedure outlined in Appendix 1. Family and unrelated-individual data were drawn from Miller (1966) for 1947 to 1960 and from the U.S. Bureau of the Census (1988) for 1960 to 1985.

[2]Nonwhites are not confined to blacks.

Table A3–10
Middle-Quintile Share by Race, 1947–1985

	White			Nonwhite[2]		
	Total White	Families	Unrelated Individuals	Total Nonwhite	Families	Unrelated Individuals
1947[1]	.173	.170	.127	.154	.161	.155
1948	.172	.173	.141	.160	.169	.149
1949	.172	.173	.145	.163	.169	.157
1950	.173	.174	.140	.165	.176	.151
1951	.172	.176	.145	.167	.172	.155
1952	.175	.176	.150	.169	.177	.154
1953	.176	.180	.137	.166	.173	.157
1954	.174	.178	.136	.160	.175	.122
1955	.175	.178	.134	.164	.178	.146
1956	.176	.178	.135	.165	.173	.145
1957	.178	.181	.138	.161	.173	.138
1958	.176	.179	.133	.156	.165	.138
1959	.175	.178	.134	.153	.166	.137
1960	.174	.178	.140	.152	.165	.120
1961	.189	.175	.134	.155	.161	.126
1962	.191	.177	.130	.157	.168	.132
1963	.193	.177	.129	.158	.163	.139
1964	.192	.178	.129	.160	.162	.139
1965	.199	.178	.137	.162	.166	.139
1966	.197	.178	.138	.163	.169	.137
1967	.198	.179	.135	.166	.168	.138
1968	.198	.178	.139	.156	.166	.137
1969	.199	.178	.139	.170	.169	.144
1970	.198	.177	.138	.169	.168	.138
1971	.198	.176	.140	.167	.165	.134
1972	.198	.175	.139	.168	.163	.137
1973	.197	.176	.141	.169	.163	.139
1974	.197	.176	.147	.168	.164	.140
1975	.197	.176	.148	.167	.167	.135
1976	.197	.177	.149	.165	.165	.140
1977	.197	.176	.148	.163	.159	.144
1978	.197	.176	.151	.167	.163	.135
1979	.202	.175	.155	.162	.159	.144
1980	.196	.176	.154	.161	.160	.143
1981	.197	.175	.154	.159	.160	.140
1982	.195	.172	.153	.160	.158	.145
1983	.195	.172	.154	.160	.156	.138
1984	.196	.171	.153	.168	.154	.141
1985	.197	.169	.154	.168	.157	.144

[1]All total white and nonwhite data were computed as a weighted average of family and unrelated-individual components from the procedure outlined in Appendix 1. Family and unrelated-individual data were drawn from Miller (1966) for 1947 to 1960 and from the U.S. Bureau of the Census (1988) for 1960 to 1985.

[2]Nonwhites are not confined to blacks.

Table A3–11
Second-Quintile Share by Race, 1947–1985

	White			Nonwhite[2]		
	Total White	Families	Unrelated Individuals	Total Nonwhite	Families	Unrelated Individuals
1947[1]	.107	.122	.061	.092	.104	.080
1948	.110	.125	.076	.092	.104	.082
1949	.108	.123	.074	.091	.100	.087
1950	.108	.124	.071	.088	.103	.072
1951	.112	.128	.071	.092	.104	.077
1952	.114	.128	.076	.102	.107	.088
1953	.112	.129	.066	.094	.107	.091
1954	.107	.125	.072	.083	.100	.072
1955	.110	.127	.072	.089	.104	.082
1956	.112	.129	.072	.092	.105	.080
1957	.113	.131	.073	.085	.102	.085
1958	.111	.129	.070	.086	.100	.080
1959	.109	.127	.072	.084	.097	.082
1960	.109	.127	.075	.081	.097	.077
1961	.115	.123	.072	.085	.099	.076
1962	.117	.126	.075	.088	.106	.087
1963	.119	.125	.075	.091	.104	.084
1964	.119	.124	.071	.093	.105	.081
1965	.128	.126	.075	.096	.108	.084
1966	.125	.128	.078	.096	.109	.082
1967	.126	.128	.075	.095	.106	.082
1968	.128	.127	.078	.090	.107	.083
1969	.128	.127	.078	.097	.109	.079
1970	.126	.125	.079	.095	.106	.081
1971	.125	.124	.082	.095	.104	.082
1972	.127	.122	.083	.096	.100	.080
1973	.129	.123	.087	.098	.101	.080
1974	.126	.123	.090	.096	.100	.085
1975	.122	.121	.092	.094	.101	.086
1976	.123	.121	.090	.094	.099	.086
1977	.122	.120	.091	.095	.096	.085
1978	.123	.120	.092	.092	.096	.083
1979	.124	.119	.094	.091	.095	.082
1980	.120	.119	.094	.091	.095	.086
1981	.120	.117	.091	.090	.094	.085
1982	.118	.116	.091	.090	.090	.082
1983	.119	.115	.091	.087	.088	.079
1984	.119	.114	.091	.093	.088	.082
1985	.120	.112	.091	.092	.091	.082

[1]All total white and nonwhite data were computed as a weighted average of family and unrelated-individual components from the procedure outlined in Appendix 1. Family and unrelated-individual data were drawn from Miller (1966) for 1947 to 1960 and from the U.S. Bureau of the Census (1988) for 1960 to 1985.

[2]Nonwhites are not confined to blacks.

Table A3–12
Lowest-Quintile Share by Race, 1947–1985

	White			Nonwhite[2]		
	Total White	Families	Unrelated Individuals	Total Nonwhite	Families	Unrelated Individuals
1947[1]	.037	.055	.019	.031	.043	.027
1948	.037	.054	.025	.030	.039	.027
1949	.035	.049	.024	.030	.034	.029
1950	.034	.048	.023	.029	.035	.024
1951	.036	.055	.023	.030	.036	.025
1952	.038	.053	.026	.035	.049	.028
1953	.034	.050	.022	.030	.039	.031
1954	.033	.049	.025	.027	.035	.024
1955	.035	.052	.025	.029	.040	.027
1956	.036	.055	.027	.029	.038	.027
1957	.037	.055	.026	.027	.036	.031
1958	.037	.056	.024	.027	.038	.027
1959	.036	.054	.014	.027	.040	.019
1960	.036	.052	.017	.026	.037	.021
1961	.039	.050	.023	.028	.040	.019
1962	.040	.054	.027	.030	.042	.029
1963	.038	.054	.026	.025	.045	.023
1964	.040	.055	.025	.026	.044	.031
1965	.043	.056	.029	.029	.047	.029
1966	.045	.059	.034	.030	.049	.030
1967	.045	.058	.031	.035	.048	.030
1968	.047	.060	.033	.031	.048	.036
1969	.047	.059	.033	.035	.048	.035
1970	.047	.058	.035	.035	.045	.036
1971	.047	.058	.035	.037	.047	.033
1972	.049	.058	.034	.037	.046	.028
1973	.051	.058	.039	.037	.047	.028
1974	.051	.058	.044	.039	.047	.037
1975	.050	.057	.042	.038	.047	.036
1976	.050	.058	.041	.038	.046	.035
1977	.051	.056	.043	.039	.044	.036
1978	.051	.056	.043	.037	.042	.036
1979	.051	.057	.043	.035	.041	.030
1980	.049	.056	.043	.036	.041	.035
1981	.049	.054	.040	.035	.040	.032
1982	.048	.052	.040	.034	.038	.026
1983	.048	.051	.038	.032	.036	.026
1984	.048	.051	.039	.036	.035	.031
1985	.048	.050	.039	.034	.036	.030

[1]All total white and nonwhite data were computed as a weighted average of family and unrelated-individual components from the procedure outlined in Appendix 1. Family and unrelated-individual data were drawn from Miller (1966) for 1947 to 1960 and from the U.S. Bureau of the Census (1988) for 1960 to 1985.

[2]Nonwhites are not confined to blacks.

Appendix 4

Regression Results

Table A4–1
Regression Results for Gini Coefficients

	Aggregate	Total Family	Husband-Wife Family Total	Wife In Labor Force	Wife Out of Labor Force	Male-Headed Family	Female-Headed Family	Total Unrelated Individual	Male Unrelated Individual	Female Unrelated Individual
Female Labor Force Participation[1]	-.002 (.39)	-.006* (3.83)	-.004 (1.71)	-.008* (3.41)	-.003 (.75)	-.012*** (10.92)	.000 (.00)	-.010*** (9.01)	-.011**** (12.83)	-.004 (1.66)
Dependency Ratio	.003**** (20.27)	.002*** (9.22)	.002*** (9.95)	.004**** (17.54)	.001* (3.82)	.001 (1.65)	.002 (1.88)	.003**** (13.19)	.002** (6.72)	.003**** (28.54)
Occupation	.146 (2.05)	.216* (3.78)	.304** (5.55)	.242 (2.37)	.251** (4.84)	-.098 (.52)	.014 (.00)	.127 (.94)	-.085 (.50)	.161 (2.24)
Industry	.342**** (14.03)	.203** (5.30)	.171* (2.79)	.231* (3.88)	.120 (1.97)	.244** (5.14)	.173 (1.14)	.299**** (8.36)	.203** (4.54)	.291**** (11.67)
Government	-.011** (4.49)	.010* (3.74)	.014** (4.97)	.010 (1.44)	.014** (5.49)	-.002 (.13)	-.019* (3.72)	-.002 (.09)	-.001 (.01)	-.016*** (9.71)
Income-Receiving Unit	-.018 (.01)	—	—	—	—	—	—	—	—	—
Total Fertility Rate	—	—	-.034**** (8.62)		.009 (1.16)	—	—	—	—	—
Constant	.050	.134	-.032	.104	.039	.768	.295	.445	.756	.167
R²	.550	.352	.374	.604	.324	.580	.340	.797	.749	.870
R̂²	.466	.253	.279	.524	.189	.517	.240	.766	.711	.851
F	6.52****	3.58***	3.94***	7.62****	2.39*	9.13****	3.41**	25.91****	19.67****	44.27****
Durbin-Watson	1.54	1.99	1.91	1.63	1.73	1.68	2.28	1.77	1.66	2.23

[1]Numbers are unstandardized regression coefficients with F-statistics in parenthesis. All independent variables are in ratios times 100. Occupation is blue-collar employment (craft, operatives, farm and nonfarm laborers) to white-collar employment (professionals, managers, clerical, sales, and farm managers). Industry is service employment to manufacturing employment. The dependency ratio is the number of individuals over 64 and under 18 to the number of individuals aged 18–64. Government is social insurance payments (social security, railroad retirement, public employment retirement, unemployment insurance, disability insurance, workers' compensation) to GNP. Income-receiving unit is female-headed units to husband-wife units. Total fertility rate is the lifetime number of children a woman would have using prevailing age-specific fertility rates. Yearly values on the dependent variable are located in Tables A3–1 to A3–6. Sources for the independent variables are located in Appendix 3.

**** p < .001
*** p < .01
** p < .05
* p < .10

Table A4-2
Regression Results for Share of Income Received by the Top Quintile

	Aggregate	Total Family	Husband-Wife Family Total	Wife In Labor Force	Wife Out of Labor Force	Male-Headed Family	Female-Headed Family	Total Unrelated Individual	Male Unrelated Individual	Female Unrelated Individual
Labor Force Participation[1]	.001 (.05)	-.005 (1.12)	-.004 (.50)	-.005 (.37)	-.015 (.08)	-.010* (3.28)	.000 (.03)	-.008* (3.31)	-.013*** (8.05)	.001 (.17)
Dependency Ratio	.002** (5.74)	.002** (4.53)	.003** (4.56)	.005*** (8.26)	.002** (4.70)	.002 (2.09)	.003 (2.55)	.004**** (19.03)	.003*** (9.71)	.004**** (29.89)
Occupation	.052 (.11)	.335* (2.99)	.402* (2.82)	.305 (1.05)	.361* (3.53)	.066 (.11)	.124 (.16)	.330* (3.75)	.040 (.05)	.316** (6.47)
Industry	.370** (6.88)	.058 (.14)	.084 (.20)	.081 (.13)	.037 (.07)	.101 (.41)	.188 (.57)	.355** (6.92)	.267* (3.53)	.205** (4.35)
Government	-.017** (4.75)	.031*** (11.15)	.030*** (6.47)	.016 (1.06)	.024** (5.45)	.017* (3.37)	-.012 (.65)	.005 (.40)	.012 (1.91)	-.007 (1.27)
Income-Receiving Unit	-.358 (.87)	—	—	—	—	—	—	—	—	—
Total Fertility Rate	—	—	—	-.059** (7.19)	-.008 (.35)	—	—	—	—	—
Constant	.206	.041	-.108	.062	-.054	.536	.075	.057	.583	-.158
R^2	.398	.414	.318	.533	.458	.283	.128	.589	.522	.704
$\hat{R}^2$	.285	.325	.214	.440	.349	.174	0	.526	.450	.659
F	3.53***	4.67****	3.07**	5.71****	4.22***	2.60**	.96	9.45****	7.21****	15.72****
Durbin-Watson	1.79	1.86	1.65	1.55	2.05	1.72	2.18	1.99	1.86	2.35

[1]Numbers are unstandardized regression coefficients with F-statistics in parenthesis. All independent variables are in ratios times 100. Occupation is blue-collar employment (craft, operatives, farm and nonfarm laborers) to white-collar employment (professionals, managers, clerical, sales, and farm managers). Industry is service employment to manufacturing employment. The dependency ratio is the number of individuals over 64 and under 18 to the number of individuals aged 18-64. Government is social insurance payments (social security, railroad retirement, public employment retirement, unemployment insurance, disability insurance, workers' compensation) to GNP. Income-receiving unit is female-headed units to husband-wife units. Total fertility rate is the lifetime number of children a woman would have using prevailing age-specific fertility rates. Yearly values on the dependent variable are located in Tables A3-1 to A3-6. Sources for the independent variables are located in Appendix 3.

**** $p \leq .001$
*** $p \leq .01$
** $p \leq .05$
* $p \leq .10$

Table A4–3
Regression Results for Share of Income Received by the Fourth Quintile

	Total Aggregate Family	Total Family	Husband-Wife Family: Total	Husband-Wife Family: Wife In Labor Force	Husband-Wife Family: Wife Out of Labor Force	Male-Headed Family	Female-Headed Family	Total Unrelated Individual	Male Unrelated Individual	Female Unrelated Individual
Female Labor Force Participation[1]	-.007 (1.81)	.001 (.04)	.003 (.17)	-.004 (.18)	-.003 (.22)	-.001 (.02)	-.001 (.02)	.000 (.02)	.007* (2.94)	-.007** (6.73)
Dependency	.000 (.04)	-.000 (.00)	-.001 (.22)	-.002 (1.06)	-.001 (.23)	.000 (.01)	-.000 (.10)	-.002** (5.78)	-.001 (.59)	-.001 (1.30)
Occupation	.058 (.12)	-.154 (.85)	-.117 (.21)	-.192 (.29)	-.161 (.56)	-.077 (.16)	-.025 (.01)	-.222 (2.66)	-.004 (.00)	-.158 (2.15)
Industry	-.072 (.24)	.188 (2.02)	.067 (.11)	.142 (.28)	.183 (1.30)	.241 (2.53)	.016 (.01)	-.131 (1.48)	-.063 (.27)	.107 (1.57)
Government	.013 (2.45)	-.027* (11.52)	-.020 (2.61)	-.009 (.21)	-.015 (1.80)	-.025** (7.27)	-.002 (.03)	-.005 (.49)	-.014* (3.38)	-.002 (.21)
Income-Receiving Unit	.540 (1.79)	—	—	—	—	—	—	—	—	—
Total Fertility Rate	—	—	—	.033 (1.51)	.015 (.83)	—	—	—	—	—
Constant	.286	.347	.309	.562	.434	.293	.321	.631	.109	.672
R^2	.114	.295	.103	.211	.247	.253	.015	.202	.195	.343
$\hat{R}^2$	0	.188	0	.054	.096	.140	0	.081	.073	.244
F	.69	2.76**	.76	1.34	1.64	2.23*	.10	1.67	1.60	3.45**
Durbin-Watson	2.58	1.96	1.80	1.67	2.50	2.30	2.49	2.08	1.94	2.39

[1] Numbers are unstandardized regression coefficients with F-statistics in parentheses. All independent variables are in ratios times 100. Occupation is blue-collar employment (craft, operatives, farm and nonfarm laborers) to white-collar employment (professionals, managers, clerical, sales, and farm managers). Industry is service employment to manufacturing employment. The dependency ratio is the number of individuals over 64 and under 18 to the number of individuals aged 18-64. Government is social insurance payments (social security, railroad retirement, public employment retirement, unemployment insurance, disability insurance, workers' compensation) to GNP. Income-receiving unit is female-headed units to husband-wife units. Total fertility rate is the lifetime number of children a woman would have using prevailing age-specific fertility rates. Yearly values on the dependent variable are located in Tables A3-1 to A3-6. Sources for the independent variables are located in Appendix 3.

**** $p \leq .001$
*** $p \leq .01$
** $p \leq .05$
* $p \leq .10$

Table A4-4
Regression Results for Share of Income Received by the Middle Quintile

	Total		Husband-Wife Family		Male-Headed Family	Female-Headed Family	Total Unrelated Individual	Male Unrelated Individual	Female Unrelated Individual
	Aggregate Family	Total	Wife In Labor Force	Wife Out of Labor Force					
Female Labor Force Participation[1]	.002 (.27)	.002 (.39)	.005 (1.52)	.002 (.42)	.005 (2.57)	-.004 (2.34)	.003** (4.30)	.003 (1.79)	.006** (4.26)
Dependency	-.001 (1.73)	-.001 (1.21)	-.001 (1.99)	-.001 (1.28)	-.000 (.45)	-.001 (1.23)	-.000 (.59)	-.001*** (7.55)	-.000 (.09)
Occupation	-.071 (.50)	-.040 (.10)	.037 (.06)	-.079 (.44)	.009 (.01)	-.035 (.13)	.001 (.00)	-.054 (.50)	.044 (.19)
Industry	-.115 (1.65)	-.033 (.11)	-.028 (.06)	-.078 (.77)	-.121 (1.99)	.045 (.34)	-.020 (.19)	-.097 (2.56)	-.101 (1.57)
Government	-.000 (.00)	-.006 (.95)	-.004 (.31)	-.005 (.61)	.000 (.00)	.003 (.49)	-.004 (2.11)	-.002 (.27)	.000 (.01)
Income-Receiving Unit	-.026 (.01)	—	—	—	—	—	—	—	—
Total Fertility Rate	—	—	.028** (6.15)	-.000 (.00)	—	—	—	—	—
Constant	.280	.217	-.020	.264	.070	.345	.055	.231	-.059
R^2	.215	.127	.384	.144	.117	.162	.468	.316	.373
$\hat{R}^2$	.068	0	.261	0	0	.035	.387	.213	.278
F	1.46	.96	3.12**	.84	.87	1.27	5.80****	3.05**	3.93***
Durbin-Watson	2.34	1.92	2.12	2.16	2.46	1.95	2.65	1.67	1.41

[1]Numbers are unstandardized regression coefficients with F-statistics in parenthesis. All independent variables are in ratios times 100. Occupation is blue-collar employment (craft, operatives, farm and nonfarm laborers) to white-collar employment (professionals, managers, clerical, sales, and farm managers). Industry is service employment to manufacturing employment. The dependency ratio is the number of individuals over 64 and under 18 to the number of individuals aged 18-64. Government is social insurance payments (social security, railroad retirement, public employment retirement, unemployment insurance, disability insurance, workers' compensation) to GNP. Income-receiving unit is female-headed units to husband-wife units. Total fertility rate is the lifetime number of children a woman would have using prevailing age-specific fertility rates. Yearly values on the dependent variable are located in Tables A3-1 to A3-6. Sources for the independent variables are located in Appendix 3.

**** p < .001
*** p < .01
** p < .05
* p < .10

170

Table A4-5
Regression Results for Share of Income Received by the Second Quintile

	Aggregate	Total Family	Husband-Wife Family			Male-Headed Family	Female-Headed Family	Total Unrelated Individual	Male Unrelated Individual	Female Unrelated Individual
			Total	Wife in Labor Force	Wife Out of Labor Force					
Female Labor Force Participation[1]	.002 (2.23)	.001 (.40)	.002 (1.28)	.002 (.71)	.002 (1.21)	.004* (3.91)	.001 (.42)	.002 (.50)	.001 (1.12)	.000 (.08)
Dependency	-.001***** (19.61)	-.001***** (12.88)	-.001*** (7.96)	-.001 (1.74)	-.001* (4.06)	-.001** (4.72)	-.001** (4.48)	.000 (.01)	-.000 (2.58)	-.001** (4.69)
Occupation	-.054 (1.53)	-.106* (3.89)	-.086 (1.25)	-.071 (.52)	-.094 (2.38)	-.001 (.00)	-.064 (.71)	.008 (.01)	.046 (1.14)	-.097 (2.67)
Industry	-.110*** (7.92)	-.137*** (10.30)	-.126** (4.28)	-.074 (1.01)	-.113** (6.13)	-.141** (5.59)	-.136** (5.04)	-.052 (.44)	-.014 (.16)	-.085* (3.27)
Government	.002 (.65)	.002 (.37)	-.001 (.13)	-.004 (.69)	-.003 (1.09)	.003 (.61)	.006 (2.40)	.004 (.67)	.003 (1.84)	.004 (1.61)
Income-Receiving Unit	-.119 (1.26)	–	–	–	–	–	–	–	–	–
Total Fertility Rate	–	–	–	.002 (.05)	-.004 (.69)	–	–	–	–	–
Constant	.225	.314	.261	.207	.254	.077	.203	-.002	.016	.220
R^2	.587	.402	.281	.168	.480	.327	.285	.386	.671	.609
$\hat{R}^2$	.510	.311	.173	.001	.377	.225	.177	.293	.621	.550
F	7.59****	4.43***	2.59**	.101	4.62***	3.21**	2.64**	4.15****	13.48****	10.28****
Durbin-Watson	2.23	2.23	2.21	2.65	1.73	2.49	2.45	1.91	2.26	1.31

[1]Numbers are unstandardized regression coefficients with F-statistics in parenthesis. All independent variables are in ratios times 100. Occupation is blue-collar employment (craft, operatives, farm and nonfarm laborers) to white-collar employment (professionals, managers, clerical, sales, and farm managers). Industry is service employment to manufacturing employment. The dependency ratio is the number of individuals over 64 and under 18 to the number of individuals aged 18-64. Government is social insurance payments (social security, railroad retirement, public employment retirement, unemployment insurance, disability insurance, workers' compensation) to GNP. Income-receiving unit is female-headed units to husband-wife units. Total fertility rate is the lifetime number of children a woman would have using prevailing age-specific fertility rates. Yearly values on the dependent variable are located in Tables A3-1 to A3-6. Sources for the independent variables are located in Appendix 3.

**** P < .001
*** P < .01
** P < .05
* P < .10

171

Table A4–6
Regression Results for Share of Income Received by the Lowest Quintile

	Aggregate	Total Family Total	Husband-Wife Family Total	Wife In Labor Force	Wife Out of Labor Force	Male-Headed Family	Female-Headed Family	Total Unrelated Individual	Male Unrelated Individual	Female Unrelated Individual
Female Labor Force Participation[1]	.002** (5.60)	.000 (.00)	.001 (1.23)	.002 (2.02)	.000 (.14)	.002** (5.48)	.000 (.09)	.001 (.60)	.002** (4.84)	.000 (.07)
Dependency	-.0005**** (15.30)	-.001 (.45)	-.0005**** (7.41)	-.001*** (8.52)	-.0003* (3.28)	-.0004** (4.79)	-.0005** (5.23)	-.002**** (55.85)	-.001**** (16.59)	-.002**** (71.78)
Occupation	-.001 (.00)	-.109 (.67)	-.043 (2.18)	-.013 (2.14)	-.027 (.72)	.002 (.01)	-.018 (.23)	-.118** (6.54)	-.030 (.57)	-.097** (4.40)
Industry	-.058*** (9.78)	-.100 (.90)	-.061** (7.08)	-.122*** (10.73)	-.028 (1.46)	-.080**** (12.05)	-.059* (4.00)	-.145**** (15.79)	-.092**** (8.60)	-.137**** (14.04)
Government	.003** (6.28)	.002 (.13)	.001 (.66)	.001 (.26)	-.000 (.00)	.004*** (7.38)	.004** (5.07)	.004* (3.14)	.001 (.31)	.006** (6.85)
Income-Receiving Unit	-.060 (1.40)	—	—	—	—	—	—	—	—	—
Total Fertility Rate	—	—	—	-.002 (.34)	-.001 (.23)	—	—	—	—	—
Constant	.042	.217	.175	.100	.100	.018	.083	.288	.071	.308
R²	.567	.116	.345	.406	.191	.655	.414	.761	.579	.822
R̂²	.486	0	.256	.288	.029	.603	.325	.725	.515	.795
F	6.99****	3.48**	3.48**	3.42**	1.18	12.53****	4.66***	21.06****	9.06****	30.44****
Durbin-Watson	1.56	1.92	2.04	2.16	1.81	2.17	1.51	1.52	1.88	1.51

[1]Numbers are unstandardized regression coefficients with F-statistics in parenthesis. All independent variables are in ratios times 100. Occupation is blue-collar employment (craft, operatives, farm and nonfarm laborers) to white-collar employment (professionals, managers, clerical, sales, and farm managers). Industry is service employment to manufacturing employment. The dependency ratio is the number of individuals over 64 and under 18 to the number of individuals aged 18–64. Government is social insurance payments (social security, railroad retirement, public employment retirement, unemployment insurance, disability insurance, workers' compensation) to GNP. Income-receiving unit is female-headed units to husband-wife units. Total fertility rate is the lifetime number of children a woman would have using prevailing age-specific fertility rates. Yearly values on the dependent variable are located in Tables A3–1 to A3–6. Sources for the independent variables are located in Appendix 3.

**** $p \leq .001$
*** $p \leq .01$
** $p \leq .05$
* $p \leq .10$

Table A4–7
Regression Results for Gini Coefficient by Race

	Total		Families		Unrelated Individuals	
	Nonwhite[2]	White	Nonwhite	White	Nonwhite	White
Labor Force Participation[1]	-.013****	-.008****	-.007***	-.003***	-.003	-.009***
	(30.00)	(19.09)	(10.40)	(11.74)	(.91)	(9.61)
Dependency Ratio	.000	-.001****	-.001*	-.000	.002***	.001**
	(.09)	(12.97)	(3.37)	(.52)	(8.60)	(5.26)
Occupation	-.209***	-.185***	-.171**	.056	.206	-.019
	(8.47)	(9.94)	(4.97)	(2.23)	(2.73)	(.03)
Industry	-.035	-.002	.156**	.171****	.207**	.198**
	(.30)	(.00)	(6.55)	(32.77)	(4.41)	(5.81)
Government	.002	-.006*	-.004	-.002	.002	-.005
	(.28)	(3.84)	(1.22)	(1.70)	(.160)	(1.20)
Income-receiving Unit	.738****	.383**	–	–	–	–
	(17.86)	(7.21)	–	–	–	–
Constant	.875	.844	.801	.376	.155	.658
R^2	.649	.870	.611	.767	.249	.815
$\hat{R}^2$	.583	.845	.552	.732	.135	.786
F	9.85****	35.55****	10.36****	21.71****	2.19*	28.98****
Durbin-Watson	1.64	1.17	1.38	1.26	1.64	1.52

[1]All total white and nonwhite data were computed as a weighted average of family and unrelated-individual components from the procedure outlined in Appendix 1. Family and unrelated-individual data were drawn from Miller (1966) for 1947 to 1960 and from the U.S. Bureau of the Census (1988) for 1960 to 1985.

[2]Nonwhites are not confined to blacks.

****$p \leq .0001$
***$p \leq .01$
**$p \leq .05$
*$p \leq .10$

Table A4–8
Regression Results for the Top Quintile by Race

	Total		Families		Unrelated Individuals	
	Nonwhite[2]	White	Nonwhite	White	Nonwhite	White
Labor Force Participation[1]	-.013**** (26.39)	-.001 (.11)	-.005**** (11.00)	-.002** (6.97)	-.004 (1.86)	-.006** (6.13)
Dependency Ratio	-.000 (.17)	-.001** (5.29)	-.000 (.56)	-.000 (.58)	.022**** (10.75)	.011** (4.91)
Occupation	-.198** (6.51)	-.077 (1.10)	-.071 (1.36)	.075** (6.22)	.215* (3.31)	.014 (.02)
Industry	-.072 (1.09)	-.071 (1.17)	.149**** (9.68)	.131**** (30.03)	.207** (4.88)	.126 (2.68)
Government	.005 (1.64)	-.004 (1.09)	-.001 (.11)	-.002 (1.18)	.007 (1.49)	.001 (.02)
Income-receiving Unit	.736**** (15.2)	.143 (.64)	-- --	-- --	-- --	-- --
Constant	.946	.603	.657	.380	.188	.589
R^2	.668	.575	.619	.779	.338	.685
$\hat{R}^2$	.605	.495	.562	.745	.238	.637
F	10.71****	7.20****	10.74****	23.22****	3.37**	14.35****
Durbin-Watson	1.76	7.60	1.30	1.32	1.89	1.39

[1]All total white and nonwhite data were computed as a weighted average of family and unrelated-individual components from the procedure outlined in Appendix 1. Family and unrelated-individual data were drawn from Miller (1966) for 1947 to 1960 and from the U.S. Bureau of the Census (1988) for 1960 to 1985.

[2]Nonwhites are not confined to blacks.

****p $\leq$ .0001
***p $\leq$ .01
**p $\leq$ .05
*p $\leq$ .10

Table A4-9
Regression Results for the Fourth Quintile by Race

	Total		Families		Unrelated Individuals	
	Nonwhite[2]	White	Nonwhite	White	Nonwhite	White
Labor Force Participation[1]	.002* (3.24)	-.008***** (20.86)	.001 (.79)	-.000 (1.07)	.002 (1.95)	.000 (.03)
Dependency Ratio	.0004** (4.13)	-.000 (.17)	-.0005** (7.23)	.000 (2.29)	-.001** (5.92)	-.000 (.02)
Occupation	.022 (.48)	-.127** (5.48)	-.082*** (7.88)	-.009 (.69)	-.116* (4.07)	-.044 (.64)
Industry	.050* (3.14)	.020 (.08)	-.055** (5.74)	.009 (1.18)	-.080* (3.10)	.024 (.29)
Government	-.002 (2.56)	-.002 (1.62)	-.001 (.70)	.000 (.84)	-.006** (5.47)	-.007** (6.86)
Income-Receiving Unit	-.105 (1.85)	.413***** (10.46)	—	—	—	—
Constant	.153	.534	.357	.241	.392	.295
R^2	.723	.753	.334	.791	.380	.418
$\hat{R}^2$	.671	.706	.233	.759	.286	.329
F	13.91****	16.24****	3.30**	24.94****	4.05***	4.73***
Durbin-Watson	1.97	.68	1.31	1.02	2.34	1.20

[1]All total white and nonwhite data were computed as a weighted average of family and unrelated-individual components from the procedure outlined in Appendix 1. Family and unrelated-individual data were drawn from Miller (1966) for 1947 to 1960 and from the U.S. Bureau of the Census (1988) for 1960 to 1985.

[2]Nonwhites are not confined to blacks.

****p $<$ .0001
***p $|\vee|$ .01
**p $|\vee|$ .05
*p $|\vee|$ .10

Table A4-10
Regression Results for the Middle Quintile by Race

	Total		Families		Unrelated Individuals	
	Nonwhite[2]	White	Nonwhite	White	Nonwhite	White
Labor Force Participation[1]	.005**** (25.77)	.003*** (9.55)	.002** (5.19)	.001** (5.76)	.001 (.89)	.002*** (9.01)
Dependency Ratio	-.000 (.48)	.001**** (19.33)	-.000 (.50)	.000 (.46)	-.001*** (7.74)	-.001**** (16.11)
Occupation	.052* (3.21)	.101*** (8.98)	.008 (.09)	-.018 (2.59)	-.008 (.03)	-.005 (.03)
Industry	.011 (.17)	.022 (.54)	-.045** (4.64)	-.038**** (18.35)	-.014 (.15)	-.036 (2.68)
Government	-.003** (5.02)	.003 (2.69)	-.001 (1.30)	.000 (.12)	-.003 (2.25)	-.001 (.50)
Income-receiving Unit	-.251**** (12.74)	-.143* (3.07)	-- --	-- --	-- --	-- --
Constant	.022	-.073	.134	.179	.178	.126
R^2	.491	.859	.681	.712	.500	.815
$\hat{R}^2$	.395	.832	.633	.668	.424	.787
F	5.14****	32.36****	14.12****	16.32****	6.60*****	29.12****
Durbin-Watson	1.44	1.03	1.35	.95	2.02	1.37

[1]All total white and nonwhite data were computed as a weighted average of family and unrelated-individual components from the procedure outlined in Appendix 1. Family and unrelated-individual data were drawn from Miller (1966) for 1947 to 1960 and from the U.S. Bureau of the Census (1988) for 1960 to 1985.

[2]Nonwhites are not confined to blacks.

**** $p \leq .001$
*** $p \mid \vee \mid \vee .01$
** $p \mid \vee \mid \vee .05$
* $p \mid \vee .10$

Table A4–11
Regression Results for the Second Quintile by Race

	Total		Families		Unrelated Individuals	
	Nonwhite[2]	White	Nonwhite	White	Nonwhite	White
Labor Force Participation[1]	.004**** (16.84)	.005**** (26.68)	.002** (6.76)	.001*** (10.95)	-.000 (.42)	.001** (6.16)
Dependency Ratio	.000 (.59)	.0005*** (10.58)	.0004*** (7.53)	.000 (.74)	-.0003* (3.54)	-.000** (6.86)
Occupation	.082*** (8.80)	.079*** (8.71)	.072*** (7.40)	-.018* (3.05)	-.059** (4.33)	-.001 (.01)
Industry	.026 (1.12)	.002 (.01)	-.021 (1.00)	-.044**** (28.10)	-.032 (1.99)	-.050*** (7.81)
Government	-.001 (.46)	.000 (.07)	-.000 (.01)	-.001 (2.53)	.001 (.29)	.003*** (9.63)
Income-receiving Unit	-.225*** (11.07)	-.213*** (10.73)	— —	— —	— —	— —
Constant	-.075	-.102	-.049	.126	.186	.055
R^2	.408	.779	.702	.913	.161	.899
$\hat{R}^2$	.297	.737	.657	.899	.033	.884
F	3.68***	18.74****	15.58****	69.02****	1.26	58.91****
Durbin-Watson	1.40	1.03	1.27	1.33	1.86	1.92

[1]All total white and nonwhite data were computed as a weighted average of family and unrelated-individual components from the procedure outlined in Appendix 1. Family and unrelated-individual data were drawn from Miller (1966) for 1947 to 1960 and from the U.S. Bureau of the Census (1988) for 1960 to 1985.

[2]Nonwhites are not confined to blacks.

**** p ≤ .001
*** p ≤ .01
** p ≤ .05
* p ≤ .10

Table A4-12
Regression Results for the Lowest Quintile by Race

	Total		Families		Unrelated Individuals	
	Nonwhite[2]	White	Nonwhite	White	Nonwhite	White
Labor Force Participation[1]	.003**** (29.93)	.003**** (28.18)	.001** (3.89)	.001** (6.71)	.001* (3.25)	.003**** (14.07)
Dependency Ratio	-.0002** (7.10)	.000 (.04)	.0005**** (9.88)	.000 (.21)	-.000 (1.57)	-.000 (1.97)
Occupation	.041**** (7.51)	.044**** (8.12)	.078**** (9.74)	.007 (.16)	-.003 (.01)	.037 (2.19)
Industry	-.018 (1.84)	-.018 (1.73)	-.026 (1.75)	-.050**** (12.80)	-.062** (6.73)	-.067*** (11.19)
Government	.002** (7.28)	.003**** (12.54)	.004**** (9.54)	.002*** (5.22)	.002 (2.32)	.004*** (11.09)
Income-receiving Unit	-.160**** (19.07)	-.131**** (12.30)	-- --	-- --	-- --	-- --
Constant	-.043	-.065	-.110	.015	.012	-.070
R²	.803	.910	.551	.517	.359	.854
R̂²	.767	.893	.483	.444	.262	.832
F	21.80****	53.69****	8.09****	7.08****	3.69***	38.60****
Durbin-Watson	1.90	.98	1.24	.97	1.35	1.01

[1] All total white and nonwhite data were computed as a weighted average of family and unrelated-individual components from the procedure outlined in Appendix 1. Family and unrelated-individual data were drawn from Miller (1966) for 1947 to 1960 and from the U.S. Bureau of the Census (1988) for 1960 to 1985.

[2] Nonwhites are not confined to blacks.

**** $p \leq .001$
*** $p \leq .01$
** $p \leq .05$
* $p \leq .10$

Bibliography

Aaron, Henry. 1982. *Economic Effects of Social Security*. Washington, DC: Brookings Institution.

Adamchak, Donald J., and Edward G. Stockwell. 1978. Trends in the Relationship between Infant Mortality and Socioeconomic Status. *Sociological Focus* 11: 47–52.

AFL-CIO. 1984. *Deindustrialization and the Two Tier Society*. Washington, DC: Industrial Union Department.

Aigner, Dennis, and Glen Cain. 1977. Statistical Theories of Discrimination in Labor Markets. *Industrial and Labor Relations Review* 30 (January): 175–186.

Aigner, Dennis, and A. J. Heins. 1967. A Social Welfare View of the Measurement of Income Equality. *Review of Income and Wealth* (March): 12–25.

Akerlof, George, and Janet Yellen. 1986. *Efficiency Wage Models of the Labor Market*. New York: Cambridge University Press.

Albelda, Randy P. 1986. Occupational Segregation by Race and Gender, 1958–1981. *Industrial and Labor Relations Review* 39 (April): 404–411.

Alderfer, Evan, and H. E. Michl. 1942. *Economics of American Industry*. New York: McGraw-Hill.

Allison, Paul D. 1978. Measures of Inequality. *American Sociological Review* 43 (December): 865–880.

Anderson, W. H. Locke. 1964. Trickling Down: The Relationship between Economic Growth and the Extent of Poverty among American Families. *Quarterly Journal of Economics* 78 (November): 511–524.

Ando, Albert, and Franco Modigliani. 1963. The "Life-Cycle" Hypothesis of Saving: Aggregate Implications and Tests. *American Economic Review* 53 (March): 55–84.

Arrow, Kenneth. 1972. Models of Job Discrimination. In Anthony H. Pascal (ed.). *Discrimination in Economic Life*. Lexington, MA: D. C. Heath.

Ashenfelter, Orley. 1978. Union Relative Wage Effects: New Evidence and a Survey of Their Implications for Wage Inflation. In Richard Stone and William Peterson (eds.), *Econometric Contributions to Public Policy*. New York: Macmillan.

———. 1970. Changes in Labor Market Discrimination Over Time. *Journal of Human Resources* 5 (Fall): 403–430.

Atkinson, Anthony. 1976. *The Personal Distribution of Income*. Boulder, CO: Westview Press.

———. 1970. On the Measure of Inequality. *Journal of Economic Theory* 2 (September): 244–263.

Averitt, Robert. 1968. *The Dual Economy: The Dynamics of American Industrial Structure*. New York: W. W. Norton.

Baily, Martin Neil. 1977. Unemployment Insurance as Insurance for Workers. *Industrial and Labor Relations Review* 30 (July): 495–504.

Baily, Martin Neil, and Alok K. Chakrabarti. 1985. Innovation and Productivity in U.S. Industry. *Brookings Papers on Economic Activity* (2): 609–632.

Bane, Mary Jo. 1986. Household Composition and Poverty. In Sheldon H. Danziger and Daniel H. Weinberg (eds.), *Fighting Poverty: What Works and What Doesn't*. Cambridge, MA: Harvard University Press.

Bane, Mary Jo, and David Ellwood. 1986. Slipping Into and Out of Poverty: The Dynamics of Spells. *Journal of Human Resources* 21 (Winter): 1–23.

Baron, Paul A., and Paul M. Sweezy. 1966. *Monopoly Capital*. New York: Modern Reader Paperbacks.

Barrett, Nancy S. 1979. Women in the Job Market: Unemployment and Work Schedules. In Ralph E. Smith (ed.), *The Subtle Revolution*. Washington, DC: Urban Institute.

Barro, Robert J. 1978. *The Impact of Social Security on Private Savings: Evidence from the U.S. Time Series*. Washington, DC: American Enterprise Institute.

———. 1974. Are Government Bonds Net Wealth? *Journal of Political Economy* 82 (November-December): 1095–1117.

Bartlett, Robin L., and Charles Poulton-Callahan. 1982. Changing Family Structures and the Distribution of Family Income: 1951–1976. *Social Science Quarterly* 63 (March): 28–37.

Bassi, Laurie J., and Orley Ashenfelter. 1986. The Effect of Direct Job Creation and Training Programs on Low-Skilled Workers. In Sheldon H. Danziger and Daniel H. Weinberg (eds.), *Fighting Poverty: What Works and What Doesn't*. Cambridge, MA: Harvard University Press.

Baum, Sandra R., and Jane Sjogren. 1988. Cost-of-Living Adjustments for Social Security Benefits: Their Impact on the Incomes of the Elderly. In Sheldon H. Danziger and Kent E. Portney (eds.), *The Distributional Impacts of Public Policies*. New York: St. Martin's Press.

Beck, E. M. 1980. Labor Unionism and Racial Income Inequality: A Time-Series Analysis of the Post-World War II Period. *American Journal of Sociology* 85 (4): 791–814.

Beck, E. M., Patrick M. Horan, and Charles M. Tolbert, II. 1980. Industrial Segmentation and Labor Market Discrimination. *Social Problems* 28 (December): 113–130.

———. 1978. Stratification in a Dual Economy: A Sectoral Model of Earnings Determination. *American Sociological Review* 43 (October): 704–720.

Becker, Gary S. 1981. *A Treatise on the Family*. Cambridge, MA: Harvard University Press.
———. 1975. *Human Capital*. New York: Columbia University Press.
———. 1971. *The Economics of Discrimination*. Chicago: University of Chicago Press.
Becker, Gary S., and Lewis H. Gregg. 1973. On the Interaction between the Quantity and Quality of Children. *Journal of Political Economy* 81 (March/April, part 2): S279–S288.
Bell, Linda A., and Richard B. Freeman. 1986. The Facts about Rising Industrial Wage Dispersion in the U.S. *Industrial Relations Research Association Series, Proceedings of the Thirty-Ninth Annual Meeting*. December: 331–337.
Beller, Andrea. 1985. Changes in the Sex Composition of U.S. Occupations, 1960–1981. *Journal of Human Resources* 20 (Spring): 233–250.
———. 1982. Occupational Segregation by Sex: Determinants and Changes. *Journal of Human Resources* 17 (Summer): 371–392.
———. 1980. The Effect of Economic Conditions on the Success of Equal Employment Opportunity Laws: An Application to the Sex Differential in Earnings. *Review of Economics and Statistics* 62 (August): 379–387.
Ben-Porath, Yoram. 1982. Individuals, Families and Income Distribution. *Population and Development Review* 8 (Supplement): 1–16.
———. 1980. The F-Connection: Families, Friends, and Firms and the Organization of Exchange. *Population and Development Review* 6 (March): 1–30.
Berger, Mark C. 1985. The Effect of Cohort Size on Earnings Growth: A Reexamination of the Evidence. *Journal of Political Economy* 93 (June): 561–591.
———. 1984. Cohort Size and the Earnings Growth of Young Workers. *Industrial and Labor Relations Review* 37 (July): 582–591.
———. 1983. Changes in Labor Force Composition and Male Earnings: A Production Approach. *Journal of Human Resources* 17 (Spring): 177–196.
Berger, Suzanne, and Michael Piore. 1980. *Dualism and Discontinuity in Industrial Societies*. New York: Cambridge University Press.
Bergmann, Barbara. 1974. Occupational Segregation, Wages, and Profits When Employers Discriminate by Race or Sex. *Eastern Economic Journal* 1 (April-July): 103–110.
———. 1971. The Effect on White Incomes of Discrimination in Employment. *Journal of Political Economy* 79 (January-February): 294–313.
Bergmann, Barbara, Judith R. Devine, Patrice Gorden, Diane Reedy, Lewis Sage, and Christina Wise. 1980. The Effect of Wives' Labor Force Participation on Inequality in the Distribution of Family Income. *Journal of Human Resources* 19 (Summer): 452–455.
Bergmann, Barbara, and Jerolyn R. Lyle. 1971. The Occupational Standing of Negroes by Areas and Industries. *Journal of Human Resources* 6 (Fall): 412–432.
Berk, Richard A., and Sarah Fenstermaker Berk. 1983. Supply-Side Sociology of the Family: The Challenge of the New Home Economics. *Annual Review of Sociology* 9: 375–395. Palo Alto, CA: Annual Reviews.
Berry, William D., and Stanley Feldman. 1985. *Multiple Regression in Practice*. New York: Sage Publications.
Betson, David, and Jacques Van Der Gagg. 1984. Working Married Women and the Distribution of Income. *Journal of Human Resources* 16 (Fall): 532–543.
Betson, David, Jennifer L. Warlick, and Timothy M. Smeeding. 1988. The Effects of

Taxing Unemployment Insurance Benefits Accounting for Induced Labor Supply Responses. In Sheldon H. Danziger and Kent E. Portney (eds.), *The Distributional Impacts of Public Policy*. New York: St. Martin's Press.

Bianchi, Suzanne M. 1980. Racial Differences in Per Capita Income, 1960–1976: The Importance of Household Size, Headship, and Labor Force Participation. *Demography* 17 (May): 129–143.

Bianchi, Suzanne M., and Reynolds Farley. 1979. Racial Differences in Family Living Arrangements and Economic Well-Being: An Analysis of Recent Trends. *Journal of Marriage and the Family* 41 (August): 537–551.

Bianchi, Suzanne M., and Daphne Spain. 1984. *American Women: Three Decades of Change*. Washington, DC: USGPO.

Blackburn, McKinley L., and David E. Bloom. 1987. Earnings and Income Inequality in the United States. *Population and Development Review* 13 (December): 575–609.

―――. 1985. What's Happening to the Middle Class? *American Demographics* (January): 19.

Blalock, Hubert M. 1979. *Social Statistics*. New York: McGraw-Hill.

Blank, Rebecca, M., and Alan S. Blinder. 1986. Macroeconomics, Income Distribution, and Poverty. In Sheldon H. Danziger and Daniel H. Weinberg (eds.), *Fighting Poverty: What Works and What Doesn't*. Cambridge, MA: Harvard University Press.

Blau, David M., and Philip K. Robins. 1986. Labor Supply Response to Welfare Programs: A Dynamic Analysis. *Journal of Labor Economics* 4 (January): 82–104.

Blau, Francine D., and Andrea H. Beller. 1988. Trends in Earnings Differentials by Gender, 1971–1981. *Industrial and Labor Relations Review* 41 (July): 513–529.

Blau, Francine D., and Marianne Ferber. 1987. Occupations and Earnings of Women Workers. In Karen Koziara, Michael Moskow, and Lucretia Tanner (eds.), *Working Women*. Washington, DC: Bureau of National Affairs.

Blau, Francine D., and Lawrence M. Kahn. 1981. Causes and Consequences of Layoffs. *Economic Inquiry* 19 (April): 279–296.

Blinder, Alan S., Roger H. Gordon, and Donald E. Wise. 1980. Reconsidering the Work Disincentive Effects of Social Security. *National Tax Journal* 33 (December): 431–442.

Bluestone, Barry. 1970. The Tripartite Economy: Labor Markets and the Working Poor. *Poverty and Human Resources Abstracts* 5 (July-August): 15–33.

Bluestone, Barry, and Bennett Harrison. 1988. The Growth of Low-Wage Employment: 1963–1986. *American Economic Review* 78 (May): 124–128.

―――. 1982. *The Deindustrialization of America*. New York: Basic Books.

Bluestone, Barry, and Mary Huff Stevenson. 1981. Industrial Transformation and the Evolution of Dual Labor Markets. In Frank Wilkinson (ed.), *The Dynamics of Labor Market Segmentation*, New York: Academic Press.

Bonacich, Edna. 1976. Advanced Capitalism and Black/White Race Relations in the United States: A Split Labor Market Interpretation. *American Sociological Review* 41 (February): 34–51.

―――. 1972. A Theory of Ethnic Antagonism: The Split Labor Market. *American Sociological Review* 37 (October): 547–559.

Bouvier, Leon F., and Anthony J. Agresta. 1985. The Fastest Growing Minority. *American Demographics* 7 (May): 31–33.

Bouvier, Leon F., and Jean van der Tak. 1976. Infant Mortality—Progress and Problems. *Population Bulletin* 31 (April).

Bowen, William G., and T. Aldrich Finegan. 1969. *The Economics of Labor Force Participation.* Princeton, NJ: Princeton University Press.

Bradbury, Katharine L. 1986. The Shrinking Middle Class. *New England Economic Review* (September/October): 41–55.

Bradbury, Katharine L., Sheldon Danziger, Eugene Smolensky, and Paul Smolensky. 1979. Public Assistance, Female Headship, and Economic Well-Being. *Journal of Marriage and the Family* (August): 519–535.

Braverman, Harry. 1974. *Labor and Monopoly Capital.* New York: Monthly Review Press.

Brimmer, Andrew F. 1988. Income, Wealth, and Investment Behavior in the Black Community. *American Economic Review* 78 (May): 151–155.

Brofenbrenner, Martin. 1970. Radical Economics in America: A 1970 Survey. *Journal of Economic Literature* 8 (September): 755–768.

Browning, Edgar. 1979. On the Distribution of New Income: Reply. *Southern Economic Journal* 45 (January): 945–959.

———. 1976. The Trend Towards Equality in the Distribution of Net Income. *Southern Economic Journal* 42 (September): 912–923.

Browning, Robert X. 1988. Priorities, Programs, and Presidents: Assessing Patterns of Growth in US Social Welfare Programs, 1950–1985. In Sheldon H. Danziger and Kent E. Portney (eds.), *The Distributional Impacts of Public Policy.* New York: St. Martin's Press.

Burggraf, Shirley P. 1984. Womenyouthandminorities and the Case of the Missing Productivity. *American Economic Review* 74 (May): 254–259.

Burkhauser, Richard, and John A. Turner. 1978. A Time Series Analysis of Social Security and Its Effect on Market Work of Men at Younger Ages. *Journal of Political Economy* 86 (August): 701–715.

Burstein, Paul. 1979. Equal Employment Opportunity Legislation and the Income of Women and Nonwhites. *American Sociological Review* 44 (June): 367–391.

Butler, Richard J. 1983. Direct Estimates of the Demand for Race and Sex Discrimination. *Southern Economic Journal* 49 (April): 975–990.

Butler, Richard J., and James J. Heckman. 1977. The Impact of the Government on the Labor Market Status of Black Americans: A Critical Review of the Literature and Some New Evidence. In Leonard S. Hausman (ed.), *Equal Rights and Industrial Relations.* Madison, WI: Industrial Relations Research Association.

Butler, Richard J., and James B. McDonald. 1986. Income Inequality in the United States, 1948–1980. *Research in Labor Economics* 8: 85–140. Greenwich, CT: JAI Press.

Butz, William P., and Michael P. Ward. 1979a. The Emergence of Countercyclical U.S. Fertility. *American Economic Review* 69 (June): 318–328.

———. 1979b. Will U.S. Fertility Remain Low? An Economic Interpretation. *Population and Development Review* 5 (December): 663–668.

Cain, Glen G. 1976. The Challenge of Segmented Labor Market Theories to Orthodox Theory: A Survey. *Journal of Economic Literature* 14 (December): 1215–1257.

Cain, Glen G., and Douglas A. Wissoker. 1987. Do Income Maintenance Programs Break Up Marriages: A Reevaluation of SIME-DIME. *Focus* 10 (Winter): 1–15.

Carlson, Leonard A., and Caroline Swartz. 1988. The Earnings of Women and Ethnic

Minorities, 1959–1979. *Industrial and Labor Relations Review* 41 (July): 530–546.

Champernowne, D. G. 1974. A Comparison of Measures of Inequality of Income Distribution. *Economic Journal* (December): 787–816.

Chiswick, Barry R. 1973. Racial Discrimination in the Labor Market: A Test of Alternative Hypotheses. *Journal of Political Economy* 81 (November-December): 1330–1352.

Chiswick, Barry R., and Jacob Mincer. 1972. Time-Series Changes in Personal Income Inequality in the United States from 1939, with Projections to 1985. *Journal of Political Economy* 80 (May/June): S34–S66.

Christensen, L., D. Cummings, and D. Jorgensen. 1982. An International Comparison of Growth of Productivity, 1947–1973. In *New Developments in Productivity Measurement and Analysis*. Chicago: University of Chicago Press.

Clogg, Clifford C. 1982. Cohort Analysis of Recent Trends in Labor Force Participation. *Demography* 19 (November): 459–480.

Cloutier, Norman R. Who Gains from Racism? The Impact of Racial Inequality on White Income Distribution. *Review of Social Economy* 45 (October): 152–162.

Cogan, John. 1982. The Decline in Black Teenage Employment: 1950–1970. *American Economic Review* 72 (September): 621–638.

Colin, Clark. 1940. *The Conditions of Economic Progress*. New York: Macmillan.

Comanor, William S. 1973. Racial Discrimination in American Industry. *Economica* 40 (November): 363–378.

Congressional Budget Office. 1988. *Trends in Family Income: 1970–1986*. Washington, DC: USGPO.

Connelly, Rachel. 1986. A Framework for Analyzing the Impact of Cohort Size on Education and Labor Earnings. *Journal of Human Resources* 21 (Fall): 543–562.

Cramer, James C. 1987. Social Factors and Infant Mortality: Identifying High-Risk Groups and Proximate Causes. *Demography* 24 (August): 299–322.

———. 1980. Fertility and Female Employment: Problems of Causal Direction. *American Sociological Review* 45 (April): 167–190.

Craves, Richard E., Walter B. Wriston, and James R. Schlesinger. 1980. The Structure of Industry. In Martin Feldstein (ed.), *The American Economy in Transition*. Chicago: University of Chicago Press.

Creedy, J., and P. E. Hart. 1979. Age and the Distribution of Earnings. *Economic Journal* 89 (June): 280–293.

D'Amico, Ronald J. 1982. Explaining the Effects of Capital Sector for Income Determination. *Work and Occupations* 9 (November): 411–439.

D'Amico, Ronald J., and Thomas N. Daymont. 1982. Industrial Organization, Economic Conditions, and the Labor Market Success of Young Men: An Overview and Extension. *Social Science Research* 11 (September): 201–226.

D'Amico, Ronald J., and Jeff Golon. 1986. The Displaced Worker: Consequences of Career Interruption among Young Men. In Stephen Hills (ed.), *The Changing Labor Market: A Longitudinal Study of Young Men*. Lexington, MA: D. C. Heath.

D'Amico, Thomas F. 1987. The Conceit of Labor Market Discrimination. *American Economic Review* 77 (May): 310–315.

Danziger, Sheldon. 1988. Introduction. *Focus* 11 (Spring): 1–4.

———. 1980. Do Working Women Increase Family Income Inequality? *Journal of Human Resources* 15 (Summer): 444–451.

Danziger, Sheldon, and Peter Gottschalk. 1986a. Families with Children Have Fared Worst. *Challenge* (March/April): 40–47.

———. 1986b. Work, Poverty, and the Working Poor: A Multifaceted Problem. *Monthly Labor Review* 109 (September): 17–21.

———. 1986c. Do Rising Tides Lift All Boats: The Impact of Secular and Cyclic Changes on Poverty. *American Economic Review* 76 (May): 405–410.

———. 1985. The Poverty of Losing Ground. *Challenge* (May-June): 32–38.

Danziger, Sheldon, Robert Haveman, and Robert Plotnick. 1986. Antipoverty Policy: Effects on the Poor and Nonpoor. In Sheldon H. Danziger and Daniel H. Weinberg (eds.). *Fighting Poverty: What Works and What Doesn't.* Cambridge, MA: Harvard University Press.

———. 1981. How Income Transfer Programs Affect Work, Savings, and the Income Distribution: A Critical Review. *Journal of Economic Literature* 19 (September): 975–1028.

Danziger, Sheldon, Robert Haveman, and Eugene Smolensky. 1977. The Measurement and Trend of Inequality: Comment. *American Economic Review* 67 (June): 505–512.

Danziger, Sheldon, and Robert Plotnick. 1977. Demographic Change, Government Transfers, and Income Distribution. *Monthly Labor Review* 102 (April): 7–11.

Danziger, Sheldon, and Kent E. Portney. 1988. *The Distributional Impacts of Public Policy.* New York: St. Martin's Press.

Danziger, Sheldon, and Michael K. Taussig. 1979. The Income Unit and the Anatomy of Income Distribution. *Review of Income and Wealth* 25 (December): 365–375.

Danziger, Sheldon, and Daniel H. Weinberg. 1986. *Fighting Poverty: What Works and What Doesn't.* Cambridge, MA: Harvard University Press.

Darby, Michael R. 1984. The U.S. Productivity Slowdown: A Case of Statistical Myopia. *American Economic Review* 74 (June): 301–322.

Darity, William A., Jr. 1982. The Human Capital Approach to Black-White Earnings Inequality: Some Unsettled Questions. *Journal of Human Resources* 17 (Winter): 72–93.

———. 1975. Economic Theory and Racial Economic Inequality. *Review of Black Political Economy* (Spring): 225–248.

Darity, William A., Jr., and Samuel L. Myers, Jr. 1987. Do Transfer Payments Keep the Poor in Poverty? *American Economic Review* 77 (May): 216–222.

———. 1984. Does Welfare Dependency Cause Female Headship? The Case of the Black Family. *Journal of Marriage and the Family* 46 (November): 765–779.

———. 1980. Changes in Black-White Income Inequality, 1968–1978: A Decade of Progress? *Review of Black Political Economy* (Summer): 355–379.

Darity, William A., Jr., and Rhoda M. Williams. 1985. Peddlers Forever?: Culture, Competition and Discrimination. *American Economic Review* 75 (May): 256–261.

Datcher-Loury, Linda. 1986. Racial Differences in the Stability of High Earnings among Young Men. *Journal of Labor Economics* 3 (July, part 1): 301–316.

Davidson, Carlos, and Michael Reich. 1988. Income Inequality: An Inter-Industry Analysis. *Industrial Relations* 27 (Fall): 263–286.

Davis, Howard. 1980. Employment Gains of Women by Industry, 1968–1978. *Monthly Labor Review* 103 (June): 3–9.

Daymont, Thomas N. 1980a. Pay Premiums for Economic Sector and Race: A Decomposition. *Social Science Research* 9 (September): 245–272.

————. 1980b. Racial Equity or Racial Equality. *Demography* 17 (November): 379–393.

Denison, Edward. 1985. *Trends in American Economic Growth, 1929–1982*. Washington, DC: Brookings Institution.

Derthick, Martha. 1979. *Policymaking for Social Security*. Washington, DC: Brookings Institution.

DeTray, Dennis N. 1973. Child Quality and the Demand for Children. *Journal of Political Economy* 81 (March-April), part 2): S71–S95.

Devens, Richard M. 1986. Displaced Workers One Year Later. *Monthly Labor Review* 109 (July): 40–43.

Dickens, William T., and Kevin Lang. 1988. The Reemergence of Segmented Labor Market Theory. *American Economic Review* 78 (May): 129–134.

Doeringer, Peter B. 1986. Internal Labor Markets and Noncompeting Groups. *American Economic Review* 76 (May): 48–52.

Doeringer, Peter B., and Michael J. Piore. 1971. *Internal Labor Markets and Manpower Analysis*. Lexington, MA: D. C. Heath.

Dooley, Martin, and Peter Gottschalk. 1985. The Increasing Proportion of Men with Low Earnings in the United States. *Demography* 22 (February): 25–34.

————. 1984. Earnings Inequality among Males in the United States: Trends and the Effect of Labor Force Growth. *Journal of Political Economy* 92 (February): 59–89.

Dorn, James A. 1986. Introduction: The Transfer Society. *Cato Journal* 6 (Spring/Summer): 1–17.

Duncan, Beverly. 1979. Change in Worker/Nonworker Ratios for Women. *Demography* 16 (November): 535–547.

Duncan, Greg J. 1984. *Years of Poverty, Years of Plenty*. Ann Arbor: University of Michigan Press.

Duncan, Greg J., and Saul Hoffman. 1983. A New Look at the Causes of the Improved Economic Status of Black Workers. *Journal of Human Resources* 17 (Spring): 268–281.

Duncan, Otis Dudley. 1969. Inheritance of Poverty or Inheritance of Race? In Daniel P. Moynihan, *On Understanding Poverty*. New York: Basic Books.

Durden, Garey C., and Ann V. Schwarz-Miller. 1982. The Distribution of Individual Income in the U.S. and Public Sector Employment. *Social Science Quarterly* 63 (March): 39–47.

Easterlin, Richard A. 1987. The New Age Structure of Poverty in America: Permanent or Transient? *Population and Development Review* 13 (June): 195–208.

————. 1980. *Birth and Fortune: The Impact of Numbers on Personal Welfare*. New York: Basic Books.

Easterlin, Richard A., and Eileen M. Crimmins. 1985. *The Fertility Revolution*. Chicago: University of Chicago Press.

Easterlin, Richard A., Victor R. Fuchs, and Simon Kuznets. 1980. American Population since 1940. In Martin Feldstein (ed.), *The American Economy in Transition*. Chicago: University of Chicago Press.

Eberts, Randall, and Erica Groshen. 1988. Do the Earnings of Manufacturing and Service Workers Grow at the Same Rate over Their Careers? *Economic Review* 24 (4): 2–10.

The Economist. 1988. America's Shrinking Middle. *Economist*, November 12.

Edmondson, Brad. 1987. Colleges Conquer the Baby Bust. *American Demographics* 9 (September): 26–31.

Edwards, Richard C. 1979. *Contested Terrain.* New York: Basic Books.

Ehrenreich, Barbara. 1986. Is the Middle Class Doomed? *New York Times Magazine* (September): 44.

Ellwood, David T., and Lawrence H. Summers. 1986. Poverty in America: Is Welfare the Answer or the Problem? In Sheldon H. Danziger and Daniel H. Weinberg (eds.), *Fighting Poverty: What Works and What Doesn't.* Cambridge, MA: Harvard University Press.

England, Paula. 1985. Occupational Segregation: Rejoinder to Polachek. *Journal of Human Resources* 20 (Summer): 441–443.

———. 1984. Wage Appreciation and Depreciation: A Test of Neoclassical Economic Explanations of Occupational Sex Segregation. *Social Forces* 62 (March): 726–749.

———. 1982. The Failure of Human Capital Theory to Explain Occupational Sex Segregation. *Journal of Human Resources* 17 (Summer): 358–370.

England, Paula, and George Farkas. 1986. *Households, Employment, and Gender: A Social, Economic and Demographic View.* Hawthorne, NY: Aldine Publishing.

Espenshade, Thomas J. 1985. Marriage Trends in America: Estimates, Implications, and Underlying Causes. *Population and Development Review* 11 (June): 193–245.

Farkas, George. 1977. Cohort, Age, and Period Effects upon the Employment of White Females: Evidence for 1957–1968. *Demography* 14 (February): 33–42.

Farley, Reynolds. 1984. *Blacks and Whites: Narrowing the Gap?* Cambridge, MA: Harvard University Press.

———. 1977. Trends in Racial Inequalities: Have the Gains of the 1960s Disappeared in the 1970s? *American Sociological Review* 42 (April): 189–208.

Farley, Reynolds, and Albert I. Hermalin. 1971. Family Stability: A Comparison of Trends between Blacks and Whites. *American Sociological Review* 36 (February): 1–17.

Feldstein, Martin. 1980. *The American Economy in Transition.* Chicago: University of Chicago Press.

———. 1974. Social Security, Induced Retirement and Aggregate Capital Accumulation. *Journal of Political Economy* 82 (September-October): 905–926.

Fienberg, Stephen E., and William M. Mason. 1979. Identification and Estimation of Age-Period-Cohort Models in the Analysis of Discrete Archival Data. *Sociological Methodology.* San Francisco: Jossey-Bass.

Fisher, Allan. G. B. 1935. *The Clash of Progress and Security.* New York: Macmillan.

Flaim, Paul O., and Ellen Sehgal. 1985. Displaced Workers of 1979–1983: How Will They Fare? *Monthly Labor Review* 108 (June): 3–16.

Flanagan, Robert J. 1973. Segmented Market Theories and Racial Discrimination. *Industrial Relations* 12 (October): 253–273.

Fortune, J. Neil. 1987. Some Determinants of Labor Productivity. *Applied Economics* 19 (June): 839–843.

Fossett, Mark A., Omer R. Gallee, and William R. Kelly. 1986. Racial Occupational Inequality, 1940–1980: National and Regional Trends. *American Sociological Review* 51 (June): 421–429.

Freeman, Richard B. 1980a. The Facts about the Declining Economic Value of College. *Journal of Human Resources* 15 (Winter): 124–142.

————. 1980b. Employment Opportunities in the Doctorate Manpower Market. *Industrial and Labor Relations Review* 33 (January): 185–187.

————. 1980c. Unionism and the Dispersion of Wages. *Industrial and Labor Relations Review* 34 (October): 3–23.

————. 1979. The Effect of Demographic Factors on Age-Earning Profiles. *Journal of Human Resources* 14 (Summer): 291–318.

————. 1978. Black Economic Progress since 1964. *Public Interest* 52 (Summer): 51–68.

————. 1977. The Decline in the Economic Rewards to College Education. *Review of Economics and Statistics* 59 (February): 22–32.

————. 1976a. *The Overeducated American*. New York: Academic Press.

————. 1976b. A Cobweb Model of the Supply and Starting Salary of New Engineers. *Industrial and Labor Relations Review* 29 (January): 236–248.

————. 1973. Changes in the Labor Market for Black Americans, 1948–1972. *Brookings Papers on Economic Activity* 1: 67–129.

Freeman, Richard B., and James Medoff. 1984. *What Do Unions Do?* New York: Basic Books.

————. 1981. The Impact of the Percent Organized on Union and Nonunion Wages. *Review of Economics and Statistics* 63 (November): 553–560.

Freeman, Richard B., John T. Dunlop, and R. F. Shubert. 1980. The Evolution of the American Labor Market, 1948–1980. In Martin Feldstein (ed.), *The American Economy in Transition*. Chicago: University of Chicago Press, 84–85.

Friedan, Betty. 1963. *The Feminine Mystique*. New York: Norton.

Friedlander, Daniel, Barbara Goldman, Judith Gueron, and David Long. 1986. Initial Findings from the Demonstration of State Work/Welfare Incentives. *American Economic Review* 76 (May): 224–229.

Fuchs, Victor. 1986. The Feminization of Poverty? Working Paper No. 1934. Cambridge, MA: National Bureau of Economic Research.

————. 1981. Economic Growth and the Rise of Service Employment. In Herbert Giersch (ed.), *Towards an Explanation of Economic Growth: Symposium 1980*. Tübingen: J.C.B. Mohr.

————. 1968. *The Service Economy*. New York: Columbia University Press.

Fulco, Lawrence J. 1986. U.S. Productivity Growth since 1982: The Post-Recession Experience. *Monthly Labor Review* 109 (December): 18–22.

Fullerton, Howard N., Jr. 1987. Labor Force Projections: 1986 to 2000. *Monthly Labor Review* 110 (September): 19–29.

Garfinkel, Irwin. 1988. The Evolution of Child Support Policy. *Focus* 11 (Spring): 11–16.

Gibson, Campbell. 1976. The U.S. Fertility Decline, 1961–1975: The Contribution of Changes in Marital Status and Marital Fertility. *Family Planning Perspectives* 8 (September-October): 250–255.

Gilman, Harry J. 1965. Economic Discrimination and Unemployment. *American Economic Review* 55 (December): 1077–1096.

Glenn, Norval D., and Patricia Ann Taylor. 1984. Education and Family Income: A Comparison of White Married Men and Women in the U.S. *Social Forces* 63 (September): 169–183.

Glick, Paul, and Arthur J. Norton. 1973. Perspectives on the Recent Upturn in Divorce and Remarriage. *Demography* 10 (August): 300–315.

Goldfield, Michael. 1987. *The Decline of Organized Labor in the United States*. Chicago: University of Chicago Press.

Goldscheider, Frances K., and Linda J. Waite. 1986. Sex Differences in the Entry to Marriage. *American Journal of Sociology* 92: 91–109.

Gordon, David. 1972. *Theories of Poverty and Underemployment*. Lexington, MA: D. C. Heath.

Gordon, David, Richard Edwards, and Michael Reich. 1982. *Segmented Work, Divided Workers: The Historical Transformation of Labor in the United States*. New York: Cambridge University Press.

Gordon, Roger H., and Alan S. Blinder. 1980. Market Wages, Reservation Wages, and Retirement Decisions. *Journal of Public Economics* 14 (October): 277–308.

Gordus, Jeanne, Paul Farley, and Louis Ferman. 1981. *Plant Closing and Economic Dislocation*. Kalamazoo, MI: W. E. Upjohn Co.

Gottfredson, Denise C. 1981. Black-White Differences in the Educational Attainment Process: What Have We Learned? *American Sociological Review* 46 (October): 542–557.

Gottschalk, Peter, and Sheldon Danziger. 1985. A Framework for Evaluating the Effects of Economic Growth and Transfers on Poverty. *American Economic Review* 75 (March): 153–161.

Greenstein, Robert. 1985. Losing Faith in "Losing Ground." *New Republic* (March 25): 12–16.

Groneau, Reuben. 1988. Sex-Related Wage Differentials and Women's Interrupted Labor Careers: The Chicken or the Egg? *Journal of Labor Economics* 6 (July): 277–301.

———. 1982. Inequality of Family Income: Do Wives' Earnings Matter? *Population and Development Review* 8 (Supplement): 119–136.

Grossman, Michael, and Victor Fuchs. 1973. Intersectoral Shifts and Aggregate Productivity Change. *Annals of Economic and Social Measurement*. New York: National Bureau of Economic Research.

Gwartney, James. 1970. Changes in the Nonwhite/White Income Ratio—1939–1967. *American Economic Review* 60 (December): 872–883.

Haessel, Walter, and John Palmer. 1978. Market Power and Employment Discrimination. *Journal of Human Resources* 13 (Fall): 545–560.

Hagenaars, Aldi, and Klaas de Vos. 1988. The Definition and Measurement of Poverty. *Journal of Human Resources* 23 (Spring): 211–222.

Hamermesh, Daniel S. 1979. Entitlement Effects, Unemployment Insurance and Employment Decisions. *Economic Inquiry* 17 (July): 317–332.

———. 1977. *Jobless Pay and the Economy*. Baltimore, MD: Johns Hopkins University Press.

Handler, Joel F. 1988. Consensus on Redirection—Which Direction. *Focus* 11 (Spring): 29–34.

Hanoch, Giora, and Marjorie Honig. 1978. The Labor Supply Curve Under Income Maintenance Programs. *Journal of Public Economics* 9 (February): 1–16.

Harrington, Michael, and Mark Levinson. 1985. The Perils of a Dual Economy. *Dissent* (Fall): 417–426.

Harris, R. J., and J. J. Hedderson. 1981. Effects of Wife's Income on Family Income Inequality. *Sociological Methods and Research* 10: 211–232.

Harrison, Bennett. 1972. Education and Underemployment in the Urban Ghetto. *American Economic Review* 62 (December): 796–811.

———. 1971. Human Capital, Black Poverty and "Radical" Economics. *Industrial Relations* 10 (October): 277–281.

Harrison, Bennett, and Barry Bluestone. 1988. *The Great U-Turn*. New York: Basic Books.

Harrison, Bennett, Chris Tilly, and Barry Bluestone. 1986. Wage Inequality Takes a Great U-Turn. *Challenge* (March-April): 26–32.

Haveman, Robert H. 1977. *A Decade of Federal Antipoverty Programs*. New York: Academic Press.

Haveman, Robert H., and Barbara Wolfe. 1984. The Decline in Male Labor Force Participation: Comment. *Journal of Political Economy* 92 (June): 532–541.

Heilbroner, Robert L. 1966. *The Limits of American Capitalism*. New York: Harper and Row.

Henle, Peter, and Paul Ryscavage. 1980. The Distribution of Earned Income among Men and Women, 1958–1977. *Monthly Labor Review* (April): 3–10.

Hicks, John R. 1966. *The Theory of Wages*. New York: St. Martin's Press.

Hirsch, Barry, 1982. The Interindustry Structure of Unionism, Earnings and Earnings Dispersion. *Industrial and Labor Relations Review* 36 (October): 22–39.

Hirsch, Barry, and John T. Addison. 1986. *The Economic Analysis of Unions*. Boston: Allen and Unwin.

Hodge, Robert W., and Patricia Hodge. 1965. Occupational Assimilation as a Competitive Process. *American Journal of Sociology* 71: 249–264.

Hodson, Randy. 1978. Labor in the Monopoly, Competitive, and State Sectors of Production. *Politics and Society* 8 (4): 429–480.

Hodson, Randy, and Robert L. Kaufman. 1982. Economic Dualism: A Critical Review. *American Sociological Review* 47 (December): 727–739.

Hoerr, John P. 1988. *And the Wolf Finally Came*. Pittsburgh: University of Pittsburgh Press.

Hoffman, Saul D. 1979. Black-White Life Cycle Earnings Differences and the Vintage Hypothesis: A Longitudinal Analysis. *American Economic Review* 69 (September): 855–867.

Horrigan, Michael W., and Steven E. Haugen. 1988. The Declining Middle-Class Thesis: A Sensitivity Analysis. *Monthly Labor Review* 111 (May): 3–13.

Hovarth, F. W. 1980. Working Wives Reduce Inequality in the Distribution of Family Earnings. *Monthly Labor Review* 103 (April): 51–53.

Howe, Wayne J. 1988. Education and Demographics: How Do They Affect Unemployment Rates? *Monthly Labor Review* 111 (January): 3–9.

Hudson Institute. *Workforce 2000: Work and Workers in the Twenty-First Century*. Washington, DC: USGPO.

Hutchens, Robert. 1984. The Effects of the Omnibus Budget Reconciliation Act of 1981 on AFDC Recipients: A Review of the Studies. Institute for Research on Poverty Discussion Paper No. 764–84.

Hyclack, Thomas. 1979. The Effect of Unions on Earnings Inequality in Local Labor Markets. *Industrial and Labor Relations Review* 33 (October): 77–84.

Jencks, Christopher. 1972. *Inequality*. New York: Harper and Row.

Johnson, William R. 1977. The Measurement and Trend of Inequality: Comment. *American Economic Review* 67 (June): 502–504.

Jud, Donald G., and James L. Walker. 1982. Racial Differences in the Returns to Schooling and Experience among Prime Age Males: 1967–1975. *Journal of Human Resources* 17 (Fall): 622–631.

Kaufman, Bruce, and Paula E. Stephan. 1985. The Determinants of Wage Growth among Industries in the 1970s. Mimeo.

Kendrick, John W., and Beatrice N. Vaccara. 1980. *New Developments in Productivity Measurement and Analysis*. Chicago: University of Chicago Press.

Killingsworth, Mark R. 1983. *Labor Supply*. New York: Cambridge University Press.

———. 1976. Must a Negative Income Tax Reduce Labor Supply? A Study of the Family's Allocation of Time. *Journal of Human Resources* 11 (Summer): 354–365.

Kindleberger, Charles P. 1980. The Economic Aging of America. *Challenge* 22 (January/February): 48–49.

———. 1974. An American Economic Climacteric? *Challenge* 16 (January/February): 35–44.

Kniesner, Thomas J., Marjorie B. McElroy, and Steven P. Wilcox. 1988. Getting into Poverty Without a Husband and Getting Out With or Without One. *American Economic Review* 78 (May): 86–90.

Kobrin, Frances E. 1976. The Fall in Household Size and the Rise of the Primary Individual in the United States. *Demography* 13 (February): 127–138.

Kosters, Marvin H., and Murray N. Ross. 1988. A Shrinking Middle Class? *Public Interest* 6 (Winter): 3–27.

Kruger, Anne O. 1963. The Economics of Discrimination. *Journal of Political Economy* 71 (October): 481–487.

Kurien, John. 1977. The Measurement and Trend of Inequality: Comment. *American Economic Review* 67 (June): 517–519.

Kutscher, Ronald E. 1987. Overview and Implications of the Projections to 2000. *Monthly Labor Review* 110 (September): 3–9.

Kutscher, Ronald E., and Jerome A. Mark. 1983. The Service-Producing Sector: Some Common Perceptions Reviewed. *Monthly Labor Review* 106 (April): 21–24.

Kutscher, Ronald E., and Valerie A. Personick. 1986. Deindustrialization and the Shift to Services. *Monthly Labor Review* 109 (June): 3–13.

Kuttner, Robert. 1985. A Shrinking Middle Class Is a Call for Action. *Business Week* (September 16): 16.

———. 1983. The Declining Middle. *Atlantic Monthly* (July): 60–72.

Kuznets, Simon. 1976. Demographic Aspects of the Size Distribution of Income: An Exploratory Survey. *Economic Development and Cultural Change* 25 (1): 1–94.

———. 1930. *Secular Movements in Production and Prices—Their Nature and Their Bearing upon Cyclic Fluctuations*. Boston: Houghton Mifflin.

Lam, David. 1986. The Dynamics of Population Growth, Differential Fertility and Inequality. *American Economic Review* 76 (December): 1103–1116.

Lawrence, Robert Z. 1984a. *Can America Compete?* Washington, DC: Brookings Institution.

———. 1984b. Sectoral Shifts and the Size of the Middle Class. *Brookings Review* (Fall): 3–11.

Layard, Richard, and Antoni Zabalza. 1979. Family Income Distribution: Explanation and Policy Evaluation. *Journal of Political Economy* 87 (Part 2, October): S133–S161.

Lazear, Edward. 1979. The Narrowing of Black-White Wage Differentials Is Illusory. *American Economic Review* 69 (September): 553–564.

Lazer, William, and Eric H. Shaw. 1987. How Older Americans Spend Their Money. *American Demographics* 9 (September): 36–41.

Lehrer, Evelyn, and Marc Nerlove. 1984a. The Impact of Female Work on Family Income Distribution in the United States: Black-White Differentials. *Review of Income and Wealth* 27 (December): 423–431.

———. 1984b. A Life-Cycle Analysis of Family Income Distribution. *Economic Inquiry* 22 (July): 360–374.

Leigh, Duane E. 1976. The Occupational Mobility of Young Men, 1965–1970. *Industrial and Labor Relations Review* 30 (October): 68–78.

Leigh, Wilhemina A. 1988. The Social Preference for Fair Housing: During the Civil Rights Movement and Since. *American Economic Review* 78 (May): 156–162.

Leonard, Jonathan S. 1986. What Was Affirmative Action? *American Economic Review* 76 (May): 359–363.

———. 1985a. What Promises Are Worth: The Impact of Affirmative Action Goals. *Journal of Human Resources* 20 (Winter): 1–20.

———. 1985b. Affirmative Action as Earnings Redistribution: The Targeting of Compliance Reviews. *Journal of Labor Economics* 3 (July): 363–384.

Leontief, Wassily. 1983. Technological Advance, Economic Growth, and the Distribution of Income. *Population and Development Review* 9 (September): 403–410.

Levine, Phillip B., and Olivia S. Mitchell. 1988. The Baby Boom's Legacy: Relative Wages in the Twenty-First Century. *American Economic Review* 78 (May): 66–75.

Levy, Frank. 1987a. *Dollars and Dreams: The Changing American Income Distribution*. New York: Basic Books.

———. 1987b. Changes in the Distribution of American Family Incomes, 1947–1984. *Science* (May 22): 923–926.

Levy, Frank, and Richard C. Michel. 1986a. Work for Welfare: How Much Good Will It Do? *American Economic Review* 76 (May): 399–404.

———. 1986b. An Economic Bust for the Baby Boom. *Challenge* (March-April): 33–39.

———. 1985. Are Baby Boomers Selfish? *American Demographics* 7 (December): 38–41.

Lewis, H. Gregg. 1986. *Union Relative Wage Effects: A Survey*. Chicago: University of Chicago Press.

Lewis-Beck, Michael S. 1980. *Applied Regression: An Introduction*. New York: Sage Publications.

Link, Charles, Edward Ratledge, and Kenneth Lewis. 1976. Black-White Differences in Returns to Schooling: Some New Evidence. *American Economic Review* 66 (March): 221–223.

Loveman, Gray W., and Chris Tilly. 1988. Good Jobs or Bad Jobs: What Does the Evidence Say? *New England Economic Review* (January/February): 46–65.

Madden, Janice. 1988. The Distribution of Economic Losses among Displaced Workers: Measurement Methods Matter. *Journal of Human Resources* 23 (Winter): 93–107.

———. 1987. Gender Differences in the Cost of Displacement: An Empirical Test of

Discrimination in the Labor Market. *American Economic Review* 77 (May): 246–252.

Mangum, Garth, Donald Mayall, and Kristin Nelson. 1985. The Temporary Help Industry: A Response to the Dual Internal Labor Market. *Industrial and Labor Relations Review* 38 (July): 599–611.

Mansfield, Edwin. 1988. *Microeconomics*. New York: W. W. Norton.

Mansfield, Edwin, Ruben F. Mettler, and David Packard. 1980. Technology and Productivity in the United States. In Martin Feldstein (ed.), *The American Economy in Transition*. Chicago: University of Chicago Press.

Mark, Jerome A. 1982. Measuring Productivity in Service Industries. *Monthly Labor Review* 106 (June): 3–8.

Mark, Jerome A., and W. H. Waldorf. 1983. Multifactor Productivity: A New BLS Measure. *Monthly Labor Review* 106 (December): 3–5.

Marshall, Ray. 1974. The Economics of Racial Discrimination: A Survey. *Journal of Economic Literature* 12 (September): 849–871.

Martin, Phillip L. 1983. *Labor Displacement and Public Policy*. Lexington, MA: Lexington Books.

Masnick, George, and Mary Jo Bane. 1980. *The Nation's Families*. Boston: Auburn House.

Mason, Karen, William M. Mason, H. H. Winsborough, and W. K. Poole. 1973. Some Methodological Issues in Cohort Analyses of Archival Data. *American Sociological Review* 38: 242–258.

Masters, Stanley. 1975. *Black-White Income Differentials*. New York: Academic Press.

Matthews, Glenna. 1987. *Just a Housewife*. New York: Oxford University Press.

Maxwell, Nan L. 1989a. Labor Market Effects from Involuntary Job Losses in Layoffs and Plant Closings: The Role of Human Capital in Facilitating Reemployment and Reduced Wage Losses. *American Journal of Economics and Sociology* 48 (April): 129–142.

———. 1989b. Demographic and Economic Determinants of United States Income Inequality. *Social Science Quarterly* 70 (June): forthcoming.

Maxwell, Nan L., and Ronald J. D'Amico. 1986. Employment and Wage Effects of Involuntary Job Separation: Male-Female Differences. *American Economic Review* 76 (May): 373–377.

McCrate, Elaine. 1988. Gender Difference: The Role of Endogenous Preferences and Collective Action. *American Economic Review* 78 (May): 235–239.

McLanahan, Sara. 1985. Family Structure and the Reproduction of Poverty. *American Journal of Sociology* 90: 873–891.

McMahon, Patrick J., and John H. Tschetter. 1986. The Declining Middle Class: A Further Analysis. *Monthly Labor Review* 109 (September): 22–27.

Mellor, Earl F., and William Parks, II. 1988. A Year's Work: Labor Force Activity from a Different Perspective. *Monthly Labor Review* 111 (September): 13–18.

Michael, Robert T., Victor R. Fuchs, and Sharon R. Scott. 1980. Changes in the Propensity to Live Alone: 1950–1976. *Demography* 17 (February): 39–53.

Michel, Richard C., Frank S. Levy, Marilyn L. Moon, and Isabel V. Sawhill. 1984. Are We Better Off in 1984? *Challenge* (September/October): 10–17.

Milkman, Ronald. 1976. Women's Work and Economic Crisis: Some Lessons of the Great Depression. *Review of Radical Political Economics* 8: 73–97.

Miller, Herman. 1966. *Income Distribution in the United States.* 1960 Census Monograph, Washington, DC: USGPO.

Minarik, Joseph. 1977. The Measurement and Trend of Inequality: Comment. *American Economic Review* 67 (June): 513–516.

Mincer, Jacob. 1974. *Schooling, Experience, and Earnings.* New York: National Bureau of Economic Research.

———. 1970. The Distribution of Labor Incomes: A Survey. *Journal of Economic Literature* 8 (March): 1–26.

Mincer, Jacob, and Haim Ofek. 1982. Interrupted Work Careers: Depreciation and Restoration of Human Capital. *Journal of Human Resources* 17 (Winter): 3–24.

Mincer, Jacob, and Solomon Polachek. 1974. Family Investments in Human Capital: Earnings of Women. *Journal of Political Economy* 82 (March/April): 576–608.

Mirvis, Philip H., and Edward J. Hackett. 1983. Work and the Work Force in the Nonprofit Sector. *Monthly Labor Review* 106 (April): 3–12.

Moffitt, Robert. 1986. Work Incentives in the AFDC System: An Analysis of the 1981 Reforms. *American Economic Review* 76 (May): 219–223.

Moffitt, Robert, and Walter Nicholson. 1982. The Effect of Unemployment Insurance on Unemployment: The Case of Federal Supplemental Benefits. *Review of Economics and Statistics* 64 (February): 1–11.

Moore, Kristin A., and Sandra L. Hofferth. 1979. Women and Their Children. In Ralph E. Smith (ed.), *The Subtle Revolution: Women at Work.* Washington, DC: Urban Institute.

Moore, Maurice J., and Martin O'Connell. 1978. Perspectives on American Fertility. U.S. Bureau of the Census, *Current Population Reports,* Series P–23 (70). Washington, DC: USGPO.

Moore, William J., and John Raisain. 1983. The Level and Growth of Union/Nonunion Wage Effects, 1967–1977. *Journal of Labor Research* 4 (Winter): 65–79.

Morley, Samuel A. 1981. The Effect of Changes in the Population on Several Measures of Income Distribution. *American Economic Review* 71 (June): 285–294.

Mott, Frank L. 1982. Women: The Employment Revolution. In Frank L. Mott (ed.), *The Employment Revolution: Young American Women of the 1970s.* Cambridge, MA: MIT Press.

Mott, Frank L., and David Shapiro. 1982. Continuity of Work Attachment among New Mothers. In Frank L. Mott (ed.), *The Employment Revolution: Young American Women of the 1970s.* Cambridge, MA: MIT Press.

Moynihan, Daniel Patrick. 1987. *Family and Nation.* New York: Harcourt Brace Jovanovich.

Munnell, Alicia H. 1982. *The Economics of Private Pensions.* Washington, DC: Brookings Institution.

Murray, Charles. 1984. *Losing Ground: American Social Policy, 1950–1980.* New York: Basic Books.

Namboodiri, Krishnan, 1981. On Factors Affecting Fertility at Different Stages in the Reproductive History: An Exercise in Cohort Analysis. *Social Forces* 59: 1114–1129.

National Center for Health Statistics. 1980. Advance Report Final Mortality Statistics, 1978. *Monthly Vital Statistics Report,* 29 (September Supplement). Washington, DC: USGPO.

————. 1979. Advance Report Final Mortality Statistics, 1977. *Monthly Vital Statistics Report* 28 (May Supplement). Washington, DC: USGPO.

National Commission of State Workmen's Compensation Laws. 1973. *Compendium on Workmen's Compensation*. Washington, DC: USGPO.

Nelson, Eric R. 1977. The Measurement and Trend of Inequality: Comment. *American Economic Review* 67 (June): 497–501.

Nelson, Richard R., and Felicity Skidmore. 1983. *American Families and the Economy*. Washington, DC: National Academy Press.

Nordhaus, William. 1972. The Recent Productivity Slowdown. *Brookings Papers on Economic Activity*. Washington, DC: Brookings Institution.

Norton, R. D. 1986. Industrial Policy and American Renewal. *Journal of Economic Literature* 24 (March): 1–40.

Noyelle, Thierry. 1987. *Beyond Industrial Dualism: Market and Job Segmentation in the New Economy*. Boulder, CO: Westview Press.

Olson, Mancur. 1982. *The Rise and Decline of Nations: Economic Growth, Stagflation, and Social Rigidities*. New Haven, CT: Yale University Press.

O'Neil, June. 1985. The Trend in Male-Female Wage Gap in the United States. *Journal of Labor Economics* 3 (January): S91–S116.

Opitz, Wolfgang, and Frank D. Bean. 1988. Household Composition Change and Household Income among Hispanics in the United States. Paper presented at the Annual Meeting of the Population Association of America.

Orshansky, Mollie. 1965. Counting the Poor: Another Look at the Poverty Profile. *Social Security Bulletin* 28: 3–29.

Oster, Sharon M. 1970. Are Black Incomes more Unequally Distributed? *American Economist* 14 (Fall): 6–20.

Paglin, Michael. 1977. The Measurement and Trend of Inequality: Reply. *American Economic Review* 67 (June): 520–531.

————. 1975. The Measurement and Trend of Inequality: A Basic Revision. *American Economic Review* 65 (September): 598–609.

Pampel, Fred C. 1983. Changes in the Propensity to Live Alone: Evidence from Consecutive Cross-Sectional Surveys, 1960–1976. *Demography* 20 (November): 433–447.

Parsons, Donald O. 1984. Disability Insurance and Male Labor Force Participation: A Response to Haveman and Wolfe. *Journal of Political Economy* 92 (June): 542–549.

————. 1982. The Labour Force Participation Decision: Health, Reported Health, and Economic Incentives. *Economica* 49 (February): 81–91.

————. 1980a. The Decline in Male Labor Force Participation. *Journal of Political Economy* 88 (February): 117–134.

————. 1980b. Racial Trends in Male Labor Force Participation. *American Economic Review* 70 (December): 911–920.

Pechman, Joseph A. 1985. *Who Pays the Taxes?* Washington, DC: Brookings Institution.

Pellechio, Anthony J. 1978. The Effect of Social Security on Retirement. Cambridge, MA: National Bureau of Economic Research.

Pencavel, John, and Catherine Hartsog. 1984. A Reconsideration of the Effects of Unionism on Relative Wages and Employment in the United States, 1920–1980. *Journal of Labor Economics* 2 (April): 193–232.

Personick, Valerie A. 1987. Industry Output and Employment Through the End of the Century. *Monthly Labor Review* 110 (September): 30–45.

Pfeffer, Jeffrey, and James N. Baron. 1988. Taking the Workers Back Out: Recent Trends in the Structuring of Employment. *Research in Organizational Behavior* 10: 257–303. Greenwich, CT: JAI Press.

Pfeffer, Jeffrey, and Jerry Ross. 1982. The Effects of Marriage and a Working Wife on Occupational Wage Attainment. *Administrative Science Quarterly* 27 (March): 66–80.

Phelps, Edmund S. 1972. The Statistical Theory of Racism and Sexism. *American Economic Review* 62 (September): 659–661.

Piore, Michael J. 1975. Notes for a Theory of Labor Market Stratification. In Richard C. Edwards, Michael Reich, and David M. Gordon (eds.), *Labor Market Segmentation*. Lexington, MA: D. C. Heath.

Piore, Michael J., and Charles F. Sabel. 1984. *The Second Industrial Divide: Possibilities for Prosperity*. New York: Basic Books.

Plotnick, Robert. 1982. Trends in Male Earnings Inequality. *Southern Economic Journal* 48 (January): 724–732.

Podgursky, Michael, and Paul Swaim. 1987. Job Displacement and Earnings Loss: Evidence from the Displaced Worker Survey. *Industrial and Labor Relations Review* 41 (October): 17–29.

Polachek, Solomon. 1985. Occupational Segregation: A Defense of Human Capital Predictions. *Journal of Human Resources* 20 (Summer): 437–440.

———. 1981. Occupational Self-Selection: A Human Capital Approach to Sex Differences in Occupational Structure. *Review of Economics and Statistics* 63 (February): 60–69.

———. 1979. Occupational Segregation among Women: Theory, Evidence and a Prognosis. In Cynthia B. Lloyd, E. Andrews, and C. C. Gelray (eds.), *Women in the Labor Market*. New York: Columbia University Press.

———. 1975. Differences in Expected Post-School Investment as a Determinant of Market Wage Differential. *International Economic Review* 16 (June): 451–469.

Porter, Peter K., and Daniel Slottje. 1985. A Comprehensive Analysis of Inequality in the Size Distribution of Income for the United States, 1952–1981. *Southern Economic Journal* 52 (October): 412–421.

Pullum, T. W. 1980. Separating Age, Period and Cohort Effects in White U.S. Fertility, 1920–1970. *Social Science Research* 9: 225–244.

Pyatt, Graham. 1976. On the Interpretation and Disaggregation of Gini Coefficients. *Economic Journal* 86 (June): 243–255.

Quester, Aline O., and William H. Greene. 1985. The Labor Market Experience of Black and White Wives in the Sixties and Seventies. *Social Science Quarterly* 66 (December): 854–885.

Radner, Daniel B. 1982. Distribution of Family Income: Improved Estimates. *Social Security Bulletin* 45 (July): 13–21.

Reich, Michael. 1982. *Racial Inequality*. Princeton, NJ: Princeton University Press.

Reimers, Cordelia W. 1984. Sources of the Family Income Differentials among Hispanics, Blacks, and White Nonhispanics. *American Journal of Sociology* 89 (January): 889–903.

Richards, Toni, Michael J. White, and Amy Ong Tsui. 1987. Changing Living Arrangements: A Hazard Model of Transitions among Household Types. *Demography* 24 (February): 77–97.

Rindfuss, Ronald R., and James A. Sweet. 1977. *Postwar Fertility Trends and Differentials in the United States*. New York: Academic Press.

Robins, Philip K. 1985. A Comparison of the Labor Supply Findings from the Four Negative Income Tax Experiments. *Journal of Human Resources* 20 (Fall): 567–582.

Rosenthal, Neal. 1985. The Shrinking Middle Class: Myth or Reality? *Monthly Labor Review* 108 (March): 3–10.

Ross, Christine, Sheldon Danziger, and Eugene Smolensky. 1987. The Level and Trend of Poverty in the United States, 1939–1979. *Demography* 24 (November): 587–600.

Ross, Heather L., and Isabel V. Sawhill. 1975. *Time of Transition: The Growth of Families Headed by Women*. Washington, DC: USGPO.

Rubin, Beth A. 1988. Inequality in the Working Class: The Unanticipated Consequences of Union Organization and Strikes. *Industrial and Labor Relations Review* 41 (July): 553–566.

Ruggles, Patricia, and Roberton Williams. 1986. Transitions In and Out of Poverty: New Data from the Survey of Income and Program Participation. Presented at the Annual Meeting of the Allied Social Science Associations.

Russell, Louise B. 1982. *The Baby Boom Generation and the Economy*. Washington, DC: Brookings Institution.

Sahota, Gian Sing L. 1978. Theories of Personal Income Distribution: A Survey. *Journal of Economic Literature* 16 (March): 1–55.

Sammartino, Frank J., and Richard A. Kasten. 1988. Distributional Analyses of Three Deficit Reduction Options Affecting Social Security Cash Benefits. In Sheldon H. Danziger and Kent E. Portney (eds.), *The Distributional Impacts of Public Policy*. New York: St. Martin's Press.

Saunders, Norman C. 1987. Economic Projections to the Year 2000. *Monthly Labor Review* 110 (September): 10–18.

Sawhill, Isabel V. 1988. Poverty in the U.S.: Why Is It so Persistent? *Journal of Economic Literature* 26 (September): 1073–1119.

Schiller, Bradley R. 1976. *Poverty and Discrimination*. Englewood Cliffs, NJ: Prentice-Hall.

———. 1971. Class Discrimination vs. Racial Discrimination. *Review of Economics and Statistics* 53 (August): 263–269.

Schoen, Robert, William Urton, Karen Woodrow, and John Baj. 1985. Marriage and Divorce in Twentieth Century American Cohorts. *Demography* 22 (February): 101–114.

Schultz, Theodore W. 1974. *Economics of the Family*. Chicago: University of Chicago Press.

Schumpeter, Joseph. 1942. *Capitalism, Socialism, and Democracy*. New York: Harper and Brothers.

Schwartz, Joe. 1988. Hispanics in the Eighties. *American Demographics* 10 (January): 43–45.

Schwartz, Saul. 1986. Earnings Capacity and the Trend in Inequality among Black Men. *Journal of Human Resources* 21 (Winter): 44–63.

Shackett, Joyce R., and D. J. Slottje. 1987. Labor Supply Decisions, Human Capital

Attributes, and Inequality in the Size Distribution of Earnings. *Journal of Human Resources* 22 (Winter): 82–100.

Shapiro, David, and Steven Sandell. 1985. Age Discrimination in Wages and Displaced Older Men. *Southern Economic Journal* 52 (July): 90–102.

Sheets, Robert G., Stephen Nord, and John J. Phelps. 1987. *The Impact of Service Industries on Underemployment in Metropolitan Economies.* Lexington, MA: D. C. Heath.

Shelp, Kent. 1981. *Beyond Industrialization: Ascendency of the Global Services.* New York: Praeger.

Sheshinski, Eytan. 1978. A Model of Social Security and Retirement Decisions. *Journal of Public Economics* 10 (December): 337–360.

Shipp, Stephanie. 1988. How Singles Spend. *American Demographics* 10 (April): 22–27.

Silvestri, George T., and John M. Lukasiewicz. 1987. A Look at Occupational Employment Trends to the Year 2000. *Monthly Labor Review* 110 (September): 46–63.

Singelmann, Joachim. 1978. *From Agriculture to Services.* Beverly Hills, CA: Sage Publications.

Slesinger, Doris P. 1980. Rapid Changes in Household Composition among Low Income Mothers. *Family Relations* 29 (April): 221–228.

Slottje, Daniel J. 1987. Relative Price Changes and Inequality in the Size Distribution of Various Components of Income. *Journal of Business and Economic Statistics* 5 (January): 19–26.

Smeeding, Timothy M. 1982. An Anti-Poverty Effect of In-Kind Transfers: A "Good Idea" Gone Too Far? *Policy Studies Journal* 10 (3): 499–522.

———. 1979. On the Distribution of New Income: Comment. *Southern Economic Journal* 45 (January): 932–944.

Smeeding, Timothy M., and Marilyn Moon. 1980. Valuing Government Expenditures: The Case of Medical Care Transfers and Poverty. *Review of Income and Wealth* 26 (September): 305–324.

Smith, D. P. 1981. A Reconsideration of Easterlin Cycles. *Population Studies* 35 (July): 247–264.

Smith, James P. 1979. The Distribution of Family Earnings. *Journal of Political Economy* 87 (Part 2, October): S163–S192.

Smith, James P., and Michael P. Ward. 1985. Time-Series Growth in the Female Labor Force. *Journal of Labor Economics* 3 (Part 2, January): S59–S90.

———. 1984. *Women's Wages and Work in the Twentieth Century.* Research Report R–3119-NICHD. Santa Monica, CA: Rand Corporation.

Smith, James P., and Finis Welch. 1987. Race and Poverty: A Forty-Year Record. *American Economic Review* 77 (May): 152–158.

———. 1981. No Time to Be Young: The Economic Prospects for Large Cohorts in the United States. *Population and Development Review* 7 (March): 71–83.

———. 1979. Inequality: Race Differences in the Distribution of Earnings. *International Economic Review* 20 (June): 515–526.

———. 1977. Black-White Male Wage Ratios: 1960–1970. *American Economic Review* 67 (June): 323–338.

Smuts, Ronald W. 1971. *Women and Work in America.* New York: New York University Press.

Snyder, David, and Paula M. Hudis. 1976. Occupational Income and the Effects of

Minority Competition and Segregation: A Reanalysis and Some New Evidence. *American Sociological Review* 41 (April): 209–234.

Social Security Bulletin. 1987. Social Security Programs in the United States, 1987. *Social Security Bulletin* 50 (April): 5–66.

Spence, A. Michael. 1973. Job Market Signaling. *Quarterly Journal of Economics* 87 (August): 355–374.

Stanback, Thomas M., Jr. 1979. *Understanding the Service Economy: Employment, Productivity, Location.* Baltimore, MD: Johns Hopkins University Press.

Stapleton, David C., and Douglas J. Young. 1984. The Effects of Demographic Change on the Distribution of Wages, 1967–1990. *Journal of Human Resources* 19 (Spring): 175–201.

Steinberg, Bruce. 1983. The Mass Market Is Splitting Apart. *Fortune* (November): 76.

Stiglitz, Joseph E. 1975. The Theory of "Screening," Education, and the Distribution of Income. *American Economic Review* 65 (June): 293–300.

Strauss, Robert P., and Francis W. Horvath. 1976. Wage Rate Differences by Race and Sex in the US Labour Market: 1960–1970. *Economica* 43: 287–298.

Sweet, James A. 1984. Components of Change in the Number of Households: 1970–1980. *Demography* 21 (May): 129–140.

———. 1971. The Employment of Wives and the Inequality of Family Income. *Proceedings of the American Statistical Association,* 1–5.

Taeuber, Alma F., Karl E. Taeuber, and Glen G. Cain. 1966. Occupational Assimilation and the Competitive Process: A Reanalysis. *American Journal of Sociology* 72 (November): 273–289.

Thurow, Lester. 1987. A Surge in Inequality. *Scientific American* 256 (May): 30–37.

———. 1986. The Hidden Sting of the Trade Deficit. *New York Times* (January 19).

———. 1984. The Disappearance of the Middle Class. *New York Times* (February 4).

———. 1980. *The Zero Sum Society.* New York: Basic Books.

———. 1975. *Generating Inequality: Mechanisms of Distribution in the U.S. Economy.* New York: Basic Books.

———. 1970. Analyzing the American Income Distribution. *American Economic Review* 60 (May): 261–269.

———. 1969. *Poverty and Discrimination.* Washington, DC: Brookings Institution.

Thurow, Lester, and Robert E. B. Lucas. 1972. *The American Distribution of Income: A Structural Problem.* Washington, DC: USGPO.

Tienda, Marta, and Jennifer Glass. 1985. Household Structure and Labor Force Participation of Black, Hispanic, and White Mothers. *Demography* 22 (August): 381–394.

Tilly, Chris, Barry Bluestone, and Bennett Harrison. 1986. What Is Making American Wages More Unequal? *Industrial Relations Research Association Series, Proceedings of the Thirty-Ninth Annual Meeting* (December): 338–348.

Torrey, Barbara Boyle, and Timothy Smeeding. 1988. Poor Children in Rich Countries. Paper presented at the annual Population Association Meeting, April.

Treas, Judith. 1987. The Effect of Women's Labor Force Participation on the Distribution of Income in the United States. *Annual Review of Sociology* 13: 259–288. Palo Alto, CA: Annual Reviews.

———. 1983. Trickle Down or Transfers? Postwar Determinants of Family Income Inequality. *American Sociological Review* 48 (August): 546–559.

Treas, Judith, and Robin Jane Walther. 1978. Family Structure and the Distribution of Family Income. *Social Forces* 56 (March): 866–880.

Tschetter, John. 1988. An Evaluation of BLS Projections of the 1985 Economy. *Monthly Labor Review* 111 (September): 24–33.

Urquhart, Michael. 1984. The Employment Shift to Services: Where Did It Come From? *Monthly Labor Review* 107 (April): 15–22.

U.S. Bureau of the Census. 1988. Money Income of Households, Families, and Persons in the United States. *Current Population Reports,* Series P–60. Washington, DC: USGPO.

———. 1987. After Tax Money Income Estimates of Households, 1985. *Current Population Reports,* Series P–20, Number 151. Washington, DC: USGPO.

———. 1986a. *Statistical Abstract of the United States: 1987* (107th edition). Washington, DC: USGPO.

———. 1986b. Population Estimates and Projections. *Current Population Reports,* Series P–25, Number 971. Washington, DC: USGPO.

———. 1986c. Projections of the Number of Households and Families: 1986 to 2000. *Current Population Reports,* Series P–25, Number 986. Washington, DC: USGPO.

———. 1984. Projections of the Population of the United States by Age, Sex, and Race: 1983 to 2080. *Current Population Reports,* Series P–25, Number 952. Washington, DC: USGPO.

———. 1983. *1980 Census of Population, Characteristics of the Population, General Population Characteristics* 1 (Chapter B): B1–B5. Washington, DC: USGPO.

———. 1980. Illustrative Projections of Money Income Size Distributions for Households: 1980 to 1995. *Current Population Reports,* Series P–60, Number 122, Washington, DC: USGPO.

———. 1975. *Historical Statistics of the United States, Colonial Times to 1970.* Bicentennial Edition. Washington, DC: USGPO.

U.S. Department of Labor. 1976. *Employment and Training Report of the President, 1976.* Washington, DC: USGPO.

Von Weizsacker, R. K. 1988. Age Structure and Income Distribution Policy. *Journal of Population Economics* 1 (Spring): 33–55.

Voydanoff, Patricia. 1986. Women's Work, Family, and Health. In Karen Koziara, Michael Moskow, and Lucretia Tanner (eds.), *Working Women.* Washington, DC: Bureau of National Affairs.

Wachter, Michael L. 1974. Primary and Secondary Labor Markets: A Critique of the Dual Approach. *Brookings Papers on Economic Activity* 3: 637–693.

Wallace, Phyllis A. 1988. A Decade of Policy Developments in Equal Opportunities in Employment and Housing. In Robert H. Haveman (ed.), *A Decade of Federal Antipoverty Programs.* New York: Academic Press.

Weiss, Leonard W. 1966. Concentration and Labor Earnings. *American Economic Review* 56 (March): 96–117.

Weiss, Noel S. 1976. Recent Trends in Violent Deaths among Young Adults in the United States. *American Journal of Epidemiology* 103: 416–422.

Welch, Finis. 1979. Effects of Cohort Size on Earnings: The Baby Boom Babies' Financial Bust. *Journal of Political Economy* 87 (October, Part 2): S565–S597.

———. 1973. Black-White Differences in Returns to Schooling. *American Economic Review* 63 (December): 893–907.

———. 1967. Labor Market Discrimination in the Rural South. *Journal of Political Economy* 75 (June): 225–240.

Wessel, David. 1986. U.S. Rich and Poor Increase in Numbers: Middle Loses Ground. *Wall Street Journal* (September 22): 1.

Westcott, Diane Nilsen. 1982. Blacks in the 1970's: Did They Scale the Job Ladder? *Monthly Labor Review* 105 (June): 29–38.

Westoff, Charles. 1979. The Decline of Fertility. *American Demographics* 1 (February): 16–19.

Williamson, Samuel H., and Warren L. Jones. 1983. Computing the Impact of Social Security Using the Life Cycle Consumption Function. *American Economic Review* 73 (December): 1036–1052.

Willis, Robert J. 1973. A New Approach to the Economic Theory of Fertility Behavior. *Journal of Political Economy* 81 (March-April, part 2): S14–S69.

Wilson, William Julius. 1987. *The Truly Disadvantaged*. Chicago: University of Chicago Press.

————. 1980. *The Declining Significance of Race*. Chicago: University of Chicago Press.

Wilson, William Julius, and Kathryn M. Neckerman. 1986. Poverty and Family Structure: The Widening Gap between Evidence and Public Policy Issues. In Sheldon H. Danziger and Daniel H. Weinberg (eds.), *Fighting Poverty: What Works and What Doesn't*. Cambridge, MA: Harvard University Press.

Winegarden, C. R. 1987. Women's Labour Force Participation and the Distribution of Household Incomes: Evidence from Cross-National Data. *Economica* 54 (May): 223–236.

Wojtkiewicz, Roger A. 1988. Household Composition Change and Economic Welfare Inequality. Paper presented at the Population Association of America Meeting.

Wolf, Wendy, and Rachael Rosenfeld. 1978. Sex Structure of Occupations and Job Mobility. *Social Forces* 56 (March): 823–844.

Wolff, Edward N. 1986. The Productivity Slowdown and the Fall in the U.S. Rate of Profit, 1947–1976. *Review of Radical Political Economics* 18 (1&2): 87–109.

Wolpin, Kenneth I. 1977. Education and Screening. *American Economic Review* 67 (December): 949–958.

Wright, Erik Olin. 1978. Race, Class, and Income Inequality. *American Journal of Sociology* 83 (6): 1368–1397.

Zucker, Lynne, and Carolyn Rosenstein. 1981. Taxonomies of Institutional Structures: Dual Economy Reconsidered. *American Sociological Review* 46 (December): 869–884.

Index

Wolfe, Barbara, 70, 95
Wolff, Edward N., 50
Wolpin, Kenneth I., 53
Worker's Compensation, 85, 86, 88, 90, 94
Wright, Erik Olin, 119

Yellen, Janet, 53
Youth, 37, 59, 60, 116, 134, 140;

dependency, 6, 66; income levels, 28, 57, 130–133; Neighborhood Youth Corps, 108; proportion in population, 62, 129, 138; unrelated individuals, 32

Zabalza, Antoni, 13
Zucker, Lynne, 53

About the Author

NAN L. MAXWELL is Associate Professor in the Department of Economics at California State University, Hayward. Her articles have been published in the *American Economic Review*, the *American Journal of Economics and Sociology*, the *Journal of Economic Education*, and the *Southern Economic Journal*.